WE
Marched Through Hell

**A Rural High School's Service
in the Vietnam War
and Life in its Aftermath**

Steven D. Schultz

outskirts
press

DEDICATION

This book is dedicated to those who honorably served during the Vietnam War. More specifically, this book is dedicated to the young men who graduated in the 1960s from Porterville High School in Porterville, California, and then marched through the hell of the Vietnam War and did what our country asked them to do.

ACKNOWLEDGEMENTS

Since this is the first book that I have ever written, I entered this project with some apprehension. I really didn't know what to expect. Without the support and assistance from the following individuals, I doubt I would have been able to complete this project.

First and foremost, I have to thank my family. I am very blessed to have the family that I do – my wife, Deina, and sons, Jonathan and Jacob. They provided me with encouragement throughout this project and my wife was often my sounding board for various aspects of the book. Their ongoing support was paramount to my ability to finish writing this book.

Certainly, I must acknowledge all of those who were interviewed for the book. Each of them gave of their personal time to be part of this project, and I appreciated their willingness and openness when telling me their stories. Almost every time I came home from an interview, I was overwhelmed with what I had heard. Their dedication during the war was extraordinary, and I hope others have an opportunity to talk with them as freely as I did. The Vietnam War veterans I interviewed included Alfred Alba, John Alba, Vince Arcure, Geary Baxter, Dan Boydstun, Melvin Braziel, Ron Crabtree, Don Dowling, Tony Forner, Roger Gibson, Greg Goble, Louis Gurrola, Felix Hernandez, Roland Hill, Robert Johnson, Ron McCarville, Chuck Migalski, Todd Pixler, Brian Rattigan, Jim Rouch, John Schultz, Joe Souza, Russell Vossler, Richard Walker, and Don Wolfram. The family and friends I contacted included Bobbie Barber, Steve Cha, Steve Durtsche, Susie

Goble, Lance Goble, Beverly Jackson, Jerry Jackson, Joan Jackson, Carol Vossler, Diane Johnson (fictitious name), Cheryl McCarville, and Reba Wolfram.

Since I am technologically ignorant and my eyes grew weary after re-reading the manuscript so many times, I needed assistance from someone with technological skills and another pair of eyes with a knowledge of English who could catch writing errors. My thanks to Mark Johnson who helped me with the enhancement of the pictures in the book and other areas relating to technology, and Kellie Sanders who served as the editor of the book and my additional set of eyes.

And, finally, I must thank my brother, John. Without a doubt, I would not have been able to finish this book without his assistance. As a graduate of Porterville High School during the 60s, and a Navy veteran who served periodically off the coast of Vietnam, John was instrumental in making contacts with the Vietnam War veterans he went to school with that might be interested in being interviewed for this book. From this group of veterans, others were referred to me or heard about the book and volunteered to participate. Since the bulk of the information in this book came from the veterans themselves, this book would have not been possible without John's assistance - thanks brother.

FAMILY TIES TO VIETNAM SCHOLARSHIP

After publishing-related expenses, all royalties from the sale of this book that would normally be paid to the author will be donated to the **Family Ties to Vietnam Scholarship** at Porterville College. The scholarship is for academically qualified students enrolled at Porterville College who have a family member that served in Vietnam during the war.

Table of Contents

Introduction

YOU WERE STANDING right next to him and didn't even notice.

Why should you have? He looked like any other seventy-year-old man in the community. His hair was gray, with some, if not most of it gone on top. His face was wrinkled with bags under his eyes. He wore glasses to see better and hearing aids to hear better. He walked a little slower than most, sometimes with a limp or a struggle. He seemed a little distant or even agitated about something, but most old folks do at that age. But if you would have taken a closer look, maybe even asked him a few questions, you might have noticed that this man was different than most his age.

His hair had turned prematurely gray due to the stress and fear of near-death experiences he faced when he was only a teenager. His face was wrinkled from the lack of sleep over the years from having nightmares and flashbacks. His ears were deaf due to exposure to intense and damaging sounds. His limp was from an injury that's never healed. His slow walk was from worn out knees that were overloaded years ago carrying friends on his back. He was agitated because our government, and many of its people, failed him earlier in his life and he still can't shake that betrayal. Who was this man?

A Vietnam War veteran.

Purpose of the Book

The city of Porterville is located in the southern part of the San Joaquin Valley in California. According to the 1960 United States census data, Porterville had a population of 7,991 at about the time when some of the future Vietnam War veterans from the area were beginning to enter high school. Ten years later, when these local veterans had either already returned home from the war or were beginning to, Porterville had grown in population to 12,602.[1] At that time, the main industry in the area was related in large part to agriculture. As you can see, the lives of these veterans were molded in a small, rural area of the world that was far removed from the influence of a small country in Southeast Asia.

But that small country soon impacted the lives of these veterans in unimaginable ways.

An article in the *Porterville Recorder* on November 14, 2013 referenced a United Press International (UPI) report in 1967 that, based on per capita data, the number of men killed in action up to that point during the Vietnam War from the city of Porterville was four times the national average.[2] Porterville then became known as the city that paid one of the highest prices in Vietnam. By the end of the war, another town earned the unwelcomed distinction of the largest per capita death rate, but Porterville certainly suffered more than most.

When the UPI report was published in 1967, many young men from Porterville, most of them really only boys at the time, had just graduated from or were currently attending Porterville High School, the only high school in town back then. Obviously for them, this data was rather disturbing as they began to think of life after high school. By the time the war in Vietnam concluded, 40 young men from the Porterville community would eventually have their names etched in the stone at the Vietnam Veterans Memorial located at Veterans Park in Porterville, listing those who had been killed in action during the war.

Too many from Porterville High School in the 1960s were killed in Vietnam. Too many were injured. Too many still live with the effects of the war. With that, the focus of this book are the young men that graduated from Porterville High School in the 1960s whose lives were undeniably impacted by the Vietnam War. They were seventeen or eighteen-year-old teenagers who were forced to think about and worry about finding themselves in the middle of a war eight thousand miles away after they graduated from high school. They were teenagers who watched too many times another classmate coming home in a flag-draped box, or seeing friends coming home with bodies that had been mutilated from an enemy's bullet or minds that had been damaged by the atrocities they experienced.

We Marched Through Hell is a book that is not just about war stories that merely catalogues experiences in combat. Rather, this is a book that takes the reader through the totality of being a soldier from Porterville during the Vietnam War by sharing stories and experiences at the various stages these men went through from being drafted, entering the military, becoming a soldier, leaving home, fighting through the war, coming back home again, and then living in the aftermath of such a terrible experience. It's not just about experiences, but also about their feelings and emotions. And the book is not just about them, but also about their families and friends and how the war affected them.

During the initial years of the war the public generally supported the war and its efforts to stem the tide of communism. But as the war dragged on with no outright victory in sight, the initial conviction and optimism were replaced with indifference and pessimism. And by the time these young men came home to Porterville after their experiences in Vietnam, many of them faced hostile and jeering crowds at the airports they flew into and a country that had turned its back on them.

The Vietnam War veterans soon found out that they had become scapegoats of a nation that was tired and weary of the war. The nation had grown angry of the lies, deception, misery, and death, and its people needed someone to take this anger out upon - the Vietnam veterans became their target.

Since they had become scapegoats and targets on which people expressed their anger and bitterness about the war, the Vietnam veterans were told to keep their mouths shut when they came home, blend into society, and forget the war ever happened in the first place. Hunker down, don't make waves, and everything will be alright. With that, many of these war veterans never spoke of their experiences in Vietnam. Sometimes, this silence actually exasperated the psychological wounds many of them brought back from the war. At other times, their silence kept their experiences from a public that should have really known, and, with their silence, a part of our country's history was not being told. And that history, and those stories, need to be told.

This book attempts to do that.

Although this book contains information obtained from various literary sources, the vast majority of the information came from the mouths of the veterans who were there. Personal interviews were conducted with the veterans, most of them in their homes, giving them an opportunity to tell their story. The veterans spoke openly about their time in Vietnam, some drawing back on remembering their experiences through pictures, letters, or words on citations. Then, a follow-up visit was scheduled to check the content of my notes and review with them the information they provided me in the first interview. Some of the experiences they remembered may be clouded by the fog of war or tainted by the passage of time. I did not question the accuracy of the information they shared with me and I hope the stories that I have provided accurately reflect their experiences.

The veterans were open, honest, and sometimes emotional when speaking about their experiences. I was humbled and moved by their stories and my respect for them grew exponentially by the time the interviews were concluded. To be honest with you, I was more than just humbled and moved. I was overwhelmed.

Some veterans that were contacted about the book declined to be interviewed because of not wanting to relive something they have been trying to forget. And that was okay, too. Not wanting to talk about their experiences in Vietnam is a story in and of itself. In addition, a few of the Porterville High School classmates who served in Vietnam have died, some only recently. Those who have died were there in Vietnam, too. They went to boot camp and Advanced Individual Training (AIT). They said their good-byes to their parents at the airport. They came back to protesters and they lived with the war long after it was over. So, this book is their book too; these stories are their stories too.

Although this book may highlight those who served in combat, it should be noted that most Americans who served in Vietnam were in non-combat assignments. The contributions of these men and women were substantial and they have stories to tell too. Even though their responsibilities may have been in a supporting role rather than in direct combat, many of them accepted assignments that put them in vulnerable locations exposing them to enemy attacks, injury, and even death.

Despite the unpopularity of the war, these young men from Porterville High School continued to serve their country with the same strength, the same courage, the same heroism, the same dedication, and the same professionalism as their fathers displayed in World War II (WWII). And like their fathers before them, the Vietnam veterans from Porterville High School have their unique stories to tell, and each of us needs to hear them.

And hearing their stories is the purpose of this book.

This Was Their Generation's War

The fathers of many of these men were WWII veterans. When you think of WWII, you think of epic battles like the Battle of the Bulge, the raising of the flag at Iwo Jima, or the storming of the beaches at Normandy. You think of great military leaders like generals Dwight Eisenhower, Omar Bradley, or George Patton. You think of heroes like Audie Murphy, or larger than life fictional war characters played in movies by John Wayne. But Vietnam was not like the war of their fathers.

This war was different.

In Vietnam, there were no parades for liberating soldiers, no raising of the flag to signify another territorial conquest, no famous men who young boys can emulate while playing in their back yards. When you ask someone today to name an important battle won during the Vietnam War, you'll receive a blank stare. Most battles in Vietnam were over hills with numbers and not cities with names. When you ask someone to name one of the most influential generals of the war, you'll get a shrug of the shoulders. Okay, Westmoreland, but who else? When you ask someone today to name a hero that came from the war, you'll get a look of confusion. Lieutenant Calley is a name some may remember but he certainly was no hero.

Rather than protracted battles like in WWII with known and respected military leaders jostling back and forth for advantages like in a chess match, the war in Vietnam was marked more often by small-scale engagements, with troops defending against an ambush, wading in rice patties, lying in elephant grass, and walking into minefields. The enemy would often engage, fight for a while, and then retreat into the jungles, down into tunnels, or across the border into Laos or Cambodia. And then, they'd do it all over again.

The vast weaponry and tremendous air power capacity of the American military were not always enough in battles with an enemy who fought close-up, hidden in tunnels, and behind foliage and termite hills. Victories in Vietnam were not determined by the conquests of territory or the liberation of people and their besieged cities, but rather by an obscure method of body count. Estimating the kill ratio to determine which side won that battle.

True, this war was not like their fathers' war, but it was still their generation's war.

Why Vietnam?

Our involvement in Vietnam did not begin as a reaction to some significant event like a terrorist attack or invasion by an enemy. The United States entered WWII mainly because of the attack by the Japanese on Pearl Harbor. We entered the war in Iraq because of Saddam Hussein's invasion of Kuwait. We entered the war in Afghanistan because of the terrorist attack in New York City and Washington D. C.

So, what was the reason we entered Vietnam?

The main answer to that question, and probably the only one that most people can think of, centers around the general feeling about the fear of communism being spread throughout the region. The "domino theory," as it was called, where smaller, unsuspecting countries would be swallowed up, one after the other, by the communist menace. That was the fear, and we couldn't let that happen. Since that may be the answer, you can see that our involvement in Vietnam wasn't spurred by some drastic event that rallied the unbridled patriotism of the public like responding to attacks or terrorism on our soil.

At the beginning of our involvement in Vietnam the American people may have known of Vietnam, but most probably couldn't find it on a map. During the initial years of the war, the American public supported the rationale for our involvement there. This support, however, would later change and, eventually, their fear of the domino theory was never realized.

Events that Changed the Perceptions of the War

When the Vietnam War first started, there was a general sense of purpose behind our involvement in the war and an attitude that we were there for a worthy and noble cause. Although not the only reasons, two events helped to change the perception of the war in the minds of many people. One was the Tet Offensive in January 1968 and the other was the televised report from Walter Cronkite, CBS newscaster, on his assessment of the war in Vietnam.

In January 1968, the North Vietnamese and Viet Cong broke a ceasefire at the start of the Tet Lunar Year by launching surprise attacks on cities and American and South Vietnamese territories across South Vietnam, including an attack on the American Embassy in Saigon. This became known as the Tet Offensive, or simply Tet.[3]

The assault was massive and caught the American and South

Vietnamese forces by surprise. However, the Americans eventually repelled the attacks, and many would claim the Tet Offensive to be a military victory for the American forces. However, if the American military scored a victory, then why did the Tet Offensive prove to be a negative turning point in the perceptions about the war in the minds of the American public?

In the months leading up to the Tet Offensive, political leaders and military officials were insisting that the war was nearly over. With a little more patience, a few more dollars, and a lot more troops, the war will be over soon. And the United States would be victorious. The public bought this assessment, but then came the Tet Offensive.

After watching on television and reading about this massive assault by the North Vietnamese and Viet Cong, people began to realize that the war was not almost over as they had been told. In fact, it became obvious that the war was increasing in terms of its scope and intensity. The public began to wonder if it could really believe that which they were being told about the progress of the war from our political and military leaders.

Some called Vietnam the "living room war" because the war was on television every night and newscasts help shaped public opinions about the war and the political and military officials who led them. One of the most famous and trusted newscasters at that time was Walter Cronkite from CBS News. Unlike many of the journalists and newscasters of today, Cronkite was known then as a straight shooter, independent, someone who was committed to reporting events with truth and honesty.

Since the reports about the successes of the Tet Offensive were suspect to some and confusing to others, Cronkite went to Vietnam to see for himself. He visited several battle sites and spoke with many soldiers and military leaders about their experiences and perceptions of the war's progress. Then, on February 27, 1968, CBS aired its "Report from Vietnam: Who, What, When, Where, Why?" At the end of its broadcast, Cronkite delivered his verdict about the war:

"Tonight, back in more familiar surroundings in New York, we'd like to sum up our findings in Vietnam, an analysis that must be speculative, personal, subjective. Who won and who lost in the great Tet Offensive against the cities? I'm not sure. The Viet Cong did not win by a knockout but neither did we.

"Then, with as much restraint as I could, I turned to our own leaders whose idea of negotiation seemed frozen in memories of General McArthur's encounter with the Japanese aboard the battleship Missouri.

"We've been too often disappointed by the optimism of the American leaders both in Vietnam and Washington to have faith any longer in the silver linings they find in the darkest clouds...For it seems now more certain than ever, that the bloody experience of Vietnam is to end in a stalemate...To say that we are closer to victory today is to believe in the face of the evidence, the optimists who have been wrong in the past.

"To say that we are mired in stalemate seems the only realistic, if unsatisfactory conclusion. On the off chance that military and political analysts are right, in the next few months we must test the enemy's intentions, in case this is indeed his last big gasp before negotiations.

"But it is increasingly clear to this reporter that the only rational way out then will be to negotiate, not as victors, but as an honorable people who lived up to their pledge to defend democracy and did the best they could. This is Walter Cronkite. Good night."[4]

Little did Cronkite know that when he made this report, calling the war a stalemate and suggesting negotiation as a way out of Vietnam, our combat troops would continue fighting in Vietnam for another five years.

The impact of those words of Cronkite touched the community of Porterville and, especially, the young men from Porterville High School who were currently serving or who would soon be called to serve in a war that was already being declared a stalemate by one of the nation's most respected journalists. If the war is a stalemate already, why go and fight in it?

The Casualties of War

The writing of this book began in the year 2018 which is the 50th anniversary of something that most people don't know. However, this anniversary is a significant one for many across this nation, and, especially, for the group of young men who graduated from Porterville High School in the 1960s and then went to the war in Vietnam.

The year 1968 was the deadliest year of the Vietnam War. Approximately 17,000 Americans died in the Vietnam War that year.[5] It was an ugly, costly, and terrible year. And so was the war.

Currently, there are two monuments in Porterville that list the names of those from the Porterville area who lost their lives in Vietnam. One is at Hillcrest Cemetery and the other at Veterans Park. The monument at Hillcrest Cemetery lists 28 names, the one at Veterans Park lists 40. Why the disparity?

When speaking with one of the organizers of the memorial at Veterans Park, he said the reason for the disparity is because the Veterans Park memorial is a broader memorial, listing names of some of those who were killed from adjacent towns to Porterville. In addition, some names are of those who were not born in Porterville or even the area, but maybe spent a large part of their life living in Porterville or in an adjacent community. In fact, both monuments list names that do not have Porterville listed as their city of origin on the Virtual Wall website. But that really doesn't matter.

Regardless of which list of names is the most accurate, there are too many names listed on both monuments. In fact, one is too many, but 28, or 40? In addition to those killed, there are many who were injured, and many still suffer from those injuries today, along with family members and friends who have suffered along with them in their rehabilitation from the war. The casualties are endless.

The End Result

Although the Americans won the most battles on the ground and in the air, winning battles does not mean winning a war.

There has been much debate regarding if America won, lost, or tied the war in Vietnam. Certainly, as the world watched on television the fall of Saigon in 1975, few can argue that America won the war in Vietnam. But did we lose it? Tie it, or what? Or does it even matter anymore? Well, to some of the Vietnam War veterans that were interviewed for this book it certainly does matter. Russell Vossler, one of the veterans interviewed for this book, said, "If you want to piss off a Vietnam veteran, tell him we lost the war in Vietnam." I certainly won't tell him that.

Several years ago, I spotted a Vietnam veteran wearing a shirt that said, "We did not lose the Vietnam War, we withdrew from it." That is an assessment that is shared by many of the Porterville High School veterans who fought there, and maybe it's the most accurate one. It is also an assessment that I will address again later in this book. Regardless if you feel we won, lost, or tied, the debate regarding the outcome of the war may never end with a definite answer.

America's involvement in Vietnam did not end with a final, significant victory lap that resulted in the raising of Old Glory in the country's capital. Our exit came as the result of a de-escalation rather than a resounding event marking a final, hard fought victory. To mark the end of the war, there was no ticker tape parade down Manhattan Boulevard in New York City. There was no ceremony in Washington D. C. where crowds of people were waving American flags and cheering the success of our efforts to stop communism. No, there was only a sigh of relief among the people of this country that this difficult chapter in our nation's history had finally been closed. The end of the Vietnam War was as anticlimactic as the beginning.

When talking about the end result of the war, Roger Gibson, one of the Porterville High School Vietnam War veterans interviewed for this book, very clearly and succinctly summed up the end result of the Vietnam War when he said:

"Too many were killed. Too many were injured. And too many still suffer. And for what?"

SECTION ONE
Before Vietnam – Their Stories

1

Profiles of the Porterville High School Patriots

"This nation will remain the land of the free only
so long as it is the home of the brave."

Elmer Davis

THE FOLLOWING PROFILES are of the Vietnam War veterans from Porterville High School who were interviewed for this book. I want to introduce each of them to you before you read about them. Their stories are interspersed throughout the various chapters of this book, and each of their stories is unique. Some of these men went to Vietnam right out of high school, while others went after spending a year or two at work or in college.

This bunch of veterans is a diverse group, with various experiences relating to their distinct assignments or military branches they served in during the Vietnam War. They served in the Army, Navy, Air Force, and Marine Corps. Six were in the infantry, three were airborne paratroopers, one was a tunnel rat, four were heavy equipment operators or truck drivers, one was a Military Policeman (MP), one was in supply, two were helicopter pilots, one was an advisor before the war, three were helicopter maintenance mechanics, two were enginemen, one was in artillery, one was a construction builder, one was an Air Police/K-9 handler, one was an air cargo specialist, two were in armor, one was in demolition and also served in special forces, and another was a shipfitter. Each assignment was an integral part of the total military effort during the Vietnam War.

When most of these veterans were still teenagers, they answered the call of their country, either through enlisting or being drafted, and then marched through hell, fighting on the battlefields or providing troop support often in harm's way. Some of their friends and high school classmates died in the war, others were physically injured, and many came back with psychological challenges they still face even today. They served our country with honor, strength, and courage.

For some of these Porterville High School students, our country's slow progression into war was not really significant in their lives until they read their draft notice in the mail. For others, the war was on their televisions every night and they worried about what they would be facing after graduation. Even though the events that led up to the war were happening almost unnoticed back home, these events would greatly impact their lives for the next 50 years and beyond.

To put it in perspective, some of the major events that began our country's slow creep into a war in Vietnam, events such as President Eisenhower's speech when he first used the term "domino theory'" to justify our involvement in Vietnam, and the Geneva Accords that divided North and South Vietnam, happened when most of these guys were around six years old.

Little did they know at the time, that as they were having recess on the playgrounds of Olive Street School, St. Anne's, Doyle Colony, Zion Lutheran, Terra Bella, Burton, Rockford, Woodville, Pleasant View, Pioneer, Saucelito, Belleview, or Bartlett elementary or middle schools, things were happening in Washington D.C. and in a country eight thousand miles from home that would eventually place these kids in the middle of a war.

Please meet these veterans.

Alfred Alba

Branch Served:	Army
MOS:	Helicopter/fixed wing mechanic
Years Served:	1965-67
PHS graduation:	1964

Alfred Alba's senior picture

Alfred Alba was born in Porterville and raised in Woodville. He was one of six children, having three brothers and two sisters. His youngest brother recently passed away and was not born until Alba was a freshman in high school. He attended Woodville Elementary School and graduated from Porterville High School in 1964. Alba's father was a farm labor contractor and his mother worked in the fields. His father served during WWII and was a prisoner of war (POW) for 28 months. His father went into the military with a friend, and they got captured together and got out together. Now that is the buddy system at its best. Alba, his father, and two of his brothers were all drafted. When he was in high school Alba did not have a lot of time for after-school activities or partying since he was expected to work with his family in the fields. Alba eventually saved enough money to buy his first car, a 1951 Plymouth. He bought the car for $25. The car needed some mechanic work done to it, including a new piston. The mechanic who installed the new piston charged Alba $30 for parts and labor. Alba said, "I paid more for the piston than I did the car." Alba's father got the mail one day, and it included Alba's draft notice. His dad, knowing what was in the envelope, handed it to Alba and said, "Here you go."

John Alba

Branch Served:	Army
MOS:	Armor
Years Served:	1968-69
PHS graduation:	1966

John Alba's senior picture

John Alba was born in Porterville and raised in Woodville. He was the middle child of six children with three brothers and two sisters. His father was a farm labor contractor and his mother was a stay-at-home mom but also worked in the fields. His father served in WWII and was a POW for 28 months, captured in Africa. One of his brothers served in the Army, stationed in Germany and the other also served in Vietnam. Alba attended Woodville Elementary School before he went to Porterville High School. When he was in high school, he didn't have much time for partying and sports. Although he did a little drinking, most of his weekend hours were spent working with his dad. As he was getting closer to graduation and thinking about the Vietnam War, he thought to himself, "If I have to go, I'll go. If my dad went, I can go, too." When Alba's mom got the mail one day and found his draft notice in the mail, she knew what it was. She sadly looked at the letter and said, "The government got another one of my sons."

Vince Arcure

Branch Served:	Marine Corps
MOS:	Infantry
Years Served:	1966-68
PHS graduation:	1966

Vince Arcure's senior picture

Vince Arcure was born in Fresno California, raised in Porterville, and graduated from Porterville High School in 1966. He had a younger brother and their parents managed a wholesale business where they sold groceries to stores in the area. Prior to high school, he attended Bartlett Middle School where he said, "That's where I became a prick." When he was subjected to constant bullying from one of his fellow classmates at Bartlett, Arcure eventually learned that confronting the bully was a better way to deal with him than running away from him. When he finally confronted the bully, the bully quickly learned that Arcure was not the person to direct his attention to. Arcure was never bullied again. When he was in high school, he played football and wrestled, and one of his friends said he was a "tough son-of-a-bitch." As a good looking, well-built teenager, his attention while in high school was often directed to girls and partying and not homework. When he was in high school, the war was intensifying as he was getting closer to graduation, and he and his friends would sometimes talk about what they were going to do after high school. Enlist? Take your chances on the draft? Move to Canada? The latter, Arcure said "was out of the question." After he confronted the bully at Bartlett Middle School, Arcure would never run from a problem again.

Geary Baxter

Branch Served:	Army
MOS:	Helicopter pilot
Years Served:	1968-71
PHS graduation:	1965

Geary Baxter's senior picture

Geary Baxter was born in Visalia and moved with his family to Porterville when he was in the third grade. His father drove a delivery truck for a local bread business and his mother was a stay-at-home mom for most of her life. He is the oldest of three children, having two younger sisters. Baxter graduated from Bartlett Middle School prior to his attending Porterville High School. Since he was short with a small frame, Baxter called himself a "runt." And to emphasize his size, or lack of it, he said, "I couldn't go to a men's clothing store." Baxter remembers one time, however, when he felt tall. While on the bus ride to school, the bus driver wanted the girls to get off first. So the boys had to stand up and let the girls off. While the girls were filing out, Baxter was able to see the top of one girl's head that walked by him. Sure, she was short, too, but he appreciated knowing there was someone even shorter than him. After graduating from high school, Baxter attended Porterville College to get a deferment from the service, but he eventually withdrew. And at that point, the war was beginning to heat up and he knew he'd probably end up in Vietnam. He wanted to fly, so he enlisted in the Army and volunteered for flight school. The flying he did in Vietnam was some of the most terrifying and difficult assignments one could ever imagine.

Dan Boydstun

Branch Served:	Air Force
MOS:	Air Cargo Specialist
Years Served:	1969-72
PHS graduation:	1968

Dan Boydstun's senior picture

Dan Boydstun was born and raised in Porterville. He was the youngest of four boys, and said that as the youngest boy, he "got all the hand-me-downs." His father was a department store manager in Porterville and his mother was a stay-at-home mom, but later worked at a local packing house. He attended West Putnam Elementary School, and Bartlett Middle School prior to going to Porterville High School, where he graduated in 1968. When he was in high school, Boydstun didn't party that much since he had to work a lot after school. When he got home from school, he worked splitting wood and also in a grocery store. During his senior year in high school he began to worry about being drafted and going to Vietnam. The year 1968 was the deadliest year of the Vietnam War and he would be graduating from high school at the worse time of the war. At that time, the draft changed to the lottery draft, but Boydstun wanted to avoid the possibility of being drafted, so he enlisted in the Air Force on the buddy system with a friend. He would later learn that his draft number was a low one, and he would have been drafted anyway. Since he would have been drafted into the Marine Corps or the Army, he felt he made the right decision enlisting into the Air Force. Even though he enlisted in the Air Force, he still found himself in Vietnam.

Melvin Braziel

Branch Served:	Army
MOS:	Heavy Equipment Operator
Years Served:	1967-68
PHS graduation:	1967

Melvin Braziel's senior picture

Melvin Braziel was born in Texas, moved to Southern California when he was a few years old, and then raised in Terra Bella. His mom and dad were both workers at the State Hospital in Porterville where his dad was a mechanic and his mother was a nurse. He had an older brother, who was an Army veteran who served in Germany, and a sister, both now deceased. His sister had special needs, including epilepsy. When he was growing up, Melvin said he liked to watch people work. He would often ride his bike to where there were phone company people climbing telephone poles, or county workers operating their road graters building roads. He'd park his bike and just sit and watch. His hands and finger nails were often dirty, and his mother was used to dumping sand and Terra Bella adobe out of the cuffs of her son's blue jeans. When he was in high school, the war was on everyone's mind, including Melvin's, but it was still a subject he tried to avoid. He didn't want to think about the war, but rather thought more about the party they were planning for Friday night. As most guys in his class did, Melvin liked to party, and that consumed more of his attention than worrying about Vietnam. But that soon changed when his mom got the mail one day.

Ron Crabtree

Branch Served: Army
MOS: Infantry
Years Served: 1968-70
PHS graduation: 1966

Ron Crabtree's senior picture

Ron Crabtree was born in Arkansas and raised in Woodville. He came from a large family, being born in the middle of six brothers and three sisters. His father was an agricultural field worker and his mom worked in a packing house. Crabtree had one brother who retired from a career in the Air Force. After attending Woodville Elementary School, Crabtree graduated from Porterville High School in 1966. While in high school, he bowled a lot and partied a lot, usually running around with the older guys. When asked if he studied more or partied more when he was in high school he said, "Study? What's that?" After he graduated from high school, rather than going to college to get a deferment from the military, he worked in a few jobs around the area, and even in Los Angeles. Since the Vietnam War was now beginning to escalate, he knew that at some point he'd probably find himself in Vietnam. But even with that feeling, he said he could never dodge the draft by moving to Canada. Crabtree had an outgoing personality and a hearty laugh, which he still has today. He was drafted into the Army and eventually found himself chest-deep in water wading through the rice patties in Vietnam.

Don Dowling

Branch Served:	Army
MOS:	Demolition Supervisor – Special Forces
Years Served:	1965-88
PHS graduation:	Class of 1966 – high school diploma in 1988

A picture of Don Dowling at high school

Don Dowling was born in Colusa, California and raised in Porterville. He was the middle child of three children, with an older brother and younger sister. His father, who was a miner, served during WWII and was a POW in Germany for one year. While he was in the Army, Dowling's father was in the same unit as Audie Murphy, one of the most decorated soldiers during WWII who was awarded the Congressional Medal of Honor. Murphy later had a successful career as a movie actor. Dowling attended Doyle Colony Elementary School and was in the second graduating class of Pioneer Junior High School. After he graduated from Pioneer, Dowling said he "didn't feel good in high school." He described himself as a loner and was not involved in a lot of high school activities, although he did serve as the team manager for the basketball team. He did well in his automotive shop classes, but not very well in his other classes. So, when he was a junior at Porterville High School he enlisted in the Army. He became what he called a "professional soldier" serving in a variety of assignments and responsibilities during his 23-year career. During his time in Vietnam, he served in some of the most dangerous and challenging assignments imaginable.

Tony Forner

Branch Served:	Marine Corps
MOS:	Infantry
Years Served:	1966-69
PHS graduation:	1966

Tony Forner's senior picture

Tony Forner was born and raised in Porterville. He is the youngest of three children, with two older sisters. His father was a mechanic and his mother was a stay-at-home mom. His father served in the Army Air Corps during WWII as an airplane mechanic. His father-in-law was in the third wave of soldiers that landed on the beaches of Okinawa and his uncle was at Pearl Harbor on the day it was attacked by the Japanese on December 7, 1941. Forner graduated from St. Anne's Elementary School prior to attending Porterville High School. Forner's father didn't really believe in sports or after-school activities. But he did believe in work, and that's what Forner did on most days after school. When Forner came home from school, there were two things that his father expected his son to accomplish. And those two things were homework and work. Although he partied some with his friends, he said that "waking up at 4:00 in the morning with a hangover didn't work too well with having to work." So his partying was more limited than what his friends did. As he was getting closer to graduation from high school, he didn't worry about Vietnam that much. He knew he was going and knew he was going into the Marine Corps.

Roger Gibson

Branch Served:	Air Force
MOS:	Air Police – K-9
Years Served:	1967-71
PHS graduation:	1966

Roger Gibson's senior picture

Serving their country in the Air Force was almost a family affair for the Gibson family. Roger, the youngest of eight Gibson children, had six older brothers. Five of his older brothers served in the Air Force. He also had an older sister. His father owned and operated a car wash in Porterville while his mother worked as a seamstress. Gibson graduated from Porterville High School in 1966 and was also one of only three students in his entire high school graduating class that was African American. Only three out of almost 500 in his graduating class. While in high school he had three main priorities – sports, partying, academics. If he was to rank the order of his priorities, the first two priorities, sports and partying, were probably almost a tie, while the last priority, academics, would come in a very distant third. When he was a senior in high school, Porterville College head football coach, Sim Innes, recruited him to play at the college. Coach Inness was a world-wide known athlete in his own right. In the 1952 Summer Olympics in Helsinki, Finland, Inness won the gold medal in the discus throw. With that, being recruited to play for a well-known Olympic athlete was an honor. Gibson chose to attend Porterville College and play football. Gibson's goal to play at a four-year university was derailed when he received an injury during his first season. Since he could not play sports anymore, he decided to quit school, but quitting school meant that he no longer had a deferment from the service.

Greg Goble

Branch Served: Army
MOS: Military Police
Years Served: 1968-70
PHS graduation: 1967

Greg Goble's senior picture

Greg Goble was born in Torrance, California, lived in Redondo Beach, and moved to Porterville in the seventh grade. He attended Burton Elementary School and graduated from Porterville High School in 1967. He has one brother, stepbrother, and sister. His father was a heavy equipment engineer and his mother was a homemaker. For a few years, she also worked at the Grand View Heights packing house in Terra Bella. When Goble was growing up, he was known as the class clown. He did well enough academically but no more than he had to. He moved sprinkler pipes in the sugar beets with a friend each morning before and after school. Goble played baseball and football, but injuries in both of those sports shattered any hope of enjoying the high school sports experience. After he graduated from high school, Goble attended Porterville College. He sold his 1955 Chevy and purchased a 1966 Chevy Super Sport with a 396 under the hood. It was the love of his life. He spent most of his time working and having fun but missing too many classes eventually doomed his fate. He dropped out of Porterville College, ending any chance for a deferment from military service, thereby making him eligible for the draft. Goble was drafted into the Army in 1968. When he was drafted, he wasn't overly concerned about it. In fact, being drafted answered his confusion of not having any idea of what

15

direction to go regarding work, school, or the service. When he was drafted, he didn't think he'd end up in Vietnam, but he would learn later, however, that the place he didn't think he'd end up going, was exactly the place he was sent.

Louis Gurrola

Branch Served:	Army
MOS:	Supply
Years Served:	1969-71
PHS graduation:	1968

Louis Gurrola's senior picture

Louis Gurrola was born in El Paso, Texas and came to California with his family when he was eight years old. His family came from Tijuana, Mexico. He was the oldest of five children with three younger brothers and one younger sister. His parents were migrant farmworkers and Gurrola spent his early years working alongside his family in the fields. They worked in the orchards and fields of a variety of crops, picking, pruning, spraying or hoeing weeds, irrigation, or whatever was required to raise and care for the crops they were working on. Gurrola remembers even picking cotton by hand, before the landowners he worked for purchased mechanized cotton harvesters. It was a hard life and a dusty existence working in the fields under the blinding sun and scorching heat of California's Central Valley during the summer months. Gurrola went to Terra Bella and Rockford Elementary Schools and then graduated from Porterville High School in 1968. When he was in high school, he participated in sports, mainly basketball and some football, but he spent most of his after-school hours working in a variety of jobs around Porterville. He didn't have a lot of time to party, cruise Main Street, or hang out at Coleman's Drive-In. He was too busy working. Gurrola graduated from Porterville High School during the deadliest year of the war, 1968. He had seen it all on television and many of his classmates at high school were enlisting, being drafted, or coming back from the war. Although he didn't want to go, he soon found himself on a plane to Vietnam.

Felix Hernandez

Branch Served:	Army
MOS:	Armor
Years Served:	1968-70
PHS graduation:	1967

Felix Hernandez's senior picture

Felix Hernandez was born in Porterville and raised in Stockton. Hernandez had four sisters and two brothers. His younger brother is a veteran of the Marine Corps, who served stateside while on standby to Afghanistan. His family moved back to Porterville when he was a freshman in high school, and he graduated from Porterville High School in 1967. Hernandez's father was a truck driver and labor contractor and his mother was a stay-at-home mom. While at PHS, Hernandez played one year of football, but most of his after-school time was spent working. He said he did enough partying when he had time, but most of his time was either working with his father or working on his car. As he got closer to graduation from high school, Hernandez often spoke with his friends about enlisting, moving to Canada, being drafted, or working. To Hernandez, moving to Canada was out of the question, because he said, "I was a U.S. citizen, so I'll go where they send me." And they sent him to Vietnam. Hernandez was drafted the following year after he graduated from high school. He actually expected to get drafted, and when he got his draft notice in the mail he was not really surprised about it. In fact, Hernandez said he had a good feeling he'd be coming back, so he didn't worry that much about Vietnam. But he said, "I went to church with my mom, and I said a prayer for my family." He was concerned about his family almost more than he was concerned about himself.

Roland Hill

Branch Served: Army
MOS: Multi-engine Tandem Rotor Helicopter
                    Repairman
Years Served: 1968-71
PHS graduation: 1966

Roland Hill's senior picture

Roland Hill was born in Los Angeles and moved to Porterville with his family when he was four years old. His father was an attorney who was drafted in WWII during the latter part of war. Hill's father wanted to get his family out of the big city experience of Los Angeles, where there were irritating traffic jams, an unending maze of freeways and highways, and a sky full of smog. Hill's father had a sister who lived in Porterville, so one day he packed up his family and moved to Porterville. Roland was the oldest of four children, having two younger brothers and one younger sister. When he was growing up, Hill used to love hunting and fishing. He also preferred to play baseball with the neighborhood kids because, Hill said, "I would often get my butt kicked in football." In addition to his father serving during WWII, he also had uncles who served in Korea and pre-Vietnam. He attended St. Anne's Elementary School and then graduated from Porterville High School in 1966. While he was in high school, his grades were fine, but he was more concerned about cars, girls, cruising Main, and the party on Friday night. When Hill graduated from high school, he went to Porterville College and received a deferment from the military. He would later learn, however, that one of his classes at Porterville College ended up becoming his ticket to Vietnam.

Barry Jackson

Branch Served: Army
MOS: Transportation (unconfirmed)
Years Served: 1967-68
PHS graduation: 1964

Barry Jackson's senior picture

Barry Jackson was born in Portland, Oregon, and when he was about three years old his family moved to Terra Bella, a small farming community five miles south of Porterville. He was the second child of five children, with one older sister, two younger sisters, and one younger brother. Jackson's father was the town doctor in Terra Bella at the time when doctors still made house calls and they knew everyone in town by their first name. Dr. Jackson was also a physician in the Air Force during

19

WWII. Jackson went to Terra Bella Elementary School and graduated from Porterville High School in 1964. While he was in high school, Jackson played defensive back on the school's football team. He was a handsome young man. After he graduated from high school, Jackson attended the University of the Pacific, Chico State University, and University of California, Berkley. He studied to be a marine biologist, and certainly had the intelligence and academic abilities to be a good one. His plans were interrupted when he was drafted in the Army.

Robert Johnson

Branch Served:	Army
MOS:	Light Weapons Infantry
Years Served:	1966-69
PHS graduation:	1966

Robert Johnson's senior picture

Robert Johnson was born in Glendale, California and moved to Porterville in 1962. He had one brother, two stepsisters, and one stepbrother. His parents were farmers, so Johnson was used to hard work and long hours when he was young. His father, stepfather, and stepuncles were WWII veterans, so Johnson came from a military-conscious family. He attended elementary school in Glendale and then graduated from Porterville High School in 1966. While in high school he was much like the other guys in his class. He spent more time playing baseball, chasing girls and drinking beer than he did studying. During his early years in high school, he didn't think much about his future, or, specifically, about the war in Vietnam.

However, as he got closer to graduation he began to think more about Vietnam. In fact, he thought about it a lot. When the time came, Johnson enlisted into the Army. And he didn't request an easy assignment or a job at the back of the line. Johnson volunteered for the infantry. In addition, he volunteered to be an airborne paratrooper. If he was going into a war, he thought, he wanted to go in all the way. He eventually got what he wanted, a close-up and personal view of the war.

Ron McCarville

Branch Served:	Marine Corps
MOS:	Infantry
Years Served:	1966-68
PHS graduation:	1966

Ron McCarville's senior picture

Ron McCarville was a military brat whose father was a career pilot in the Marine Corps. McCarville was born at Camp Pendleton and spent his early years living on various bases in Florida, North Carolina, and Southern California. Since his family traveled around a lot while he was growing up, McCarville described himself as a loner, often preferring to do things by himself. He never got particularly close to any of his younger friends since he would often move to another base when his dad got new orders. McCarville had one younger brother, in addition to three other brothers who died at birth. McCarville attributes their early death to the stress his mother experienced as the wife of a husband who was a pilot in the Marine Corps. On December 1, 1954, McCarville's father was killed while flying his Fury plane solo over Japan. No one ever explained to the McCarville family the details of the mission in which he was killed, or what happened that resulted in the plane crash. McCarville may not have known about the circumstances surrounding the accident, but he did know that he wanted to be a Marine, just like his father.

Chuck Migalski

Branch Served: Navy
MOS: Engineman
Years Served: 1966-70
PHS graduation: 1966

Chuck Migalski's senior picture

Chuck Migalski was born in Illinois and moved to Porterville in 1955. He was the youngest of three children, with an older brother and sister. Both of his siblings have passed away. His brother was a Korean War veteran, serving in the Navy on a minesweeper. Migalski's mom was a maid in a local hotel, and he never knew his father. He attended Belleview and Bartlett Elementary Schools and graduate from Porterville High School in 1966. Migalski was an avid outdoorsman, spending many days backpacking in the mountains, or hunting and fishing. When he was a freshman and sophomore in high school, he was like most his age who played sports. However, the following year he found something to take the place of sports. About mid-way through his junior year, Migalski gave up sports to smoke cigarettes, drink beer, and party. He soon found that he got more enjoyment out of lighting up a Marlboro or chugging down a Coors than he did strapping on the pads and hitting football practice dummies. He became what he called a "typical red neck." Sports became a distant memory as he entered his senior year at Porterville High School. During his senior year, he began to think and worry more about Vietnam. A couple of his friends from high school had been killed in Vietnam and news of the war was constantly on television or on the front pages of the paper. In order to hopefully avoid serving in Vietnam, he joined the Navy after graduating from high school. Later, the threat of being court-martialed landed him in the middle of the war.

Todd Pixler

Branch Served: Army
MOS: Transportation
Years Served: 1968-70
PHS graduation: 1966

Todd Pixler's senior picture

Todd Pixler was born in Ft. Dodge, Iowa and moved with his younger brother, mother and father to California when he was eight years old. The main reason his father wanted to move to California was the weather in Iowa. In fact, the snow. His father was an accomplished golfer, and, obviously, it's rather difficult to play golf in the snow. He wanted to play consistently, to practice daily, and to perfect his skill. But it's hard to do that when there's three feet of snow on the ground during unsettling weather. So, he packed up the family and moved to California. His father was hired as the golf pro at the Porterville Municipal Golf Course. His mom was a real estate agent in the Porterville area. Pixler attended Olive Street Elementary School and graduated from Porterville High School in 1966. His life in high school centered around drag racing and athletics. When he was in high school, he really did not think much of Vietnam. He was more focused on attending a university after high school, running track, and using his running ability to get a deferment and guarantee that Vietnam would not be in his future. That worked, for a while at least. After attending several colleges to run track or play football, Pixler eventually dropped out of school before graduating. Vietnam began to creep into his thoughts because once he was out of school, he no longer had a deferment from the military service. Pixler may have been one of the few young men in those days to involuntarily "volunteer for the draft." Because it was his honesty with the draft board that landed him in Vietnam.

Brian Rattigan

Branch Served:	Army
MOS:	Airborne Infantry Paratrooper – 11B4P
Years Served:	1966-69
PHS graduation:	1966

Brian Rattigan's senior picture

Brian Rattigan was born in Detroit, Michigan and lived there until he was six years old. In 1954, his family moved to Porterville. He attended St. Anne's Elementary School and graduated from Porterville High School in 1966. He has one older sister, and his dad was a Certified Public Accountant (CPA) who worked in various areas in the accounting field. Rattigan's mother was an English teacher at Porterville High School. This situation was extremely disconcerting to Rattigan during his high school years. When he was in high school, Rattigan would sometimes climb the city water tower at night and then sit on the tower smoking Wolf Brothers

Old Stogies – "The Cigar That Won the West" - while contemplating life from his elevated perch. Rattigan loved hunting, being around firearms and anything related to the sport. He enlisted in the Army out of curiosity and a general sense of duty. Being in high school during the war, and reading about it or watching it on television, Rattigan felt that he knew what he was getting into. So, when high school was over with, he was ready to go. He looked at the military and the possibility of being in a war much like an experience or adventure. He certainly had an adventure jumping out of airplanes and subsequently being sent to Vietnam.

Jim Rouch

Branch Served:	Navy - Seabees
MOS:	Heavy Equipment Operator
Years Served:	1966-69
PHS graduation:	1964

Jim Rouch's senior picture

Jim Rouch and his brother and sister were born in Porterville. With the exception of a couple of years living in Reno, Rouch was raised in Porterville. His father worked in the forest service and lumber industry while his mother was a homemaker. Rouch went to Doyle Colony Elementary School and Bartlett Middle School and then graduated from Porterville High School in 1964. Since the involvement of the United States in Vietnam was predominately in an advisory capacity at that time, and not yet in combat, Vietnam was not really on the minds of Rouch and his friends at high school. He considered himself an "average partier." Sure, he liked to party and have a good time, but partying didn't consume his after-school activities like it did for so many others. He played in the high school band and was active in water polo and swimming. After he graduated from high school, Rouch attended Porterville College, but dropped out after one year. Since he was no longer enrolled at the college, he no longer had a deferment from the military. And then the war in Vietnam started to escalate. When the government sent him a letter ordering him to appear for a physical for possible entrance into the military draft, he knew then he needed to enlist because he didn't want to go into the Army or the Marine Corps. His first preference was the Air Force, but since he had a few traffic citations, the Air Force did not accept him. He eventually enlisted in the Navy and was part of the Seabees as a heavy equipment operator. This assignment, however, did not keep him from Vietnam. In fact, he later found himself in one of the bloodiest and costliest battles during the Vietnam War.

John Schultz

Branch Served:	Navy
MOS:	Shipfitter
Years Served:	1966-70
PHS graduation:	1966

John Schultz's senior picture

John Schultz was born and raised in Terra Bella and was the oldest of four boys. His father was a farmer and his mother a homemaker. Schultz was a rather rambunctious and active child, growing up to be known for some mischievous activities. When he was in high school, Schultz was involved in some sports, such as track and football, but mainly spent his years focusing on girls, partying, and how to ditch school without being caught. He attended Zion Lutheran Elementary School, and then graduated from Porterville High School in 1966. Worrying about the possibility of going to Vietnam, Schultz enlisted in the Navy. Although he never found himself in combat on the ground of Vietnam, his destroyer, the USS Nicholas, was involved in providing artillery support in the Mekong Delta region. The Nicholas would be anchored about 200 yards off the coast and fire in artillery rounds to support the troops on the ground. One day, while he was in the middle of the Pacific Ocean in a torrential storm, he received word that his father had died. And Schultz was almost killed when they were trying to pick him up during the storm to send him home to his father's funeral.

Joe Souza

Branch Served:	Army
MOS:	Communications advisor first tour, helicopter pilot second tour
Years Served:	1960-64, 1967-71
PHS graduation:	1960

Joe Souza's senior picture

Joe Souza was born and raised on a farm on the west side of Porterville, near the small town of Poplar. Back in the 60s, Poplar was known to be one of the roughest towns around. So rough, that the Tulare County Sheriff Department deputies knew almost everyone in town on a first-name basis. Souza was born in the middle of his five siblings, having one brother and four sisters. His family were farmers, raising cattle and growing alfalfa on the west side of Porterville near the towns of Poplar and Woodville. Souza's family was of Portuguese descent, and, not meaning

27

to sound stereotypical, but my elderly aunt once said that you could tell a Portuguese by his hands - rough, thick, and strong. Souza's hands certainly fit that description. Souza attended Woodville and Pleasant View Elementary Schools and then graduated from Porterville High School in 1960. His two favorite subjects in high school were football and partying and he did both of those very well. When he was in high school, the United States was not yet involved in a combat war in Vietnam. At that time, our involvement there was basically to provide military and logistical assistance to South Vietnam in an advisory capacity. So, Souza's worry was not about our increasing involvement in a country thousands of miles away from home. He served two tours of duty in Vietnam, the first as an advisor, the second as a helicopter pilot. It was during his second tour where he almost lost his life.

Russell Vossler

Branch Served:	Army
MOS:	Helicopter Maintenance
Years Served:	1967-71
PHS graduation:	1967

Russell Vossler's senior picture

Russell Vossler was born and raised in Woodville, a small farming community a couple of miles west of Porterville. He was the second of five children. His dad was drafted into the Navy during WWII, and then after the war spent his life farming in the Woodville area. Early to rise, long hard hours of manual labor in dusty fields, and early to bed. And the next day was the same, because crops took no vacations or had weekends off. That was a routine that the Vossler family was accustomed to, and one that Vossler found to be similar in Vietnam. He attended Woodville and St. Anne's Elementary Schools and graduated from Porterville High School in 1967. When he was in high school, Vossler was rather shy until he found beer, and his social life immediately improved. During his senior year in high school, one of his older friends was killed in Vietnam. And the death of this friend had a heavy impact on him. In fact, during his last term in high school, four former Porterville High School graduates were killed in Vietnam. He said it felt like they were "dropping like flies." He wanted to do something to make up for his high school friend who had died in Vietnam, so he enlisted. He felt it was his duty to go where his country sent him. And his country eventually sent him to Vietnam.

Richard Walker

Branch Served:	Navy
MOS:	Engineman
Years Served:	1966-70
PHS graduation:	1966

Richard Walker's senior picture

Richard Walker was born and raised in Terra Bella, along with his two older sisters. His father worked with the county road department while his mother worked with a local lumber company. He attended Terra Bella Elementary School, and then graduated from Porterville High School in 1966. When he was in high school, Walker was not particularly interested in sports. Not only was he not big enough, his heart just wasn't into sports. There was something else on his mind that he was more interested in. He wanted a car. So, after working part-time at a supermarket in Porterville, he saved up enough money to buy his own car. A 1952 Chevy. And the price for this wonderful set of wheels? Two hundred dollars. Sure, it might not have been the fanciest or the fastest car in town, but it was his. During his junior year in high school, Walker realized that he wasn't really interested in attending college after graduation. Since the war in Vietnam was beginning to heat up, he knew he'd eventually get drafted. If he got drafted, he'd probably go to Vietnam. So, to avoid going to Vietnam he enlisted in the Navy while he was still in high school. About a month after walking the steps to receive his high school diploma during the Porterville High School commencement ceremony, he was walking onto the base at San Diego for boot camp in the Navy. His plan to miss Vietnam by enlisting in the Navy didn't work either. He was eventually sent to Vietnam and found himself in the middle of the war.

Don Wolfram

Branch Served:	Navy - Seabees
MOS:	Builder
Years Served:	1967-70
PHS graduation:	1965

Don Wolfram's senior picture

Don Wolfram was born in Oceanside, California and raised in Terra Bella. He is the oldest of four children, having two younger brothers and a younger sister. He attended Zion Lutheran Elementary School in Terra Bella and graduated from Porterville High School in 1965. Wolfram's father was a WWII and Korean War veteran and worked as a farmer and with a local agricultural chemical business. His mother worked at Good Shepherd Lutheran Home, which was a residential facility in Terra Bella for mentally handicapped individuals, as well as working at an assembly plant in Porterville. Wolfram describes himself as quiet and somewhat of an introvert, who was involved with his church youth group when growing up. After graduating from high school, Wolfram worked on a farm and attended Porterville College. When he dropped out of college, his classification changed, and he was now eligible to be drafted. Since the Vietnam War was beginning to find itself on the front pages of the paper, Wolfram started thinking about enlisting so that he would avoid being drafted into the Army or Marine Corps. Wolfram enlisted in the Navy and went into the service on the buddy system with a friend. The only request Wolfram had when he enlisted was that he start boot camp after September 1st, which was the opening day of dove season. Little did he know at the time that his decision to join the Navy wouldn't help him avoid Vietnam.

Okay, you've met these men. At first glance, they seem like every other high school student during the 1960s. Well, they might have started out that way, but their lives took incredible turns because of the war in Vietnam.

When faced with the fear of war, these young men from Porterville High School answered their country's call, either through enlistment or through the draft. They took with them to Vietnam the values of small-town America that they learned from their lives in the rural Porterville community. Family, faith, and country were the guiding principles that had, up to this point, shaped their young lives. And these principles helped to transform these young high school students into dedicated and brave soldiers, Marines, sailors, and airmen.

The stories they shared touched on the range of emotions. Some stories are comical, some are sad, and some are of things you never knew before. But all of them are real, and most of them are unique. Certainly, not every story of every veteran could be printed in this book. I wish I could have, but to print them all, would take volumes.

And for some, this was the first time they ever had shared their stories with anyone.

When listening to their stories and hearing about the intense fear, stress, and utter terror many of these guys were faced with, I came to the following conclusion about these veterans from Porterville High School.

These guys were studs.

Before you read their stories, I would like to provide a couple of disclaimer statements.

In order to ensure and protect the privacy of individuals the veterans referenced or spoke about during our interviews, I may have changed or eliminated some names and identifying details about a person; however, the story did not change. In addition, this book contains words, language, or descriptions used by the veterans that may be considered offensive to some. With that, reader discretion is advised.

Now read their stories.

Vietnam War and Wall Facts

Total American Deaths in Vietnam [1]

Hostile Death	47,434
Non-Hostile Death	10,786
Total Deaths	58,220

Branch of Service

Army	38,224
Marine Corps	14,844
Air Force	2,586
Navy	2,559
Coast Guard	7

Year of Death – 1956-1975

1956-1959	4
1960	5
1961	16
1962	53
1963	122
1964	216
1965	1,928
1966	6,350
1967	11,363
1968	16,899
1969	11,780
1970	6,173
1971	2,414
1972	759
1973	68
1974	1
1975	62

2

Coming of Age in the 1960s

*"As for deserters, malcontents, radicals, incendiaries, the civil
and uncivil disobedients among the young...Yippies, Hippies,
Yahoos, Black Panthers, Lions, and Tigers alike, I would swap
the whole damn zoo for a single platoon of the kind of young
Americans I saw in Vietnam."*

Former Vice President, Spiro Agnew

THE PORTERVILLE HIGH School graduates who were interviewed
for this book came of age during the 1960s. During that decade,
they went from being pre-teenagers to adults. They went from riding
Schwinn bicycles to driving Ford Mustangs. They went from drinking
soft drinks to guzzling beer. They went from living in peace to serving
in a war.

The cover of LIFE's April 2019 "A Reissue of LIFE's Classic
Edition" magazine called the 1960s, "The Decade When Everything
Changed." And that is an appropriate and accurate description of that
incredible decade. Certainly, the lives of these Vietnam veterans from
Porterville High School changed during the 1960s. Their families
changed, their communities changed, their country and their world
changed. These young men lived and fought in a war during one of

the most tumultuous times in our country's history, with events that almost ripped the fabric of our country apart at the seams.

When most think of the 1960s they remember Woodstock, Charles Manson, hippies, women's liberation, the Kent State killings, forced school integration, racial tension, and television programs like *The Ed Sullivan Show* and *The Andy Griffith Show*. They remember the Beatles, the moon landing, and the assassinations of President Kennedy and his brother, Senator Robert Kennedy, and Martin Luther King, Jr. With many of these cultural and political events consuming the evening news and headlines in the paper, the focus of most people's attention in the early and mid-60s was often on something else far removed from the war in Vietnam. But that soon changed.

As the war progressed into the late 60s, public dissent grew as did violence and turmoil in our society. The politicians in Washington D. C. were asking for increasing dollars to fund a war that had no end in sight. And as more and more people watched the Vietnam War on television, the support for the war began to wane as concerns and discontent about the war increased.

One group of people who watched their televisions and read the local paper with concern were not only the young men from Porterville High School who would soon be placed in that war, but also their families. "The war was on television every night," Reba Wolfram, mother of a Vietnam veteran said, "and I was worried about my boys. Every night I saw the news and it scared me. So I prayed and prayed."

How can the mother and father of a Porterville High School student in the 1960s not be concerned when they would watch the war on television every night and listen to Walter Cronkite announce the number of men who died in combat that week? And it wasn't just one killed, or 10 or 20 killed that week, but hundreds. This is certainly not the kind of news a young man and his family wants to hear as he is nearing graduation from high school.

Back in the 60s, these young men from Porterville High School had other things on their minds than to worry about a war. They were more concerned with how to cover up a hickey so their parents, or another girlfriend, wouldn't notice. Or deciding on which liquor store they could buy a six pack of beer from to drink after the football game on Friday night. Many of their experiences up to this point in their young lives were centered on "cruising Main," starting at Coleman's Drive-In, going east on Olive Street, left on Main Street, around Gang Sue's Restaurant and then racing back to Coleman's to have a cherry Coke with French fries. And if they got lucky, taking in a movie at the Porter Theater that they did not watch because they were too busy making out with a girl in the back row while dodging the flashlight from the theater attendant. This was their simple life. But that life was about to change.

During the time in which these men served in the military, the people across the country were becoming more open about their perceptions of the war, and attitudes of the war became increasingly more negative. The mood began to shift from unease about the war, to organized anti-war protests with hundreds of thousands of protesters participating on campuses and in cities across the nation. In addition, there began a slow, yet profoundly significant and disturbing shift within the war's growing protest movement itself – a shift from protesting the war, to blaming those who fought in it.

In many ways, the GIs from the Porterville community were more fortunate than those who lived in other communities. In the 1960s, Porterville generally welcomed their returning combat veterans home with open arms and grateful hearts. Sure, not everyone in Porterville was supportive of the war, but most who disagreed with our involvement in Vietnam did not generally transfer that disagreement to those who fought there like was found in other communities. However, as you will read from some of the veterans later in this book, the city of Porterville was not immune from mistreating their returning Vietnam veterans. But for the most part, the hostility of the war remained where it should have been – on the shoulders of the political and military leaders who made the decisions the troops were obligated to follow.

While students at Porterville High School, these young men

certainly had the intellectual capacity to be scholar students, but I don't believe any of these guys, their parents, or their teachers were seriously counting on them to bring home the Nobel Prize for literature, physics, or chemistry. If the administrators at Porterville High School in the 60s were hoping these young students would fill their campus trophy case with ribbons, trophies, or plaques awarded to them for their academic prowess, they were sorely disappointed. These guys were having too much fun to concern themselves with scholastic awards.

Although they may not have been able to safely light a Bunsen burner, define an isosceles triangle, or measure angles using a protractor, they could tap a beer keg at 20 paces. If there were beer guzzling contests in the Olympics back then, these guys would have won the gold medal. As they shared in almost universal fashion during the interviews, while they were in high school, anything related to academics, studying, doing homework, or even going to class, were not high on their list of priorities. As Ron Crabtree said when asked about studying back in high school, "Study? What was that?"

When their name would not show up on the attendance list for the day, all the truant officer had to do to find them was to look in the parking lot of Coleman's Drive-In across the street from the high school or take a drive down Main Street where they'd be cruising.

If these guys were to rank their priorities in life when they were students at Porterville High School, partying would be number one, girls would be number two, and there was no number three. As Melvin Braziel said, "High school in Porterville in the 60s was a lot like the movie *American Graffiti.*" He said, "We partied, smoked cigarettes, chased girls, and raced our cars on dirt roads behind the orange groves." Their life was fun, carefree, and without a worry.

Although drugs were beginning to make their way into the local culture, most of the guys back then drank beer. Some smoked marijuana, but hard drugs were not as prevalent as they became later on high school campuses. Gangs were basically non-existent in Porterville, at least like they are in towns and cities nowadays. If a cop pulled one of these guys over for speeding or reckless driving, he would have found in the car empty beer cans, packs of Marlboro cigarettes, and a bottle of Old Spice after-shave cologne. And maybe in the pockets of a few of them, he would have found unopened packs of Trojan condoms. These guys played hard and partied hard, but they were basically harmless.

Russell Vossler said "When I was younger, I was rather shy. But when I got into high school, I discovered beer, and my shyness went away!" His social life became wrapped around a beer can, and this self-described shy young man from Woodville eventually came out of his shell thanks to a family from Colorado named Coors.

Ditching was their pastime, truancy was their art, and drinking was their specialty. Going to class, studying, and doing homework were not real interests of theirs, but, somehow, they earned enough points to graduate. Some of their antics during their high school years were creative, some were amusing, and some were, well, illegal.

John Schultz

There was one student who was concerned enough about not getting in trouble that he did something unusual to make sure he didn't. However, what he did not only got him in trouble, but also got him suspended from high school. No, it wasn't cheating. It was something far more graphic.

Each student in a physical education class at Porterville High School had a certain assigned number. And the numbers were painted on the asphalt. The bell would go off to alert students that they needed to be standing on their number, and then the instructor would walk down the line taking roll and making sure everyone was wearing their required class attire: t-shirt, gym shorts, socks, and tennis shoes.

When the bell rang one day, John Schultz was in the locker room, far away from his number on the asphalt, still getting dressed.

Realizing that he would be considered ditching if he was not on his number when the teacher walked by, he stormed out of the locker room sprinting to get to his number in time before the teacher got there.

He raced passed curious students and around those who were already standing on their numbers waiting for the inspection of their teacher. The students watched in awe and with their mouths open and jaws dropped as Schultz sped by to get to his number. After running to his place in the line, Schultz was relieved to find that his teacher had not yet made it to his number. But when the teacher did, he got the shock of his life.

Schultz was not wearing the required attire for the physical education class. In fact, he wasn't wearing anything at all. Schultz was naked.

When the bell rang, Schultz had a choice to make. "What's worse?," he thought, "Do I get in trouble for ditching for not being on my number, or do I get in trouble for not being dressed as required?" When the teacher got to Schultz as he was standing on his number in his birthday suit, the teacher laughed and asked sarcastically, "Schultz, what in the world are you doing?" Well, the teacher found some humor in what Schultz did, but the administrators didn't.

Schultz was suspended.

Even though there was some distance between where Schultz was standing naked and the administration office, the administrators felt that the female assistants in the office could have seen this naked student and been offended by it. Rumor has it, however, they did see Schultz. In fact, rumor also has it that after that incident Schultz was often asked by the secretaries in the administrative office to serve as their work-study intern. Apparently, they weren't offended at all.

Schultz was the first, and possibly only, streaker in Porterville High School history. Although there was no official diagnosis conducted by a school psychologist, a campus administrator called Schultz's mom to inform her about the incident and to let her know that he felt her son had some psychological issues he may need to deal with.

Schultz may have gotten suspended, but he won the hearts and admiration of the female staff in the administration office and became a legend in his own right.

Brian Rattigan

Not only was Brian Rattigan somewhat mischievous at times, he was also very creative in carrying out his mischief deeds.

On Tuesday, November 3, 1964, the presidential election was held between President Lyndon Johnson and Senator Barry Goldwater. Leading up to the election, Rattigan and a couple of his friends would occasionally visit the Goldwater campaign headquarters on Main Street in Porterville. Since he frequented the headquarters periodically, one of the men in the headquarters assumed Rattigan was a Goldwater supporter. Rattigan said, "He gave us a large, full-color head shot poster of Goldwater that measured about five to six feet high." However, as Rattigan admitted, unbeknownst to the man who gave him the Goldwater poster, "We were staunch LBJ supporters."

Since he now had a large poster of the candidate he was not supporting, Rattigan and his buddies got an idea and then put their creative idea into motion.

"For several weeks prior to the presidential election," as Rattigan explained, "three of us planned to alter the large Goldwater poster into a likeness of Adolph Hitler and paste the poster atop the city tower on Halloween night." This was the same tower that Rattigan climbed up occasionally during the night to contemplate life while smoking cigars. He further explained, "We purchased black crepe paper and modified the Goldwater poster with a Hitler-like hair piece and his trademark Charlie Chaplin-style mustache." Once that was done, the plan was set in motion on Halloween night.

With the doctored poster in hand, Rattigan and his friends drove to the water tower, parked their car, and began their climb up the ladder under the cloak of darkness. Well, there was a cloak of darkness for a little while, but then that darkness ended.

"Several guys on the front porch of a house north of the water tower began flashing around the darkness with a powerful flashlight," Rattigan explained. "We were about half way up when the beam zeroed in on us." They were almost like a jack rabbit caught in the beams of a car's headlights. And what happens when rabbits are hit with a light like that? They freeze. And what did Rattigan and his friends do? "We froze," Rattigan said. He further explained, "The scene was eerily reminiscent of prison escape movies where prisoners are stealthily attempting to avoid being spotted by the guard tower search lights."

Not totally sure what to do, the trio decided to keep going up the ladder. After all, it was Halloween night and the election was only a few days away. They made it to the top, attached the poster to the water tower, climbed back down the ladder, and made their getaway without incident. But when they looked back up to see the Goldwater poster on the water tower, they noticed something completely different. It didn't look like a Goldwater face at all. Rather, Rattigan said, "From the ground it looked like a large picture of Adolph Hitler."

Rattigan beamed with pride when he said that the local newspaper, the *Porterville Recorder*, highlighted noteworthy Halloween shenanigans on its front page that year, and the trio's Hitler-atop-the-city water tower operation was chosen as the "Caper of the Evening." Rattigan said, "The article recounted that police received a report that a large picture of Adolph Hitler was visible atop the city water tower. Police climbed the water tower to remove the Adolph Hitler picture." But then once the police got to the top of the tower, Rattigan said, "They were surprised to discover it was not Hitler, but rather a color picture of Barry Goldwater, adorned with a large black mustache."

Well, LBJ went on to win the election a few days later, and maybe Rattigan and his buddies had some influence in the local results.

Uncle Bill and Mexican Joe

Okay, Uncle Bill and Mexican Joe are not two of the veterans who were interviewed for this book. "So why put them in this section of the book?" you may ask. Well, these two guys became close friends with a few of these high school students and deserve to be recognized. Without their assistance, some of the Porterville High School students may not have enjoyed their weekends as much without them.

Since Brian Rattigan nor any of his friends were twenty-one when they were in high school, they couldn't buy beer, legally at least. Sometimes, they could find a clerk at a mini-mart who would sell them beer, but they couldn't always count on finding a clerk willing to take that risk. But they soon found an answer to their weekend booze-buying dilemma.

Hobos.

As Rattigan explained, "We learned by word-of-mouth that hobos encamped on the Tule River would buy beer in exchange for money to buy Tokay wine." Where and how the hobos lived back then was typical of the homeless shelters you'd find along the Tule River today. Enclosures built with boards, sticks, or pieces of broken furniture, with maybe a tarp to protect them from the elements and a dog to protect them from other hobos. But not much else.

Two of their favorite hobo contacts were guys nicknamed Uncle Bill and Mexican Joe. Uncle Bill was the older of the two hobos, probably around fifty to sixty years old. As Rattigan explained. "He looked much older and was very frail and had very few visible teeth." Since he was at least a decade or so younger and in much better shape, Mexican Joe helped take care of Uncle Bill as best he could.

Rattigan explained, "We would drive down to Tony's Liquor store on South Main at Orange Street and either Uncle Bill or Mexican Joe would buy us Coors beer. He'd then buy cheap, fortified Tokay wine and cigarettes for himself and others at the campsite." Rattigan said they would sometimes buy the hobos hamburgers and sandwiches that they shared at the hobo campsite. Also, rather than dropping the hobos off at their campsite after buying the beer and cigarettes and then leaving, Rattigan and his friends would sometimes stay and chat around the campfire with Uncle Bill, Mexican Joe, and any other hobos who were there that evening.

These Porterville High School students became friends with Uncle Bill and Mexican Joe. They shared beer, food, and stories. The hobos helped these high school students enjoy a pastime that they, without the hobos' help, may not have been able to enjoy. But then the relationship came to a tragic end.

Rattigan explained, "Sometime in the late 60s, three or four thugs viciously and senselessly attacked, without any provocation, Uncle Bill and Mexican Joe in their encampment. Both men were hospitalized with severe injuries." But the tragedy doesn't end there. "Several days later," Rattigan said, "Mexican Joe died as a result of the beating."

Not only did these high school students lose a friend, but so did Uncle Bill. I hope that Uncle Bill eventually found someone like Mexican Joe who could be his friend and help take care of him.

Anonymous

Shortly after I entered high school in 1968, I heard a story that some of the "older boys" at Porterville High School did a couple of years earlier. When I asked some of the veterans I interviewed for the book if they were the culprits of this story, none of them admitted to it. Maybe because the story was too graphic or maybe they thought they committed some crime and the statute of limitations has not yet run out. Regardless, after getting to know each of these veterans during our interviews, this stunt seems like something one of these guys would have done.

The story goes like this.

During an agriculture class one day, the class took a field trip to a local ranch. On the ranch were various species of animals including horses, cattle, and sheep. The topic of discussion that day was the subject of animal castration. In other words, how to cut off animal testicles. The teachers were demonstrating to the class how to castrate sheep. It was a rather graphic demonstration which left most in the class queasy, except for one rather devious student. For some reason, this one student saw the byproducts of the demonstration, i.e. the sheep testicles, to be something he could use in a prank later. So, unbeknownst to the teacher and most of his friends in class, the student gathered up some of the sheep testicles and put them in his pants pocket.

Later that night, there was a boys' basketball game in the school gymnasium. The gymnasium included a snack bar with the usual candies, soft drinks, hot dogs, and hamburgers. But the target of this one student's prank was the popcorn machine. As the popcorn was popping in the machine, with butter slowly dripping over the ingredients creating a wonderful taste and sweet smell, the student reached into his pocket. He looked around to make sure no one was looking and took aim.

He tossed the sheep testicles into the popcorn machine.

I heard he got caught, and no attendees at the basketball game ate any of the toasted nuts. Again, none of these veterans admitted to it. But true story or not, it certainly seems like a prank that would have been conjured up by one of them.

These guys loved to party, and party they did. As previously described, if you watch the movie *American Graffiti* you will get a taste of what life was like in Porterville during the 1960s. But while these older boys were enjoying drinking booze, chasing women, and cruising Main Street, the threat of war was looming in the back of their minds.

They were a close-knit group of guys back in high school and many of them have remained friends even until today. Regardless if they admitted it or not, Vietnam was on their minds as they approached graduation. How could it not be? It was on television every night and on the front page of the *Porterville Recorder* every day.

Some of these high school students were ready to go into the service, some were apprehensive, and others were scared. And sharing in these feelings, especially the latter two, were their parents. Maybe partying was a way for some of them to mask or bury the fear of worrying about fighting in a war.

Male high school students back in the 60s often did not have the luxury of being solely responsible for making the decision to enlist or not, like those in today's all-volunteer military have. Normally, if these high school students in the 60s did not make the decision themselves, the government made it for them through the draft. Although some delayed their duty in the military by going to college, most were either drafted or decided to enlist right out of high school. Some of their classmates even moved to Canada.

At such a young age, these Porterville High School students had some major life decisions to make. And there was one common word that affected most of those decisions.

And that word was Vietnam.

Vietnam War and Wall Facts

The Most Casualties [1]

The most casualties for a single day was on January 31, 1968:
245

The most casualties for a single week was February 11-17, 1968:
543

The most casualties for a single month was May 1968:
2,415

The most casualties for a single year was 1968:
16,899

1968 was the most brutal and costly year of the Vietnam War.

3

Making the Choice: Enlist, Draft, College, or Canada

"We will not tire, we will not falter, we will not fail."

George W. Bush

GREETINGS.

According to the Merriam-Webster dictionary, the word "greetings" is defined as an "expression of good wishes or a salutation at meeting." At first glance, the word seems peaceful, welcoming, and somewhat gentle. But not to the boys from Porterville High School in the 1960s.

For these young men, the word "greetings" was a word many of them feared to read. Not just in Porterville, but in every city and state across the country. It was a word that made them lose sleep at night. It was a word that would impact their lives like no other word could. It was a word that could mean the difference between life or death.

Why? Because that polite word of goodwill was followed by fourteen words that when taken collectively together would mean they would soon be leaving their peaceful lives in Porterville and be shipped out to a place of unknown origins, spending the next two years in a life of uncertainty.

Here is the word, followed by the other fourteen.

"Greetings. You are hereby ordered for induction in the Armed Forces of the United States."

In other words, you've been drafted. A polite word of welcome followed by an order or command. A gentle and peaceful greeting and then only four short words later, a command and an order to follow. You were going into the military regardless if you wanted to or not.

For teenage boys in the mid to late 1960s, there was probably no other letter or form of communication that induced as much fear, apprehension, worry, or anxiety, than the draft notice did. This was a letter that no one wanted to receive. This was a letter that brought the war directly into the homes of families across our country. This was a letter that would forever change the life of the person it was addressed to and his family.

Remember, these guys were teenagers. They had spent the last few years of high school watching the war on television. They had been listening to the stories from their high school friends who were returning from the war. They saw their injuries. They were attending the funerals of their friends who had been killed there. So, if they decided to move to Canada to avoid that, could you really blame them, especially when the decision would have been supported by their parents?

They may not have left, but many of them thought about it.

A few of the Vietnam veterans interviewed for this book gave at least some consideration to going to Canada to avoid military service. Some even had very attractive offers and the solid support of their parents. But none of them took those offers. They all stayed home and did their duty.

Roland Hill

When he was nearing graduation from Porterville High School, Vietnam was on Roland Hill's mind, and he didn't want to go there. So, to avoid the military and the probability of going to Vietnam, Hill decided to go to college and get a deferment. He enrolled at Porterville College and began taking the regular prerequisite courses new college students take their freshman year. Little did he know at the time, but his dislike for one class would land him in the middle of Vietnam during the height of the war.

As a new student in college, Hill took the general education classes that are required for graduation and transfer. Classes such as English, Math, Science, History, Political Science and Social Science. Of the list of courses that he was required to take, there was one course he had a particular disdain for - Anthropology.

The Meriam Webster dictionary, defines Anthropology as: "The study of humans in relation to distribution, origin, classification, and relationship of races, physical character, environmental and social relations, and culture." Hill would summarize his feelings about this course in one, succinct word.

"Boring."

As Hill said, "Anthropology was one of the most incredibly boring classes I had ever taken." He would much rather be home working on the engine of his car than listening to a boring lecture on environmental and social relations. His feelings about the subject soon began to show in his progress in the course. Or, rather, his lack of progress. Missed classes, forgotten assignments, poor grades on tests.

At one point during the semester the instructor was looking at his grade sheet and told Hill he was not passing the class. Then, the instructor gave Hill some advice and said, "Roland, I'd recommend you drop the class. Otherwise, you're going to fail it." Who was he to argue? So, Hill took the advice of the instructor and dropped the class rather than receiving a failing grade.

Dropping the class gave Hill a sense of relief. He was no longer in a boring class, he could now focus more on the other courses he was enrolled into, and the extra time from not having to be in the Anthropology class gave him more time to work on his car or meet with his friends in the cafeteria. But, as Hill said, "By dropping the class I created one major problem for myself."

The following semester, on February 15, 1968 to be exact, the local draft board sent him a letter. When he went to get the mail, he noticed a letter from the government addressed to him. "I knew what it was," Hill said. Still, he opened the letter with sweating hands and butterflies in his chest, read the first few words, and, he said, "I felt like I got a stiff kick in the gut." He was drafted. He was ordered to report on March 13th, less than a month away.

This was just after the start of the Tet Offensive and during the height of the war. In fact, the week that the letter was dated was during the worst week of the Vietnam War in terms of troops killed in action – 543.[1] The news out of Vietnam was on television every night and it was awful. Not only was he concerned, but so were his parents. "Mom was terribly distraught," Hill said, "and dad would have preferred me to go to Canada."

But why was he drafted? He was enrolled at Porterville College, and, therefore, eligible for the student deferment. Or so he thought. Surely, the draft board must have made a mistake. So, with his draft notice in hand, Hill went to the local draft board to argue his case.

The draft board informed Hill that to receive a deferment from military service, he needed to be enrolled full-time each semester, which was at least 12 units. Dropping the Anthropology class brought him down to nine units. Therefore, he was no longer a full-time student and, as a result, not eligible for a deferment. "I didn't know that dropping the class would be such a big deal," Hill said. But it certainly was.

Drafted because he didn't like Anthropology.

When Hill received his draft notice and his appeal to the draft board was denied, his father hinted around to him that he'd help Hill if he wanted to avoid the draft and move to Canada. It was an attractive idea. Going to Vietnam was not where he wanted to be, especially with so many of his former classmates being killed or injured in the war.

As Hill considered the idea, he realized that he didn't want to lose his citizenship and the chance to return to his family and friends back in Porterville. Going to Canada was serious. "Sure," Hill said, "I didn't like the possibility of going to a war but leaving the United States to become of citizen of Canada was too much." Certainly, his dad would have preferred he move to Canada, but this was Hill's decision to make, and make it he did. He went into the military, and he went to Vietnam.

Todd Pixler

Todd Pixler thought his legs were his ticket out of the military, but his honesty put him in the center of the Vietnam War.

When he was growing up, Pixler was a rather rambunctious boy, somewhat quiet, and very athletic. He played baseball, but his first love was running track. And Pixler was fast, darn fast. In fact, he was one of the fastest runners in Porterville High School history and some of his track records still stand today. When he graduated from high school he accepted a full-ride, four-year athletic scholarship from the University of Utah to run track. He also had offers from the University of Oregon, University of Southern California, University of California, Los Angeles, University of California, Berkley, and Occidental College.

A lot of universities wanted Pixler, but the main reason he chose the University of Utah was because it was not in California. "I wanted to go where I could spread my own wings," Pixler said. "I wanted to get away from home and experience another world somewhere else." Well, he certainly experienced that other world, but he soon found out that Utah was not really the best choice for a budding track star.

In fact, what he experienced in Utah was the same thing that his father experienced back in Iowa. And this experience that drove his father from Iowa to California would drive Pixler from Utah and back to California as well. What was that experience? The weather. In fact, the snow. When he was at the track running in Utah, or at least trying to run, he began to ask himself, "How do they expect me to run track in the snow?" "How can I run sprints on an icy lane?" In addition to the weather, there was one other aspect of life in Utah that Pixler didn't quite fit into.

The Mormon community.

Utah is home to the Mormon church. And the Mormon lifestyle includes drinking no alcohol, no cussing, no sinful behavior, no, well, things that Pixler enjoyed on the streets of Porterville. As Pixler described himself, "I was not Mormon potential." It was hard, basically impossible, to find a bar in town to have a few beers, or a strip joint to stuff dollar bills in the G-string of a pole dancer while your college buddies scream for more action. The college lifestyle in Utah was not the same as college life on university campuses back in California. Admittedly, Pixler said, "I didn't really fit in."

Feeling that the weather was impacting his ability to properly train and compete and realizing that the social life in Utah was not what he particularly enjoyed, he moved back to California and enrolled at Occidental College, the first university that expressed an interest in him.

The athletic director and head coach of the track team at Occidental must have gotten on their knees and thanked God for the weather in Utah, because Pixler quickly established himself as an accomplished runner when he broke the freshman record in the 100 meters, a record that still stands today as well.

He considered training for the Olympic team, but that would mean he would need to spend the next few years training and training hard. When training for the Olympics, Pixler said, "You can't make the team by running or working out every few days. You have to train every day, run every day, work out every day." And to get on the Olympic team, Pixler said, "My life would need to be committed almost one-hundred percent to training." After thinking about it more, Pixler decided he was not ready to make such a commitment.

Pixler even began to reconsider his decision to enroll at Occidental in the first place. The more he thought about it, he said he realized that "Maybe I wasn't ready to be away from home just yet." So, he came back home. He enrolled at Porterville College, ran track, and played football. However, like many young people at that age, he was undecided on his major and career goals, and eventually dropped out of PC. Once he dropped out, Vietnam began to creep back into his thoughts because his classification would change if he was not enrolled in school.

In fact, Pixler may have been one of the few young men in those days to involuntarily "volunteer for the draft."

Since he was not in school at that time, Pixler was concerned about his deferment status, so he went to the local draft board to find out if he was still classified as "2-S", which was a student deferment. "I didn't really know what my classification was anymore, so I asked the draft board," Pixler said. When he asked them that question, one of the members of the draft board asked him a question that made Pixler realize that he should have kept his mouth shut. After Pixler explained his situation, the person on the draft board asked, "You mean you're not still going to school?"

"Oh, crap. They didn't know," Pixler thought, "but now they do." And because of his honesty, he was immediately reclassified as "1-A" and placed on the list to be drafted. Soon thereafter, Pixler received his draft notice in the mail.

Pixler's honesty before the draft board guaranteed him a round-trip ticket to Vietnam. He didn't want to go, but the only other choice he had was to go to Canada. His parents didn't want their son to be drafted either, and they certainly didn't want their son to be sent to Vietnam. So, they encouraged him to move to Canada.

The father of a friend of Pixler's from Utah offered him a job in Canada and Pixler's parents wanted him to take it. There, he could avoid the draft and, especially, avoid going to Vietnam. But going to Canada would also mean leaving home, for good, and being tagged as a draft dodger. He didn't want that either.

Moving to Canada would mean leaving his friends. It would

mean losing most contact with those he grew up with, family and friends alike. It would mean essentially starting his life over again. As Pixler said, "Not going to Vietnam was a good enough reason to go to Canada." But as he thought more about this offer and the ramifications of whether the offer was accepted or not, he decided to decline the offer. He soon found himself in boot camp in Ft. Lewis, Washington, the first step on his way to Vietnam.

Melvin Braziel

When he was at Porterville High School, Melvin Braziel didn't want to think about the war, but rather thought more about the party they were planning for Friday night. Who was buying the booze? Did someone remember the ice? Should he get a date or go stag? As most guys in his class did, Melvin liked to party, and that consumed more of his attention than worrying about Vietnam.

As he was getting closer to graduation, Braziel said "The anxiety began to rise within me as I thought about the possibility of going to a war." He knew the draft was a possibility, but he tried to suppress the thought of experiencing it. He could not, however, deny the reality of being an 18-year-old during a war where the draft was becoming a common occurrence. Soon, though, he had to face that reality.

During his senior year, he started to have the same questions his fellow classmates at Porterville High School had. Braziel said "I didn't know if I should enlist. Should I take my chances on the draft? Or should I go to college and try to get a deferment?" Since Braziel had some learning challenges, going to college was really not an option for him. He didn't want to move to Canada, so what should he do? Well, the answers to those questions were soon provided by the United States government.

One day, his mom had gotten the mail. And when Melvin came into the house where she was standing he could tell something was bothering her. She showed him a letter she had opened that was addressed to him. She looked at her son sadly and said, "You've been drafted."

When his mom said that, Braziel said "I went numb." What he knew was a possibility had now become a reality. His first thought was, "What do I do now?" He'd been putting off answering those questions about what to do, but he couldn't any longer. Now, it was decision time.

At first, Braziel's health, specifically high blood pressure, looked like it might be his ticket out of the military. He failed his first physical, so they gave him a second one. He failed his second physical, and then Braziel thought, "Thank God for high blood pressure. I'm not going into the service!" But not so fast. It seemed like the government didn't want to give up on Braziel just yet. He was a big guy, maybe a little cocky, and certainly possessing a lot of confidence. Just what the military wanted. So they gave him a third physical, and he passed that one. Then what happened?

He got drafted.

Ron McCarville

Making the decision to either enlist or take his chances on the draft was an easy decision for Ron McCarville. While he was still a young boy, McCarville made the decision that he wanted to eventually join the Marine Corps. In fact, McCarville said, "I even wanted to enlist my junior year in high school." For McCarville, there was really no other option.

As his friends at Porterville High School struggled with the choices in front of them, such as enrolling in college to get a deferment, getting a job and taking chances on the draft, or moving to Canada to avoid the military entirely, McCarville did not struggle making his decision. He knew what he wanted. And he wanted to be a Marine.

His country was at war, so his decision to enlist was from a sense of duty. In addition, McCarville said, "I wanted to enlist in the Marine Corps out of respect for my father." He wanted to be a Marine just like his dad. As mentioned earlier, McCarville's father was a pilot in the Marine Corps and was killed during a mission over Japan in

1954. His uncle was in the Army and fought in the Philippines during WWII. One time, his father even flew to the Philippines to meet with his brother. "I wanted to follow in my dad's and uncle's footsteps and join the military," McCarville said.

So, when he was in Porterville High School, the news about the Vietnam War did not really bother him. He knew he was going into the Marine Corps upon graduation and, most likely, would be sent to Vietnam. Since he wanted to join the Marine Corps since he was a little kid, getting closer to high school graduation meant that his goal of joining the military was getting closer, too.

Shortly after he graduated from high school, he enlisted in the Marine Corps. McCarville said, "That was my goal, and I was ready to go." And not only did McCarville go to Vietnam, but he found himself deep in the jungles experiencing the worst the war could offer while being awarded a medal for heroism in the process.

His dad would have been proud.

Louis Gurrola

Although most who dodged the draft or thought about doing so, considered Canada as the country of choice. A few men, however, considered a different place on the opposite side of our country – Mexico.

Louis Gurrola graduated from Porterville High School during the deadliest year of the war, 1968. He had seen it all on television and many of his classmates at high school were enlisting, being drafted, or coming back from the war. Some who came back were fine, others were experiencing emotional challenges, some had been injured and some had died.

Certainly, the possibility of being drafted was on his mind and the minds of his friends. Gurrola said, "I knew being drafted was a possibility, but I hoped that I'd never receive a draft notice in the mail." Although he did not really want to go to college, the thought of a student deferment was still a consideration. However, Gurrola was raised working with his hands outdoors, so "Sitting in a classroom and taking notes in college were not high on my list of priorities," he said.

In January of 1969, Gurrola came home one day and found a letter on the table. A letter sent to him from the United States government. His parents were worried about the letter and its contents. But when he saw the letter, Gurrola knew what it was. "I opened the letter, read the first few lines, and didn't know what to think or say." It was confirmed. What he hoped that would not happen, just did. He was drafted.

He had one more hope, maybe the last hope, that something else could keep him from military service. His health. When he went to get his physical, Gurrola said, "I was hoping that they would find some physical problem that would categorize me as 4-F (unfit for military service)." But no such luck. His hopes had run out. He passed his physical.

Unless he left the country, Gurrola would soon find himself in a military uniform.

Gurrola's parents were so worried about their son going to Vietnam that they discussed the possibility of him moving to Mexico. "My family had friends and relatives who lived there, so arranging for a place for me to live and work in Mexico would not be a problem." Most draft dodgers were going to Canada; however, Mexico provided a better opportunity for him since he would be among family and friends.

But Gurrola did not want to be tagged as a draft dodger, and he couldn't see himself leaving the United States and never returning. Sure, he had family and friends in Mexico, too, but Terra Bella was his home. It was here where he grew up. It was here where he worked the fields around Porterville and Terra Bella. It was here where he had his high school friends. It was here where he had his parents and siblings. So, it was here where he decided to stay.

Robert Johnson

When Robert Johnson enlisted in the military, he said, "My dad was very emotional at the thought of me going to Vietnam, so he tried to encourage me to not go into the service." Instead, Johnson's father wanted him to consider going to Canada.

His dad would provide any support he could offer if his son moved to Canada. But, as he thought about the offer, Johnson said that "Going to Canada would be an impossible burden for me to carry, especially with the military history in my family."

With his father, stepfather, and stepuncles all having served in WWII, Johnson said, "I would not be able to face the men in my family if I deserted to Canada." Johnson thought about his dad's advice, but he couldn't follow it. He decided to stay. And he decided to enlist. The Army was his choice, as well as an assignment that would place him in the middle of the war, sustaining injuries that would affect him for the rest of his life.

The fear of going to Vietnam caused many of these young men from communities across the country to volunteer in order to have a choice of which branch in the military they would serve. They joined the Navy or Air Force, with longer years of service required, so they could avoid the possibility of being sent to Vietnam. Spending four years in the Navy as compared to two years in the Army or Marine Corps was a tradeoff they were willing to take to avoid the draft and potential assignment to Vietnam.

Many young men in the country attempted to get a deferment by enrolling in college, while others fled to Canada. Some even tried to find a doctor who could verify a physical problem so they could be classified as 4-F and, thereby, be physically ineligible for the military. Others were lucky enough to have a friend on the local draft board who could personally ensure they wouldn't be drafted.

As more people began to examine the demographics of those

who were being drafted, it was felt that there was a disproportionate number of minorities and lower income men being drafted because they could not afford to attend college, did not have a doctor who could give them a medical deferment, or did not know of anyone on their local draft board that they could convince. Therefore, in an effort to make the draft fairer, a lottery draft was instituted on December 1, 1969.[2]

Under the lottery system, the order in which someone would be drafted was based on his date of birth. There were seven lotteries held. The first lottery for the years of birth from 1944-50 was held on December 1, 1969; the second lottery for the year of birth 1951 was held on July 1, 1970; the third lottery for the year of birth 1952 was held on August 5, 1971; the fourth lottery for the year of birth 1953 was held on February 2, 1972; the fifth lottery for the year of birth 1954 was held on March 8, 1973; the sixth lottery for the year of birth 1955 was held on March 20, 1974; and the seventh and final lottery for the year of birth 1956 was held on March 12, 1975.

Permit me to tell one personal story about the lottery draft.

The lottery for my year of birth (1954) was held on March 8, 1973. Luckily, the day of my lottery was about six weeks after the peace agreement was signed in Paris, France and about three weeks before the last combat troops left Vietnam. Still, hearing and reading about the lottery coming up for your year of birth was a bit disconcerting. Sure, President Nixon ended the draft about a month earlier, but you still had it in the back of your mind that anything could happen. In fact, that was the reason the government continued the lotteries after the draft was officially ended, because anything could happen, and the government needed to be ready with troops in case something did happen. So you still prayed that your number would be a high one.

The day following the lottery, those of us who had our lottery numbers drawn the night before were sitting in the cafeteria at Porterville College talking about the lottery. The numbers were printed in the paper, announced on the radio, and shown on television. My lottery number was 55, a low one since the lottery numbers being drafted during the latter part of the war were in the high 90s to low 100s.

Fifty-five. A number I will never forget.

When I told everyone that my lottery number was 55, they burst into nervous laughter, and my one friend said, "Crap, Schultz, you're going to Nam!" The rest of the day in class I couldn't concentrate. It was hard enough understanding Chief of Police Torigian talking about some complex criminology theory in my Administration of Justice class but throw in a low lottery number and my mind was not into his lecture. Or any other lecture that day.

Throughout the day in my mind I thanked President Nixon for ending the draft a month earlier because a low number like 55 was a ticket to Vietnam about two or three years earlier. On the drive home that day to Terra Bella after my classes, I prayed and prayed and prayed to God and promised Him that if He'd make sure President Nixon didn't reinstitute the draft that I'd never curse, lie, cheat, steal, or get drunk ever again.

Well, to be honest with you, God kept His promise, but I didn't.

About half of these Porterville High School students that you met were drafted, while the other half enlisted. Most of those who were drafted experienced the same feelings when opening their draft notice. As Roland Hill said when he opened his draft notice, "I felt like I got a stiff kick in the gut!" Melvin Braziel said he went numb. When reading the draft notice, the new draftee would experience fear, uncertainty, and anxiety. And their mothers and fathers felt the same.

College deferments helped some of them to avoid the war, for a while at least. And some, through their lack of understanding about the rules or regulations of college deferments, lost their deferment by not remaining as full-time students. Once they lost their deferments they were drafted and ended up in the same place they initially wanted to avoid by going to college.

Most of the young men from Porterville High School who volunteered did so to avoid being drafted into the Marine Corps or Army, and, hopefully, to avoid going to Vietnam. On the other hand, a few of them enlisted specifically to go into the Marine Corps, the Army, or to Vietnam. Ironically, almost all of those who volunteered to avoid Vietnam eventually found themselves in Vietnam anyway. Many volunteered as a sense of duty, a feeling of adventure, or because of respect to their fathers or other family members who previously served in the military.

For some of the veterans, the decision not to go to Canada or Mexico was an easy one. For others, the choice was only made after some serious consideration. Moving to Canada or Mexico would have guaranteed them a life without war, and their parents or other family members would have paid their way across the border.

But there were things that pulled them more in the direction to stay home and either enlist or be drafted, such as commitment to their families, the bond of friendship with their fellow classmates, and the sense of duty they felt compelled to honor. Sure, most didn't want to go to Vietnam, but like their fathers before them, their lives included a war their country was fighting, and it was their turn to fight in their war.

And fight they did.

Vietnam War and Wall Facts

Oldest and Youngest [3]

The youngest soldier killed in the Vietnam War was Private First Class Daniel Bullock. He was 15 years old.

The oldest soldier killed in the Vietnam War was Dwaine McGriff. He was 63 years old.

There were at least five men killed who were 16 years old.

There were at least twelve men killed who were 17 years old.

4

From Books to Boots

"America without her soldiers would be like God without his angels."
Claudia Pemberton

THE DRIVE FROM Fresno to Monterey is a beautiful and pleasant one, meandering through the vast farmlands of the San Joaquin Valley in Central California, and then along the beautiful and pristine coastline of the Pacific Ocean. This route is a familiar one for families from the valley who wish to escape the heat of the summer to vacation and relax in the cool breezes of the ocean.

Sure, this route for some of the boys from Porterville High School in the 60's who were going into the Army may have been a familiar one, but the end result for them on this drive was certainly not a vacation. Far from it. They had traded in their books from high school for boots in the Army. They were no longer at home, because their new home was something totally different.

Boot camp.

After being sworn into the military at the induction center in Fresno, they boarded a bus that would take them to Ft. Ord in Monterey for eight weeks of basic training. The drive on the bus was one of mixed emotions. Sadness for leaving home, excitement because of the new adventure, fear because of the possibility, or probability, of going to Vietnam.

As they drove, some of them sat in silence as their minds wandered in anticipation of what they were soon to experience, many of them tried to sleep, but nervousness or apprehension prevented them from doing that. Or at least prevented them from a deep and restful sleep.

About three hours after the trip began in Fresno, the bus came to a screeching halt, and their lives were now in utter chaos. The doors to the bus swung open, and someone they never knew before comes screaming in, hollering at them, calling them names, telling them how worthless they were, and ordering them to grab their gear, get the hell out of the bus, and get on the line. And who were they to argue?

Welcome to the Army!

They were marched to the reception center barracks, hollered at some more, called more names, degraded in any way possible, and then told to shut up, turn the lights off, and go to bed. The next morning, they were accosted before the sun came up by the drill instructor (DI) banging on the trash can to wake them up. The DI started and ended every sentence with the "F" word and was never one to throw a compliment in their direction.

And in just a few hours, each recruit would totally lose his personal identity and become almost a clone to his fellow soldier. They were given the same clothes, the same sheets, the same pillow, the same underwear, the same utensils, the same socks, the same shoe shine polish, and the same duffel bag and footlocker to put it all in. But then their loss of personal identity was about to be totally and thoroughly consummated.

They got their heads shaved!

No trim it up on the sides, no take a little off the top, or no taper it in the back just a little bit. Totally shaved. Some recruits came into the Army as hippies with stringy hair down their backs, some had flowing hair perfectly manicured, some had curly, some had straight, but that all changed.

Now, they all had none. It was gone. Lying on the barber's floor. If you stood side-by-side next to one of your fellow soldiers and looked in the mirror, you could almost tell no difference. You were no longer you, but rather you were a soldier in the Army, government issued (GI). Property of the United States government.

You followed orders, or you suffered the consequences. You did what they told you to do regardless if you wanted to or not. You ate what they gave you. You woke up and went to bed when they wanted you to. Your life was now in their hands, like it or not.

For those who appreciated privacy when they did basic things like go to the bathroom, that was all gone now, too. The toilets were side-by-side with no privacy walls in between them. Talk about culture shock when having to poop next to someone about two feet from you who has diarrhea. Or to take a shower next to 10 other naked guys. Community showers may seem kinky in real life, but in the military that's standard operating procedure. Going to the bathroom and taking a shower brought you closer to your fellow soldiers in a manner you never anticipated.

But then came nightfall, which was a whole other experience entirely. After a full day of physical training, orientations, classes, two-mile jogs and five-mile marches, they were ready for bed, thoroughly exhausted. However, they weren't at home sleeping in their bed in the quiet solitude of their own bedroom. They were in the Army, sleeping in a barracks with fifty other guys who all had different patterns of sleep, different snoring sounds and volume, and different nighttime schedules of bodily functions. Snoring, coughing, farting, wheezing, going to the bathroom. It was all there, all night long. And you had to learn to sleep through it.

Boot camp was similar between all branches of the military. The basic training experience for those in the Army, Navy, Air Force, or Marine Corps included scared recruits, boisterous and often belligerent DIs, training, marches, drills, Kitchen Patrol (KP) duty, early mornings, late nights, being exhausted, burned out and overloaded.

Regardless of their branch of service, the new recruits were often pushed to the limit, and the reason being, when in combat, they'd be pushed to the limit and they better be prepared for it. And there was no better place to prepare them for it than boot camp.

Ron McCarville

Regarding Marine Corps boot camp back during the Vietnam War, Ron McCarville said, "People today would not believe what went on in boot camp back then."

When he graduated from high school, Ron McCarville enlisted in the Marine Corps and went to basic training at the Marine Corps Recruit Depot in San Diego. It was here that he became acquainted with a future movie star, an actor who was even nominated for a Golden Globe Award for Best Supporting Actor. An actor who played or did voices in various movies and even had his own television series. And McCarville got to know this actor very intimately.

But this movie star was not some pretty actress like Marilyn Monroe or a handsome actor like Robert Redford. The future movie star he became acquainted with was his DI, Staff Sergeant Ronald E. Ermey. For those of you who may not be familiar with the name, Ermey played the sadistic DI in the movie, *Full Metal Jacket*. Gunnery Sergeant Hartman.

The first greeting from Ermey to McCarville and the new recruits was much like that from the movie, and his first greeting would set the tone for the whole boot camp experience. In the movie, when introducing himself to his new recruits, he said, "I am Gunnery Sergeant Hartman, your senior drill instructor. From now on you will speak only when spoken to, and the first and last words out of your filthy sewers will be 'Sir.' Do you maggots understand that?" It went downhill from there.

As McCarville described him, "Ermey was something else. A

mean son-of-a-bitch." If you ever watch the movie, McCarville said that "Ermey was the same in the movie as he was as my drill instructor." Mean, cocky, loud, rude, and, at times, sadistic. Some of the things that Ermey did during McCarville's training in boot camp are not for print here in this book but suffice it to say it was often ruthless.

McCarville explained, "Ermey would often take us out to the farthest corners of the training grounds at the base so no one could see or hear what he was doing." And then, out of the eyesight and earshot of most on the base, Ermey proceeded to violate any form of civility onto his pitiful recruits.

But McCarville also mentioned that Ermey wasn't the only one who was mean when he said, "The other DIs were just as sadistic." One time while they were at the rifle range practicing breathing and squeezing the triggers of their M14s, McCarville's group was in a circle with the DI walking inside the circle checking the recruits. The DI noticed one of the recruits playing around with the bolt on his rifle. Playing with a rifle like that was unacceptable, so the DI decided to make this recruit into an example to the others. While the others stood around watching, the DI took the recruit's rifle, pulled back the bolt, stuck the finger of the recruit into the opening of the bolt and let the bolt go.

Whack!

With great force, the bolt shut on the recruit's finger. The other recruits in the circle winced in shared pain with their fellow recruit, but, surprisingly, he did not learn his lesson. He was later caught playing with his rifle again. When caught the second time, the DI used a different part of the recruit's anatomy to be stuck in the open bolt.

His nose.

Like he did with the recruit's finger, the DI stuck the recruit's nose in the bolt and let it go. "This time," McCarville said, "there was blood all over." When I asked McCarville if he ever played with his bolt like that after what happened to that recruit, he quickly replied, "Hell no!" Okay, lesson learned. A very painful lesson learned. Heaven forbid if that recruit would have done it again. I can only imagine what part of his anatomy the DI would have stuck in the bolt the third time.

So, if you want to see what McCarville dealt with in boot camp with a DI like Ermey, watch the movie. It's not pretty.

When I asked McCarville what he would do if Ermey was still alive and he came across him today, he said, "I'd avoid him." It was obvious McCarville did not care much for his DIs, but most of the other recruits didn't either. In fact, the DI's did not really care if you liked them or not. They only expected you to respect them, not like them. And they expected you to follow orders. Nothing more, nothing less.

Regardless, welcome to Marine Corps boot camp in the 60s. And after hearing more about his basic training experience, McCarville is right. People today would not believe what went on in Marine Corps boot camp back then.

Vince Arcure

Eleanor Roosevelt, the former First Lady of the United States said this about the Marines back in 1945: "The Marines I have seen around the world have the cleanest bodies, the filthiest minds, the highest morale, and the lowest morals of any group of animals I have ever seen. Thank God for the United States Marine Corps!"[1]

First Lady Roosevelt's description may be her list of unproven stereotypes, but there are other stereotypes or adjectives that are often used to describe infantrymen in the Marine Corps: confident, maybe a little cocky, bad ass, self-assured, and always a buddy that can be counted on during battle. And one of the Marine Corps veterans that exemplifies most of these stereotypes is a graduate of Porterville High School.

Vince Arcure enlisted in the Marine Corps in 1966 because he felt he would be drafted anyway. When he told his mom that he enlisted in the Marine Corps, she said, "You tell your dad, I'm not!" Later, when he told his dad that he had enlisted, his dad warned, "You better not have!" And when Arcure assured his dad that he really did, in fact, enlist in the Marine Corps, his dad did something that most fathers don't do when confronted with such information. He punched his son. Okay, point taken, but it was too late. Arcure had already enlisted.

Now it was time to tell his grandfather. When Arcure and his father told his grandfather that he enlisted, his grandfather had basically the same reaction as Vince's father did, but he put a different twist to it - he hit Vince's dad. When he punched him, the grandfather hollered at Vince's dad saying, "Why did you let him do that?" Okay, the father and grandfather may have used a unique method to express their disapproval of his decision to enlist, and their feelings were obvious.

When he left from Fresno to his book camp in San Diego, Arcure realized that he would most likely be going to Vietnam when his basic training was over with. Because of that probability, the trip to boot camp was one in nervous anticipation of what he was about to face. Even though he was confident in what he was about to encounter, Arcure said he did something to calm his nerves that he had never done before. "I smoked two packs of cigarettes."

Along with the other guys on the bus, Arcure was dropped off at a street corner in San Diego to wait for the Marine Corps to take them to the base. A taxi driver saw the group of guys waiting on the street corner, knowing these were new recruits probably on their first step to Vietnam. So he drove up to them and made them an offer, "Give me $20 each and I'll take you across the border." Maybe for others this might have been a tempting offer, but not for Arcure.

They turned down the offer from the taxi driver and waited to be picked up by the Marine Corps. Arcure was going to be a Marine, whether that meant Vietnam was in his future or not.

When talking about his boot camp experience, Arcure described his DI in one succinct word – "asshole." But, he also said, "All the DIs in boot camp were assholes." Since there was no love-loss between Arcure and his DI, he said that if given the chance back then, he probably would have hit his DI. But when asked how he would approach him today, he said, "We're Marines. We're all the same. Every Marine is a friend."

At the end of basic training, they were told what their Military Occupational Specialty (MOS) was going to be. Arcure had put in a request to be assigned as a truck driver. As the DI was reading the names of those assigned to be truck drivers, Arcure said, "I was waiting for my name to be read, but it never was." Then, the DI said he would be reading the names of those assigned to the infantry. And the first name he read? Arcure.

From a truck driver to an infantryman. Not what he expected, not what he wanted, but he was ready for any assignment the Marine Corps would give him.

After hearing about Arcure's experiences in boot camp, infantry training, and while in the jungles of Vietnam, I'm convinced that First Lady Roosevelt's description of Marines was rather accurate.

Roger Gibson

Initially, Roger Gibson was using a student deferment to avoid the military service and the probability of going to Vietnam. But when his college football career ended with a knee injury, he decided to quit school, too. Knowing that he'd probably now be drafted, Gibson decided to enlist.

When considering which branch of the service to enlist into, one of his brothers gave him some very simple advice when he said, "Don't go into the Marines!" So, Gibson took his brother's advice, stayed with the family tradition, and enlisted in the Air Force.

He went to his basic training at Lackland Air Force Base in Lackland, Texas. Since he had come from a military family, he really wasn't worried about boot camp until he got there. Like most recruits in basic training, Gibson remembers being hollered at, constantly. Calling him names, making disparaging remarks about him, and treating him like he was dirt. But, he also noticed that they were treating all the other recruits the same way. It wasn't just him. He realized then that these DIs were serious, and he better listen, follow orders, and not cause any trouble.

He remembers his DI was "clean to the bone." The DI's shoes shined like glass, his clothes were hard pressed and creased, his hair was cut, and his face was shaved. Gibson said that "Everything the DI wore was in order, clean, pressed, or shiny." Gibson's DI also expected the recruits to have the same precision with their clothes, bunks, footlockers and boots.

In every branch of the service, DI's are known for walking up to a bunk, taking out a coin, and flipping the coin onto the bunk. Since the bunks were supposed to be made in such a way that the blanket covering the bunk was pulled tight as a drum, the DI's would expect the coin to bounce off the blanket. Well, to make sure that he was always ready for such a bed inspection, Gibson invented a different approach to ensuring he would be ready for the coin toss.

He always slept on top of the bed.

Gibson explained, "If I slept on top of the bed it wouldn't take me as long to make my bed when the hollering started for everyone to wake up." His sheets and blankets could easily be tucked in the corners as expected, and it would not take him long to make final preparations for a surprise coin toss inspection. Gibson knew that if the coin did not bounce high enough to please the DI, he would be put on detail, such as pulling KP detail or picking up cigarette butts around the barracks. He didn't want to be punished for a coin that didn't bounce so he wanted to be ready. To prepare for that, Gibson slept through basic training without the comfort of cuddling underneath the sheets.

Melvin Braziel

When Melvin Braziel was at the induction center, the recruits were placed in long lines and then at one point they were told to start counting, beginning with the guy at the front of the line. They were only supposed to count to two and then start over again. The guy at the front of the line started with shouting "one", the next guy shouted, "two", the next guy shouted "one", the next guy shouted "two" and this continued through each line. One. Two. One. Two. One. Two.

As this was happening, Braziel said, "I asked one of the guys in line what they were doing, and he told me they were counting to determine what branch of service you'd be assigned to. The number one was for the Army, and the number two was for the Marines." Braziel then looked ahead in his line, started from the front and counted back "one" and "two" in his head, and determined that he was going to be a number two. The United States Marine Corps. So, he casually switched positions with the guy next to him. Braziel "volunteered" for the Army.

Braziel went to basic training at Ft. Ord in Monterey, California. He remembers running. And running. And running. "Everywhere we went, we ran," Braziel said. He also said that "Our old commanding officer would often run right along with us." So, these young recruits really couldn't complain about the long runs if the old guys were keeping up with them, sometimes in front, sometimes at their side, but, if they were in the rear, it wasn't because they were slow. It was probably because they were yelling at some poor recruit who was dogging it while puking, gasping, wheezing and falling behind.

"Since I was the biggest guy in my platoon, they made me platoon leader," Braziel said. Sometimes, platoon leaders got special privileges, while at other times they took the full force of discipline for someone in their platoon who screwed up. Braziel remembers being hollered at constantly, not necessarily because of him, but because being hollered at was the culture of the boot camp experience. "At that time," Braziel said, "I felt that all the DIs were assholes, every single one of them." But looking back on the experience now, Braziel said, "It makes sense how, what, and why they treated us like they did."

When Braziel was in boot camp, there had been a warning about the spread of meningitis in the area. To avoid being infected with the disease, his company was basically quarantined from the other companies. Braziel explained, "We were only able to go to the Post

Exchange (PX) one time, and the rest of the time we stayed together, not interacting with anyone except those in our own company."

Fresh air was one of the things they said could protect them from the spread of meningitis, so they were required to keep the windows in the barracks open, all day and all night. They never closed. If it was freezing outside, it was freezing inside. As Braziel said, "The drill instructors didn't really care if the recruits were cold or not, the windows stayed open."

Since Ft. Ord was in Monterey, alongside the beaches of the Pacific Ocean, fog was quite common. Thick, wet fog. For those who live in the Central Valley of California and experience dense fog quite often during the winter months, they call this thick fog "pea soup fog." Sometimes, you can't see more than a few feet in front of you. Braziel remembers one time that the fog was so thick outside that it filled the inside of his barracks, too, since they had to keep the windows open. Braziel said, "You could not see from one end of the barracks to the other end because of the fog inside." Pea soup fog inside a building?

Only in the Army.

Roland Hill

Around the time he got drafted and prior to his leaving for the service, Roland Hill was at a party where one of his friends who had just returned from Vietnam attended. He remembers that during this party his friend basically just sat on the edge of the couch, staring at the wall, and sipping whiskey. Seeing this, Hill wondered to himself, "I'm going to Vietnam, will that be me when I return?"

Ft. Ord in California was temporarily closed due to the recent meningitis scare, so Hill went to basic training at Ft. Lewis, Washington. He flew from Fresno to McCord Air Force base in Washington and then took a bus to Ft. Lewis. Like all new recruits, Hill said that the first thing he was met with when the bus stopped at the base was "a hollering, screaming drill instructor."

This quiet ride ended up in almost utter chaos. Recruits running, doing pushups, while being called dirty names by fanatical drill instructors. And this was around midnight. Welcome to the Army. For a little bit at least, the Anthropology class at Porterville College was not so bad after all.

At the end of boot camp, he was offered some choices on which training program he wanted to pursue in Advanced Individual Training (AIT), and Hill chose to take the AIT program that took the longest to complete. As he explained, "The reason I chose the longer AIT was because I was thinking that maybe the war would be over with before I finished training, or at least, getting closer to being over so they would not be sending any more troops to Vietnam." Wishful thinking, sure, but thinking that gave him some hope.

Hill went to Ft. Eustis, Virginia to be trained as a multi-engine, tandem rotor helicopter repairman. During his time at Ft. Eustis, he was able visit Washington D.C. He was away from home, and the nation's capital was not that far away, so he thought he'd take advantage of the situation. But this was during the height of not only the war, but also the anti-war protest movement.

Back in the late 1960s, Washington D. C. was a magnet that attracted protesters from across the country, many of them the more radical elements of the peace movement. Even though Hill might have shed his uniform during his visit to D.C., it wasn't hard to spot someone in the military out of a crowd of people protesting the war. Clean shaven, short hair and pressed clothes as compared to beards, long hair, beads, and tattered pants. Since he stuck out like a sore thumb, Hill said he was "nervous and uncomfortable to be in such a hostile environment. It was not a relaxing visit."

But here in the nation's capital was a large contingency of angry citizens protesting our country's involvement in a war thousands of miles from home. And not just protesting, but sometimes protesting violently. And not just protesting the war but protesting those who fought in it. Hill watched what was happening, realizing that he'd probably soon be in the middle of the war that so many people were against.

About 10 days before the end of his AIT, Hill received his orders to Vietnam. It was official. "Getting orders to Vietnam was not really a surprise, I sort of expected it," Hill said. So, that which he had been hoping would never happen, was now his reality. He's going to Vietnam, because he hated Anthropology.

Greg Goble

When Greg Goble thinks back to the time when he left home to join the life in the military, he can remember being depressed about having to leave his family, his friends, and his high school sweetheart. But he also remembers being depressed for leaving one other thing. And not just leaving this thing but having to sell it.

His 1966 Super Sport car.

Like a lot of the teenagers did back then, Goble spent time racing cars out in the country. But those days of racing were soon to end, because Goble was now the property of the U.S. government, soon heading to book camp. He hated to say goodbye to his car.

Goble went to basic training at Ft. Lewis, Washington. Hearing stories about how difficult and sometimes scary Army boot camp could be, Goble said, "I wanted to get ahead of the game and be in shape. So I drank raw eggs that supposedly helped with stamina and endurance." In addition to focusing on his diet, Goble said, "I ran miles in the foothills of Terra Bella. I am glad I did."

He remembers spending most of his time training outside where it was very cold and windy. Goble said, "The screaming drill instructors showed no mercy and back then, they could be abusive verbally and physically." He said that the DIs would always find that one guy to pick on who was a little behind when learning drills. "If that guy messed up," Goble said, "the rest of us would be punished for his mistakes with extra push-ups, running or the dreaded on your back, crab position." The guy who messed up then became a candidate for what is known as a "blanket party."

A blanket party is where some unsuspecting recruit, usually one that's been a screwup or continues to get his platoon in trouble, is accosted by some other recruits. They put a blanket over his face and body while he is sleeping, hold the blanket down so the recruit can't escape, and then punch the recruit all over his body. Everyone who wants to can take a turn at punching the recruit. During this one particular instance, the person who was going to be given a blanket party was a friend of Goble's. And when he heard about this, Goble tried to save his friend from this ugly ritual. "I was able to talk a few guys from going through with it," Goble said, "but not all." He continued, "They made their move when I was on fire watch duty in another barracks."

But this blanket party ended up having unintended consequences. As Goble explained, "The blanket party, plus ongoing harassment from the DIs was too much for him. I suspect he had a nervous breakdown and was transferred to another company because I never saw him again."

Goble was not a fan of his DIs and considered them bullies. "They would sometimes mess with us for their own amusement," Goble said, "rather than for any training that was beneficial to becoming a better soldier." He described one time when they were awakened in the middle of the night and ordered to assemble outside at attention. But they didn't get to put on jackets or cold weather clothes prior to going outside either. They were only wearing their skivvies, or their underwear. "We were told an M14 rifle was not turned in from earlier drills that day," Goble explained, "and we would be there all night unless whoever it was stepped forward."

No one stepped forward.

So, for most of the night, Goble and the other recruits ran, jumped, low crawled, and waded through knee-deep water. But Goble had a suspicion. "Of course, there was no weapon missing," Goble said, "and I suspect the DIs were drinking and were having a little fun with us." And to make matters worse, Goble said, "That night of fun for the DIs resulted in some recruits who didn't graduate because they were too sick to complete the obstacle course test."

When Goble completed his basic training, he said, "I graduated from boot camp and now was the big moment when you find out what MOS was selected for you and where you would be going next for AIT." He explained that his platoon was gathered, standing at attention, and the names began to be read informing everyone of their MOS and AIT base to where they would be transferred. Since most feared the infantry MOS and the fear of being trained for combat in the jungles of Vietnam, everyone was nervous, waiting in anticipation of what they were going to be assigned to do.

"Name after name was 11 Bravo infantry or 13 Bravo artillery," Goble said, "and then came my name." This was it. The waiting was over. This was his time to find out. The anticipation was nerve-wracking. The DI said, "95 Bravo." When hearing this, Goble's first reaction was, "What the heck is that?" He found out that he was going to be an MP and his training would be at Ft. Gordon in Augusta, Georgia. He might not have been too sure what exactly an MP did, but at least he knew he was not going into the infantry.

After completion of his AIT, Goble was not sent to Vietnam like most other soldiers were. Rather, he remained stateside and was sent to Ft. McClellan in Anniston, Alabama. "When I found out I was staying stateside," Goble said, "I felt like maybe I wasn't going to Vietnam after all." So, he was feeling that his initial thought that he would not go to Vietnam was becoming a satisfying reality.

Goble's assignment as an MP on an Army base was basically like that of a police officer in civilian life. His duties included traffic control, gate duty, robberies, bar fights, drunk drivers, and domestic disputes. Back in the 1960s, Ft. McClellan was one of the largest WAC training centers in the Army. WAC stood for Women's Army Corp and was basically the women's branch of the United States Army. On a side note, the WAC as a branch was disbanded in 1978 and the women were integrated with the male units.

Thinking back on all of the disputes or problems Goble had to deal with as an MP, he had a favorite one - catching peeping toms. In fact, Goble said, he liked catching peeping toms, "especially if they were officers." For someone who may not have cared much for authority figures, busting an officer for a peeping tom violation provided Goble with a satisfying feeling of accomplishment.

Like civilian policemen, MPs are not immune to letting violators of some law or regulation off the hook now and then. Goble was no different.

One time, Goble pulled over a lady who was going 40 miles per hour (MPH) in a 15 MPH zone. Goble explained, "As she is yelling and letting me know that her husband is a captain in the Army, I am writing her ticket using the hood of her car on the driver's side." But as he was writing the ticket, Goble noticed something about himself that could have resulted in some serious consequence. "As I was writing the ticket, I didn't realize that my crotch was even with her face," Goble said, "and she informed me that my zipper was down." And to make the situation even worse, Goble said, "She threatened to report me for sexual harassment." So, what did Goble do?

"I tore the ticket up and let her go."

Goble's time at Ft. McClellan did not last very long. About 4 months after he first started there, he got orders to the place he never thought he would be assigned to - Vietnam. And his responsibilities as an MP in Vietnam were much more serious and life-threatening than catching peeping toms in Anniston, Alabama.

Jim Rouch

One day in 1966, Jim Rouch came home and found a letter from the government on the table. "I knew what it was," Rouch said, "but I didn't want to open it." He stared at if for a while. When he finally got the nerve to open the letter, his fears were confirmed. "The letter told me that I was being ordered to complete a physical for possible entrance into the military draft," Rouch said. "In other words, I'm going to get drafted eventually unless I enlist." Now, two years after he graduated from high school, Vietnam was beginning to make its way from the back pages of the paper to the front. And our country's involvement had changed from advisory to combat. "I started to worry now," he said.

When he went to get his physical, he noticed some draftees who had already passed their physicals were standing in line and someone was walking down the line counting off, "Army", "Marine," "Army," "Marine." Since being drafted in the Marine Corps or Army was almost like a guaranteed ticket to the jungles of Vietnam, he knew then that he better avoid the draft and enlist in the Air Force or Navy. His first choice was the Air Force, but since he had a number of traffic citations on his record, the Air Force didn't want him. Rouch eventually enlisted in the Navy and went to boot camp in San Diego.

During the first three weeks of boot camp they did nothing but march and physical training, but then he got meningitis. Rouch said, "I spent the next six weeks in the hospital and then was given a 30-day medical leave for being sick. And that pissed off my commanding officer." His commanding officer wanted him there, not going on leave, but going through training like everyone else.

When Rouch returned from his leave, his commanding officer did not welcome him back with open arms and a caring heart. Instead, he came up to Rouch shouting, "I don't want you!" And "I don't want you around my men!" Rouch knew then that the next few weeks of boot camp were going to be challenging, nonetheless. "Because he didn't like me," Rouch said, "my commanding officer actually gave me some pretty good assignments." This seemed rather odd that Rouch would get good assignments when his commanding officer didn't like him. Why the good assignments? Rouch said, "He gave me assignments that kept me away from his men."

One time, Rouch was assigned to assist with the Marine Corps water training test. When the Marine recruit was on the bottom of a pool, "My responsibility was to walk around the pool with a long pole poking the recruits on the bottom of the pool," he said. "If a recruit didn't move when I poked him, someone would jump in and pull the Marine out."

Like most new recruits, Rouch was often told to listen and keep his mouth shut. Since he described himself as "a very outspoken individual," it was hard for him to keep his mouth shut. "My mouth got me in trouble sometimes," Rouch admitted, "actually, a lot of times."

After boot camp, Rouch went to Port Hueneme Navy base in Ventura, California for his "A" school, or advance training school, in heavy equipment. Since the base was overcrowded at the time, Rouch had to stay at Point Mugu, which is about seven miles away. Not only did he have to live in another location, he said, "The Navy didn't even have regular, temporary barracks for us to live in." So, as they were waiting for the new battalion to be formed, "We lived in tents," Rouch said. For six weeks, they lived in tents. As Rouch explained, "Here we are, volunteers in the Navy, living in tents, in America. They didn't even have a place to put us."

Well, the Navy finally found a place to put them, but it was in the place that Rouch enlisted in the Navy to hopefully avoid. Vietnam.

Don Wolfram

Don Wolfram went to Navy basic training in San Diego. Since he was in basic training with a friend from home, the experience of boot camp and being away from home was more bearable by having a friend by his side. At the end of basic training he found out he was going into the Seabees as a builder.

There was one aspect of the military that Wolfram wished he could have avoided, not only in boot camp but at other times during his service. Something that brought chills to his body, sweat to his brow, and palpitations to his heart. No, it was not guard duty, mean DIs, mile runs, or ten-mile marches. It was something more profound, and something all military recruits were forced to endure.

Shots.

"I hated getting shots," Wolfram said. Not only did he hate shots, he was afraid of them. There was something about a person poking a needle into his arm that sent him to the floor, literally. Yes, Wolfram passed out a few times when taking shots. As he admitted, "There was no way I'd ever be a drug addict." So, maybe his fear of shots had an unintended and positive result. He stayed away from drugs.

Richard Walker

Richard Walker's mother wanted to submit an appeal that her son be excluded from having to go into the military. And what was Walker's response to his mother's idea? "No way," he said. "I would not have felt right if I didn't go into the service."

For Walker, the hard work in Navy boot camp, the long hours, the hikes, marches, and physical training were not that difficult for him. As Walker said, "I grew up in Terra Bella, so I was used to hard work." Walker, however, remembered one guy who found the rigors of boot camp unbearable. "We had this one guy in boot camp who looked like he had been pampered a lot," Walker explained. "He was a mild-mannered kid who seemed like he had been spoiled when growing up." Obviously, this guy had a hard time adjusting to the mental and physical aspects of boot camp. "Then one day," Walker said, "the kid went bonkers. He couldn't handle it anymore."

Walker remembered another recruit he first met during the initial days of boot camp. "We were getting ready to get our hair cut," Walker explained, "and I remember this one guy in line who had long, flowing hair down his back. He was one of the first guys I had ever seen with long hair," Walker said. At that point in the cultural history of Porterville and Terra Bella, most guys kept their hair short, and hippies were a few hours up the freeway in San Francisco.

Walker remembers this guy went into the barber area and the barber asked him sarcastically, "Son, how do you want your hair?" The recruit said, "Trimmed." And the barber proceeded to shave it off, right down to his scalp. This head of long, flowing hair, was now cascading onto the floor. This hippy was now completely bald. As Walker remembered, "This long-haired guy walked into the barber's chair smiling and came out bald and crying." He wasn't a hippie anymore, at least not on the outside.

Prior to the end of boot camp, they asked Walker to list 10 things he wanted to do for a job in the Navy. One of his top choices was electronics, but he did not qualify for that job and some of the other jobs, too. Why? Because he was color-blind. "The very last job I wrote on my list of 10 things to do was an engineman. I didn't really know what that was though," Walker said. And sure enough. What job did the Navy assign to him?

Engineman.

After boot camp, Walker was sent to the Illinois Naval Training Base for advanced training and then to San Diego for additional language classes and training for boats. Walker remembers one guy in his class who was rather cocky and an annoying braggart. Walker explained, "This guy would brag about wanting to go to Vietnam to kill some Viet Cong and save our country from communism." Then one day in class, the instructor was telling the class of 30 where they were going to be assigned for their next duty. In a strike of poetic justice, Walker said, "Twenty-nine of us were told we were going to Vietnam, and one was told he was staying stateside." And who was the one staying stateside?

The guy who bragged he wanted to go to Vietnam to kill some communists.

Chuck Migalski

Chuck Migalski never anticipated being in Vietnam and under fire from the enemy. He joined the Navy to avoid all of that and planned to spend his tour on a ship navigating itself through the waters of the world. But something in his demeanor changed all of that.

After graduating from Porterville High School in 1966, Migalski, like his fellow classmates, had a decision to make. A very important decision. Volunteer? Get drafted? Go to college? Work? Move to Canada? From what Migalski had been reading and watching about the war, Vietnam was the last place he wanted to go. Since getting drafted probably meant he'd end up in Vietnam, enlisting was his option of choice. Therefore, he enlisted in the Navy.

Migalski went to his boot camp and advanced training in San Diego. Since he had a hard time with authority and following orders, boot camp and his advanced training were challenging at times. When his boot camp was ending, he found out that his MOS was an engineman. Actually, being an engineman was the perfect responsibility for Migalski. Enginemen clean and maintain the engines, propellers, gears, mechanical systems, and related parts. Since his contact would be more with the engine in the belly of the ship than with an officer, Migalski could reduce the chances he'd tangle with a superior he may not have had much respect for.

After his advanced training, he was assigned to the USS Bauer, a Dealey-class destroyer escort. The ship was named after Lieutenant Colonel Harold William Bauer, a recipient of the Medal of Honor in the South Pacific during WWII.[2] At only a little over 300 feet long the Bauer was not a large vessel, but Migalski would find out later that it was about 6 times longer than the boat he would eventually find himself in on the rivers of Vietnam.

Migalski joined the Bauer while it was in Japan, and the ship would eventually find its way to San Diego. Although it may seem like the best-case scenario for a young GI in the military during the Vietnam War was to be stationed close to home, it was not in Migalski's best interest. Since he was only about a five-hour drive from home, Migalski found himself going home to Porterville more than he should. In fact, more than he had permission to. And not being one to always follow the orders of superiors, Migalski eventually found himself in trouble. So much trouble that he faced the threat of a court-martial.

"I screwed up so much the bastards gave me two choices." Migalski explained. "The first choice was to be court-martialed, and the second choice was to go to Vietnam." Being court-martialed and dishonorably discharged from the Navy would certainly have profound consequences on his life if he chose that route. But so would going to Vietnam.

He decided to take his chances and go to Vietnam.

Basic training was an existence far removed from the peaceful, quiet, and carefree life these high school students lived in Porterville, California. Their initial months in the military were spent in an environment that included harsh treatment, strict discipline and following orders. It was a life in which they were no longer individuals, but rather pieces of property owned by the United States government.

When the bus door opened to this new world of boot camp, their lives were immediately interrupted by a screaming drill instructor whose whole existence seemed to be one of intimidation, ridicule, and harassment. These new recruits were oftentimes pushed beyond their limits, but they were not alone. Their barracks were full of new recruits just like they were, and each would eventually lean on the other to help be pulled through this new life in the military.

AIT had more of a sense of normalcy, with most days consumed in classes and learning a new trade. A trade that would be their job or their MOS. Sure, there was still discipline and order, but not to the degree they faced in boot camp. But AIT brought with it a unique level of stress and worry, because it was at the conclusion of AIT when these young men would be finding out where their next stop was. And for most of them, that next stop was Vietnam.

Vietnam War and Wall Facts

The Buddies from Midvale [3]

Three boyhood friends from the town of Midvale, Utah, Tom Gonzalez, LeRoy Tafoya, and Jimmy Martinez, all served in Vietnam. They lived on three consecutive streets in Midvale, Fifth, Sixth, and Seventh street, so their houses were only yards apart.

In late 1967, all three were killed during a span of 16 days. Tafoya was killed on November 22nd, Martinez died less than 24 hours later, and Gonzalez was killed on December 7th.

5

A Black and White America

"One could leave the United States,
but one couldn't leave its racial heritage behind."

Gerald F. Goodwin

DURING THE VARIOUS wars throughout our country's history, African Americans have served in the military with honor and distinction. Their service, however, was in segregated units often under the leadership of white officers. In 1948, President Harry Truman ordered the desegregation of our nation's military. It was not until the end of the Korean War, however, that full integration was finally accomplished. Therefore, the Vietnam War was our country's first major combat engagement that included an integrated military.[1]

When our country's involvement in Vietnam was increasing, so was the intensity and unrest of the civil rights movement back home. In June of 1964, three young civil rights workers were murdered by members of the Ku Klux Klan. The public outrage over these murders provided another push for the eventual passage of the Civil Rights Act on July 2, 1964.[2] One month later, Congress also passed the Gulf of Tonkin resolution that removed most restrictions from President Johnson to escalate our involvement in Vietnam.[3] The civil rights movement and Vietnam, events that dominated our nation, were happening at the same time and our country was being pulled in two different directions.

So, men and women were entering the military with their own experiences, prejudices, and opinions relating to the civil rights movement. In most ways back home, the young men from Porterville High School were far removed from the turmoil of the civil rights movement. But some of their experiences in the military brought the issues of racism and segregation directly into their own lives, too.

Joe Souza

When he first went into the Army, Joe Souza went to basic training at Ft. Ord, California and after boot camp he went to Ft. Gordon in Georgia for his AIT training as a radio operator in the Signal Corp. Ft. Gordon is located near Augusta, deep in the South. "Living in the south during this time in our country's history, was like a whole different world to me," Souza said. Since this was the early 60s, segregation and racism were rampant across the South, and Souza was right in the middle of it.

During his two tours of duty while in the military, Souza was assigned to bases in several Southern states including Louisiana, Texas, Alabama, Oklahoma, and Georgia. The impact of the civil rights movement with the unrest, protests and violence were right at his feet. Living in the South during this time, after spending his life up to this point in the alfalfa fields near Poplar, California, was certainly like living in another world.

Souza commented, "It was strange to me seeing bathrooms designated for whites only, and how blacks were told to sit in the back of the bus. I'd never experienced anything like that before." Certainly, the world in the South that he was living in during the Army was far different than what he was exposed to in the Porterville community. Sure, there was racism back home, but nothing like this.

On the outside of the military during the early 60s, the South was segregated. But on the inside of the military, it was not. Souza learned and trained with blacks just like any other soldier. It was almost like two different worlds: one inside and the other outside of the base. Souza said, "Blacks and whites did almost everything together on the inside of the base." They lived together, took the same classes together, and wore the same clothing. They slept in the same barracks, ate in the same mess halls, and used the same bathrooms. Sometimes, however, the environment of the civilian world on the outside brought challenges to the inside of the military.

For the most part, the segregation that Souza experienced or witnessed was more outside of his base than on the inside. Souza said, "There was some racism that was felt on the base, but most of the soldiers lived and operated as part of the same team." Outside of the base, however, was a different story.

Geary Baxter

Geary Baxter went to boot camp at Ft. Lewis, Washington and then to his AIT at Ft. Rucker, Alabama. While he was at Ft. Rucker, 25 of his group were gathered together one day and offered the opportunity to attend air traffic school at Biloxi, Mississippi. And Baxter volunteered. He said this about living in Biloxi during that time, "It was scary."

The reason it was scary was because Biloxi, Mississippi was located in the heart of the South during the middle of the civil rights movement. Racial unrest was rampant across the country and segregation was easily visible in the South. Baxter said, "I remember seeing road crews of prisoners working along the roads like in the movie *Cool Hand Luke*." But the most disturbing to Baxter was what he experienced that he never would have found in Porterville.

One day, Baxter was at a gas station with some friends and they had to go to the bathroom. Noticing a bathroom nearby, they went in to use it. As Baxter explained, "When we came out of the bathroom, an old man with a heavy southern drawl said, 'I know you boys are not from here, but don't ever use that bathroom again. It's for coloreds only.'"

Another time, a group of Baxter's friends from the base went to a bar downtown. There was one guy in the group that was an African American. "As they were leaving the bar," Baxter said, "one of the white guys in the back of the group was pulled out by some of the guys in the bar and they beat him up." As Baxter explained why they beat up his white friend, he said, "They beat him up as a lesson to all of us that we shouldn't hang out with a black guy." But Baxter and his friends didn't want to heed the advice from a bunch of racists. They took action.

Word began to spread around the base about their white friend getting beaten up because they had a black friend in their group. The more the word spread, the more the anger and emotions were also spread among those on the base. Then, Baxter said, "About 300 GIs on the base (including Baxter) began to march downtown to find the guys in the bar to avenge the beating of our friend." Luckily for the guys in the bar and all involved, the local police heard about what was happening and were able to diffuse the situation.

Yes, there is power in numbers sometimes, and Baxter and his friends should be credited for taking such a brave stand against racism.

Roger Gibson

Even though he was one of only three African Americans in his high school class, Roger Gibson did not experience from his Porterville High School classmates the hatred, animosity, or disdain like was directed at African Americans in the South. "I felt like just another student at the school. My circle of friends didn't treat me any differently," Gibson said. They were friends, and it didn't matter to them what the color of someone's skin might have been. They weren't black or white, they were just friends. But it was different in Texas in the 1960s, and certainly in Vietnam, too.

Gibson said, "My friends were mostly white, and I got along with them like they were members of my family." But being in the military in the 1960s was a different story from the life he experienced in Porterville, California. Texas certainly had its share of segregation and racism, but Vietnam, according to Gibson's experiences, was much worse. In fact, Gibson said, "Vietnam was the most racist environment I had ever experienced."

While in Texas at Lackland Air Force base, they were instructed to not go off base by themselves. "You always had to go with another person," Gibson said. Texas was a neighbor state to the core of the civil rights movement, with segregated bathrooms, whites only establishments, and sitting in the back of the bus. It took some time for Gibson to get acclimated to this environment. "It was a lot different than back home in Porterville," he said.

When he was in Vietnam, Gibson was told by his fellow African American soldiers to not frequent off-base "white clubs." The off-base clubs were essentially segregated by race. "Stay away from places where the white soldiers go," he was told, "and the whites will stay away from the places we go." Gibson talked about a recreational beach area in Vietnam and said, "It was segregated and there were often fights between black and white soldiers. Guys would fight each other at the beach and then fight with each other in the jungle." In most bars or social gathering places Gibson's white friends from Porterville High School would not be welcomed with him, and neither would he be welcomed with them. This was not the world he was used to. This was crazy.

Regardless of the racist or segregated pressures he might have faced in Vietnam, Gibson said, "I could never turn my back on my friends from Porterville High School."

Brian Rattigan

Fayetteville, North Carolina is the Army town next to Ft. Bragg, the home of the 82nd Airborne Division. With its large population of military and civilian employees, the base is the life blood of the

Fayetteville business community. Brian Rattigan remembered a situation involving racism against African American soldiers in the community when he said, "Around 1968, two businesses in Fayetteville, a barbershop and a bar I seem to recall, refused to serve the division's black paratroopers or its white paratroopers who accompanied their black friends downtown." At the time, black paratroopers made up a large segment of the division.

In response to this blatant display of racism against his soldiers, Rattigan said, "The 82nd Airborne Division's commanding general put Fayetteville off-limits to his paratroopers." Since this restriction would have such a profound effect on Fayetteville's economy, its business leaders met with the commanding general to vocally object to this off-limits policy.

After meeting with the business leaders and city officials, the commanding general reconsidered his off-limits order. Rattigan said, "The commanding general then directly addressed the entire division of approximately 15,000 paratroopers and advised them of the racial discrimination issue." Rattigan also said that the commanding general, "Specifically mentioned the two offending businesses that were the impetus for his off-limits order. And he also gave out the addresses of these businesses."

The commanding officer, however, rescinded his order with some conditions. He withdrew his order with the expectation that the Fayetteville business community would not discriminate against the black soldiers. Rattigan further explained, "I think that the reason the general specifically identified the businesses that initially discriminated against the black soldiers was a signal to his paratroopers to visit the offending businesses and test whether or not these businesses were still discriminating."

The commanding general of the 82nd Airborne Division deserves a great deal of thanks for taking such a bold move against discrimination during such a tumultuous time in our nation's history.

Don Dowling

When he was at Fayetteville, North Carolina with the 82nd Airborne Division, Dowling experienced the sort of segregation that was rampant throughout the South in the 1960s. Dowling said, "There was a street called Gillespie Street that was also nicknamed 'Combat Alley.' Whites lived on one side of the street and blacks lived on the other. There was fighting all the time on both sides of the street. It was a dangerous place."

Dowling said one time he and an African American friend that he had been with through boot camp, AIT, and jump school went into town together. "We got off the bus and noticed that there were two doors, one said 'Colored' above it and the other said, 'Whites.'" And they both went in the door marked "Whites." But why did they both go in the same door marked "Whites"? Quite simple. Dowling said, "We didn't know what 'colored' meant." That certainly wasn't a term Dowling used in Porterville, and no establishments back home had signs about them directing blacks or whites through respective doors.

People in the bus station warned them not to do that again. Dowling said, "They told us, whites go in one door and coloreds go in the other." Not only were they not to enter the same doors, they should not go into the same establishments again, too. Lesson learned.

As Dowling said, "He and I were best friends and we weren't going to split up." But Dowling understood the reality of the environment in the South. "When we were off base, I went to places he couldn't, and he went to places I couldn't," Dowling said. And to sum up his experiences living in the South during the height of the civil rights movement, he said, "It was scary as hell off base."

Greg Goble

One of Greg Goble's best friends while in Vietnam was a guy named Alex. Goble said this about the relationship with his friend, "We got rank together, we ran convoys together, and we proved more than once that we had each other's back." Indeed, these two were best of friends. But there was something about their friendship that made the relationship challenging at times.

Goble was white and Alex was black.

As Roger Gibson, an African American, said before, "Vietnam was the most racist environment that I had ever experienced." Similarly, Goble and Alex experienced this same level of racism in their own relationship. Goble and Alex were each just trying to do their jobs and get home. But Goble said, "Alex was addressed behind his back as an Oreo Cookie by some and the "N" word by others." Because this white guy and black guy were friends, they sometimes had to endure consternation from other soldiers. "I received some flak for the relationship we had, too, but we did not care!" They were friends, and their skin color did not matter to them.

Goble certainly learned from his friend. As Goble explained, "The stories he told me of growing up in the South were unbelievable to me. He could not use public restrooms, had to order food from the back door of restaurants and more." Alex's life was certainly not the life that Goble experienced in Porterville, California.

Despite the ugly life of segregation and racism that he experienced, Alex still maintained a positive personality and sense of humor. Goble explained the time when he and a few in his unit were getting ready to leave Vietnam and fly back home to the world. To prepare for the flight, they were laying in lawn chairs trying to get a suntan so they'd look good for the trip back home. When they were doing that, Alex's sense of humor showed through when he said, "You white boys don't have nothing on me" and while he was saying that, he held his feet and palms up toward the sun.

Thinking back to his friend, Goble said, "I miss and think of him to this day and still read his letters." And what happened to Alex? Goble said, "He died early with stomach cancer, which I suspect was from Agent Orange, which is yet another thing our government would not admit."

Friends forever, regardless of skin color. Our society today certainly needs more of that.

What some of these men experienced in terms of segregation and racism was like living in another world to them. Their lives in Porterville were not affected much by the civil rights movement. White and African American students could share friendships without fear of reprisal. Sure, there is racism in every city or state in our country, and always will be, but what they experienced in the South during the 60s was a culture shock, to say the least.

In Porterville, you wouldn't find a segregated eating establishment where blacks and whites used separate bathrooms. You wouldn't find signs above doors that said "whites" or "coloreds" and threats from local patrons if you entered the wrong door. But in the South during the 1960s, segregation was a way of life, a standing operating procedure, and friendships or associates were often measured by the color of your skin. That is what some of these veterans found in the South. And it was hard to understand.

During the time of the Vietnam War, many African Americans were fighting two wars. One at home during the civil rights movement and the other in Vietnam. And often, the veterans from Porterville High School found themselves in the middle of both wars.

Vietnam War and Wall Facts

Draftees [4]

Approximately 25% of Vietnam veterans in country entered the military through the draft. That amount is far lower than the 66% who were drafted in WWII. And draftees accounted for 30% of combat deaths during the Vietnam War.

6

Leaving Home

*"I dream of giving birth to a child who will ask,
'Mother, what was war?'"*

Eve Merriam

FOR THESE NEW recruits entering the military after graduating from Porterville High School, the beginning of boot camp still seemed like a long way away from Vietnam. They hoped that maybe by the time boot camp and AIT were over, the war would be over or winding down enough to where they wouldn't be sent to Vietnam. In the meantime, they were too busy dealing with a mean drill instructor and the overwhelming aspects of basic training to think too much of where they would find themselves after boot camp. When AIT approached, the apprehension of their next duty station grew as their training was nearing an end.

Depending on their MOS, life during AIT included some hope that their next duty station would not be in some country called Vietnam. Maybe they'd be lucky and get sent to Germany, maybe Korea, or better yet, maybe even staying stateside. They hoped, they prayed, they made promises to God. "Keep me away from Vietnam and I'll go to church every Sunday."

During the last few days of AIT, the hopes or fears of the young recruits were finally realized. They got their orders. They found out where they would be going next. When they found out, there was either a sigh of relief, or a moan of fear and concern. Regardless of where they were assigned after AIT, most of these guys took a 30-day leave to be home with family and friends before they were shipped to their next duty station.

Then, quicker than they knew it, the 30 days were over, and now came time for the final good-byes, the final hugs, the final kisses. Leaving home. Flying away. Their parents, who watched their sons take their first steps in life 17 or 18 years before, now watched their sons take those anxiety-filled steps up a staircase and into a plane that would take them away from home and place them in the middle of a war. Maybe they'll come back home alive, maybe dead, maybe injured. Who knows? And that's what worried them.

Vince Arcure

Even though an infantry assignment in Vietnam was a ticket to combat, Arcure said he had total confidence in his abilities, his training, his instincts, and was not worried about his assignment. "I was confident," Arcure said, "that I would not be killed in Vietnam." It was that old Bartlett Middle School prick mentality coming out of him again. Sure, he was nervous during the trip to the airport, but he was also confident that his skills and training would bring him back home again, alive.

His dad, however, might not have been so confident.

His parents drove Arcure to the airport when he was going to be flying off to Vietnam. When they got to the airport, they said their goodbyes, hugged their son for the last time, and then his mom and dad got in the car and drove off. Years later, his mom told Arcure that his dad did something on their trip back from the airport that she had never before seen in her husband.

"Mom said that after they were driving for a while, my dad pulled the car over and cried." Arcure further said, "Mom had never seen him cry like that before."

Sure, he may have punched his son when he found out that he enlisted in the Marine Corps, but he cried for him when he left.

Arcure's parents were like the other parents. They were worried. They were scared. They were sad. But they went with their child to the flight out of the country, a flight that would take him to the battlefields of a war. They tried to provide some last-minute parental support and encouragement, but it was hard. Their son was going to a war, and they didn't know how he would be coming back.

And that uncertainty made Arcure's dad cry.

Todd Pixler

When it was time to leave home to Vietnam, Todd Pixler's dad took him to the bus terminal in Fresno, to catch the flight to Vietnam. "Mom did not go," said Pixler, "because she couldn't handle it emotionally." He described the car ride as very quiet, and when they got to the terminal his dad bought him a drink at a bar. Pixler was not 21 yet, but his dad wanted to buy him a drink anyway. The bartender didn't ask for Pixler's identification. Maybe he looked 21, or maybe the bartender knew that Pixler was on his way to Vietnam.

Pixler remembers something vividly about the flight to Vietnam. When the plane first took off, the passengers were laughing, joking, and having a good time. The good-looking stewardesses were bringing drinks to the GIs, helping them with whatever they needed, while having to withstand some flirtatious and suggestive comments. But all this revelry changed on their last refueling stop prior to Vietnam at Wake Island.

Pixler said, "When the plane left Wake Island, with everyone knowing that the next stop was Vietnam, there was dead silence. Total and absolute silence." There was not a peep. No one was joking anymore. No one was laughing. No one was flirting with the steward-esses. Everyone was quiet, personally reflecting, meditating, or pray-ing about the situation that lay before them. The war in Vietnam.

"It was the silence that I've never forgotten," said Pixler.

Russell Vossler

When Russell Vossler was going to leave for Vietnam, his father and brother-in-law took him to the airport in Oakland. At the airport they said their good-byes, hugged, and shook hands one last time. After leaving Vossler off at the airport, his father and brother-in-law went to pick up Vossler's mother and sister and they went to a restau-rant to eat. Vossler did not find this out until years later but he said, "While they were at the restaurant, my dad started crying and he couldn't stop." Vossler continued, "He was crying so hard that they had to get up and leave the restaurant."

"Dad was in no condition to drive," Vossler said, "so mom had to drive." And his mom later told him, "Your dad cried all the way home." The driving time between Oakland and Woodville is about four hours. That's a lot of crying.

Robert Johnson

After a 30-day leave at the end of AIT, Johnson's dad took him to Travis Air Force Base for the trip to Vietnam. Johnson said, "Mom was too worried and emotional to make the trip." Johnson remembers that it was a quiet ride, and his dad was obviously worried and apprehen-sive for his son. "I was starting to get nervous, too" Johnson said. He had been watching the war on television and the anticipation was becoming nerve-wracking. He didn't really know what to expect, but then he knew the realities of the war, too. He'd seen it on television. He had spoken with friends about it. Now, it was his turn.

He said goodbye to his father at the airport, knowing that this could very well be the last time he saw him. His flight went from

Travis, to Hawaii, to Guam. And after Guam the next, and last stop was Vietnam. Johnson said, "When the plane lifted off to Vietnam, the mood in the plane really changed." Everyone now was beginning to grasp what lie ahead.

When they landed in Vietnam, Johnson noticed that some of the passengers looked scared, some were obviously nervous, and, he said, "Some were even crying." They landed in a war zone that may take their life, or injure their bodies or minds, and that would be enough for anyone to worry and cry about.

Louis Gurrola

For Louis Gurrola, leaving the United States to fly to Vietnam was made more stressful by an old military axiom.

On the day he was to fly to Vietnam, his parents drove him from Terra Bella to the airport in Oakland. The ride was a quiet one, somber, and filled with anxiety. As his parents drove, Gurrola remembers, "Hardly a word was spoken during the trip." Their son would soon be flying into a war zone and his parents were obviously concerned and worried.

When they got to the airport, Gurrola said his painful good-byes to his parents, hugged them one last time, and headed into the terminal to board the plane. Boot camp was over with, he had been trained in his MOS at AIT, and he had said his goodbyes to his family and friends. "I guess I was ready to go," Gurrola said, "but the military wasn't."

In typical military fashion, his plane did not leave shortly after he got there. In fact, he had to wait. And not a short wait either. He waited for four hours before he boarded the plane. Four long hours. "Hurry up and wait" was a common description of life in the military and that description certainly fit his circumstances in the airport. "Here I was," Gurrola said, "sitting in the airport terminal, waiting to fly into the Vietnam War, and having the wait for four hours for the plane to finally leave." Gurrola further said, "The wait was nerve-wracking."

What else could he do for four hours other than worry? His mind began to wonder about Vietnam as he waited, and his stress level increased. What was he getting into? Would he get injured or killed like so many already have from Porterville High School? Finally, the wait was over, and Gurrola boarded the plane to Vietnam.

His route to Vietnam took him from Oakland, to Alaska, to Japan, and, finally, to Vietnam. The ride was fairly quiet the whole way, and, especially, after the last stop in Japan. "The last jog to Vietnam," Gurrola admitted, "was more nerve-wracking than the four-hour wait in the airport." The reality of being in Vietnam would soon be upon him.

Melvin Braziel

Melvin Braziel's mom took her son to the airport in Bakersfield, about a 50-minute drive south of Porterville. The trip was depressing, quiet, with little talking. Braziel usually has a lot to say, a real jokester at times. But there was no joking on this trip. They were both scared and nervous about soon boarding a plane to fly into a war.

Maybe a prophetic sign or not, but on their way to the airport their car broke down. Airlines, and especially military transports, don't wait for passengers who experienced car troubles on the way, so Braziel and his mother were worried about what to do. As Braziel said, "There were no cell phones in those days, so we couldn't call a tow truck." If Braziel missed his plane, he could have been labeled as AWOL (absent without leave) and gotten into serious trouble. "My stress level was increasing," Braziel explained.

Luckily, some man pulled over to find out what was wrong, and they explained their situation and that Braziel was flying to Vietnam. In a nod of support for a soldier in uniform, the man took Braziel to the airport and then turned around to take his mom to get the car fixed. He didn't ask for any money for his time and effort, and probably wouldn't have taken any either.

They never saw the man again.

Greg Goble

Greg Goble's mom took him to Fresno to catch his flight to Oakland. Goble said, "I was one of many kids on a military plane because the United Airlines 747 jet was full." From Oakland, he eventually landed in Okinawa, which was the final stop before Vietnam. He remembers the stewardesses were serving the passengers while enduring flirtatious comments, and the soldiers were laughing, joking, and kidding around. But, Goble explained, "All that joking stopped when one short announcement came over the plane's loudspeaker."

Goble remembers the pilot making the following announcement: "Gentlemen, I'd like to inform you that we have now entered the Republic of Vietnam." When the pilot made the announcement, Goble said that two things hit him, "Reality and fear in a matter of seconds when the pilot announced that we were now entering the Republic of Vietnam." When the announcement was made, Goble said, "It was stone cold silence." Not a word was said. Not a sound was made. You could hear a pin drop.

Goble then remembers looking out the plane's window. He said, "As we were approaching our destination in Bien Hoa late at night, it looked like a firefight was going on the ground." When he saw that, Goble said, "I am now officially scared." But he soon realized that they were not under enemy attack like he feared. "I was new," he said, "and did not realize that it was just flares being shot up in the air."

Knowing that, he calmed down a little. But regardless, the reality set in that he was about to be placed in a country that he initially felt he'd never be sent to.

Don Wolfram

After Navy boot camp, Don Wolfram attended "A" school to be trained as a builder in the Seabees. Then, his first deployment was to Midway Island. At Midway, Wolfram performed all related aspects to construction and building. He painted buildings, curbs, dumpsters, and worked on preparing base housing for the next family to live in after the previous family moved out. He spent a year at Midway and then got orders to his next duty station. "Our orders were posted on the wall," Wolfram said, "And when I looked at my name, it said I was going to Vietnam." Since the Vietnam War was beginning to escalate around this time, Wolfram said, "It didn't really surprise me that I was going to Vietnam."

Prior to leaving for Vietnam, Wolfram came home for two weeks and then went to SERE training in Virginia. SERE is an acronym that stands for Survival, Evasion, Resistance, and Escape. This training included orientations about Vietnam, a simulated POW camp where the trainers tried to break the sailors down, how to avoid capture, what to do if captured, and survival skills.

Wolfram wondered, "What did this training have to do with being a builder in the Seabees?" This was not just additional building-related training, this training was serious. Now, the thought of what could happen in Vietnam was getting more worrisome. Certainly, if the Navy was subjecting its sailors to this type of training, being captured was a remote possibility.

After SERE training, Wolfram came home for two weeks. When it was time to leave, his mom and dad drove him to Travis Air Force Base for his flight to Vietnam. "It was a quiet ride," Wolfram said, "Mom and dad didn't say too much. In fact, none of us did." And, how could they? They were driving their son to an airport where a plane was waiting for him that would take him to a war. Hopefully, his SERE training would not be necessary, but what if it was?

"It was so hard to say goodbye," Wolfram said.

Alfred Alba

Alfred Alba's boot camp was at Ft. Riley in Kansas. After boot camp, Alba went to Ft. Rucker, Alabama for his AIT as a helicopter/fixed wing mechanic. When his AIT was completed, he was sent back to Ft. Riley in Kansas for about six months. Then, he got orders to Vietnam.

After a two-week leave at home in Porterville, Alba went back to Ft. Riley to prepare for his transfer to Vietnam. Alba's flight back to Kansas started from Los Angeles, but his parents did not take him to the airport, Alba's uncle did. "When I was leaving," Alba said, "mom started crying and crying." Trying to console his wife and reassure his son, Alba's dad said, "He'll be alright. Don't baby him." And then his dad also gave him some advice from the perspective of a WWII veteran who had seen combat and was a POW for over two years. His dad said, "Whatever you do in Vietnam, remember, it's just a job. When you get out, leave it there. Don't bring it home." And that's exactly what Alba did.

But there were some differences in Alba's trip to Vietnam and the welcome he received than his fellow classmates from Porterville High School who were sent to Vietnam. First, Alba's whole division was sent to Vietnam together. There were no individual assignments, no one reading the list of names posted on a wall to find out where you were going. Everybody in his division went together. And everyone went to Vietnam.

Secondly, Alba didn't fly to Vietnam. He didn't walk up the steps at Travis Air Force Base into a plane that was going to be taking him to a war. He didn't open the doors of the plane and be slapped with heat, humidity and a horrible smell. He wasn't verbally accosted coming down the steps by soldiers who were leaving Vietnam. The way Alba got to Vietnam was different.

He went by boat. Yes, boat.

"They sent us as a division and put us on a boat out of Oakland," Alba explained, "and it took us 27 days to get to Vietnam." Not only was he on a boat for 27 days, but Alba was also in trouble for 27 days. He explained, "Just before we left from Oakland, me and some guys went to watch some go-go dancers at a strip joint. And they took roll and we weren't there." One thing about the military, and that is superiors don't like absent GIs when taking roll. Especially those who did not have permission to be gone. With that, Alba got punished. And how?

"I was put on KP duty during the whole boat ride to Vietnam," he said.

But Alba further explained, "It really wasn't so bad. A Merchant Marine cook heard that we got in trouble and said that he'd take care of us. And he did." When asked what the cook did, Alba said, "He'd cook us whatever we wanted. Steak and eggs. Whatever." And Alba said, "He even let us fish off the side of the boat, but we never caught anything."

Alba was probably the only soldier who was put on KP duty for almost four weeks straight and actually enjoyed it.

But after 27 days, and a belly full of steak and eggs, Alba's boat arrived in Saigon. "They put us on landing craft to make the trip from the boat to the shore," Alba explained, "and since the landing crafts were similar to those used in WWII when they made beach landings I thought we might have been going into a battle or something." But as the ramp went down when they touched the beaches, he wasn't met with an enemy firing bullets into the landing craft like at Normandy. And what he was met with when the ramps went down was the final difference between his trip from home to Vietnam and those of his fellow classmates.

"The Army band was waiting for us and played music," Alba said. "They were there to welcome the whole division."

Obviously, Alba's transition from being at home to being in Vietnam was different than the other veterans from Porterville High School. Go-go dancers, a 27-day boat ride, KP duty the whole ride with an understanding Merchant Marine who cooked them almost anything they wanted, sneaking off the side of the boat to fish, and being greeted by the Army band welcoming his division to Vietnam.

But his welcome would later turn into a rude awakening.

Parents often know what to say to calm their sad or hurt child. When their children were growing up and got hurt, or when picked on by some bully in school, the parents would know what words to express that might console their hurt child. But not on this trip.

These parents were taking their son to an airport that would fly him into a war, and they were often almost speechless. In the same manner, boisterous or loud mouthed teenagers who would often argue instead of listening to reason, didn't have much to say on this trip either.

What words of comfort could be said that would calm each other down?

Neither the parents or their child would say this out loud or admit to it during this car trip, but they knew deep down inside that this could very well be their last car ride together. They were flying into a war where some of their friends from Porterville High School had already returned home from after being injured or killed. The parents and their child knew the realities of what they were facing, but they tried to put their game faces on during this trip, nonetheless.

Their flights would start out like any other commercial fight to another country. But they would end up in an eerie silence when the reality of being in Vietnam came across the plane's loudspeaker.

Vietnam War and Wall Facts

Chaplains on the Wall [1]

During the war in Vietnam, chaplains offered the troops spiritual and emotional support while sharing the same discomforts experienced by those in battle. As they assisted the sick, injured or dying, they did so sometimes in places of danger and in harm's way. In all, sixteen chaplains died in Vietnam.

Two U.S. Army chaplains, Charlie Watters and Angelo Liteky were awarded the Congressional Medal of Honor, America's highest award for bravery and valor.

SECTION TWO
During Vietnam – *Their Stories*

7

First Impressions of 'Nam

*"For those who have fought for it,
life has a flavor the protected will never know."*

Guy de Maupassant

THREE WORDS SEEMED to be consistent among the veterans when asking about their first impressions of Vietnam. Those three words were: heat, humidity, and smell. Although the temperature may have hovered around the same temperature as a hot day in California's Central Valley during the summer, throw in the suffocating humidity and the weather becomes almost unbearable.

It didn't matter if it was early in the morning or late in the day. Midnight or sunrise. It could have been in the summer, fall, winter, or spring. The heat was almost always there, and the humidity made the heat into an oven of living hell. And on top of that, the place stunk.

According to the veterans, Vietnam smelled. The smell of dead fish, the smell of rice patties, the smell of diesel fuel, the smell of human waste. And if you were in the boonies, the smell of you, the smell of your buddies, the smell of napalm, the smell of death. It was all there.

The first impressions of the veterans were similar, but some were quite different.

Melvin Braziel

When asked what his first impression of Vietnam was when he was walking down the steps from the airplane when it landed in Vietnam, Braziel said something without any hesitation whatsoever. His first impression was a smell. But it was the smell of something so disgusting that he can still smell it today.

"The smell of shit. Burning shit!" Braziel remembers.

Vietnam certainly had its array of smells, but this one was the worst. The smell permeated the air because of the way the military disposed of human excrement - by burning it. The process to burn this human waste is explained in more detail later in this book, but it was an experience every Vietnam veteran would choose to forget. Absolutely disgusting. But everywhere he went in Vietnam, Braziel smelled it. And Braziel said, "I can still smell it today, fifty years later."

Now when Braziel drives through the stinky cattle dairies near Tulare, California during the hot summer months, where cows are standing shoulder-to-shoulder in piles of crap and puddles of urine, his mind goes back to the days in Vietnam when that smell was a daily experience.

Roger Gibson

Since he had a brother serving in Vietnam, Roger Gibson could have turned down an assignment to Vietnam due to his brother being there. "But while I was at Lackland," Gibson said, "I felt worthless." He talked about his assignment while at Lackland as being important, but he still felt he needed something more. Gibson said, "I really felt that I needed to go to Vietnam." And, eventually, that's where he went.

When Roger Gibson's flight arrived in Vietnam, there were three things he remembers vividly. The heat, the humidity, and a certain person standing at the bottom of the steps.

When he got on the steps to disembark the plane Gibson can still remember the wave of humidity that virtually slapped him in the face. He could not really take a deep breath due to the humidity and, because of the heat, he began sweating as soon as he left the plane. But then, looking down the steps he saw him. A familiar face in a crowd of unfamiliar people in a country at war eight thousand miles from home.

He saw his brother.

Gibson said, "Just seeing my brother waiting for me at the bottom of the steps made the stop in Vietnam a much easier one." No, this wasn't home, but having a brother by your side made the transition from the comforts of home to the uncertainty of war a little less stressful.

Roland Hill

"During the flight to Vietnam," Hill said, "the inside of the plane kept getting quieter and quieter as we got closer." When his plane flew into Vietnam air space, "There was dead silence," Hill remembers. And when the plane began to descend onto the airport runaway, it did not take long for plane load of passengers to realize that they were, in fact, in a war zone.

Shortly before their plane landed, the airport had come under rocket attack. So, rather than drop the GIs off near the main terminal, where the rockets had recently landed, Hill said, "We were dropped off on the runway as far away from the terminal as possible. Our duffle bags and other luggage were dumped on the runway, and then the plane took off." Here they were, a bunch of nervous, scared, and tired new troops standing on the runway suffocating from the heat and humidity of Vietnam with their luggage piled in a heap not knowing where to go or who was going to take them there.

Finally, a bus came out to pick them up. But this bus was no four-star Greyhound bus either. It was a beat up, ragged bus, with windows boarded up so the riders inside would be protected from any shell fragments or debris that could enter through the windows if the bus came under attack. "This was certainly not the kind of welcome to Vietnam that I was expecting," Hill said.

Louis Gurrola

When his plane landed in Vietnam, Gurrola remembers, "The weather was so nasty." But, as he later found out, the weather would be nasty like that for the next 12 months. It wasn't just hot like the days during the summer in the fields of California picking cotton. It was hot and humid. It was a sticky, suffocating, and smelly heat. "It was awful," he said.

He exited the plane with the same worries, the same fears, and the same apprehensions that his fellow soldiers in front of him or behind him in the line were experiencing at that moment. When they were off the plane, they were given some general directions and instruction, and then made their way into their temporary barracks to spend the first night in a war zone.

The day after his plane landed in Vietnam, only his first full day in the country, his fears about being in a war zone were realized.

As he was still getting settled into his temporary location, Gurrola said, "Before we had been issued any weapons, the airport came under enemy attack." Shots were being fired, people were yelling, sirens were blasting, and everyone was running into bunkers. It was scary. When all of this was happening, Gurrola thought to himself, "I'm never going to make it back home. No way in hell."

He was in supply, so this kind of action wasn't supposed to happen to him. But it was happening all around him and he was scared. He had no rifle to defend himself with, and no other weapons to return fire. So, he just hunkered down and waited. Finally, it was all over. His second day in Vietnam. "What were the next 12 months going to be like?" Gurrola wondered.

Russell Vossler

Prior to his leaving the United States to fly to Vietnam, Russell Vossler developed pneumonia. After some time to recuperate, he was scheduled to leave for Vietnam. Since he was still sick and under medication on the day he left, Vossler said, "I slept the whole way to Vietnam." He did not remember the stops the plane made, or anything about the flight itself. Which may have been a good thing. Rather than sitting during a long flight and worrying about Vietnam, building up stress and anxiety along the way, he slept. He slept the whole way. But when his plane landed the sleep ended, and he was now in a whole different world.

His first impressions of Vietnam were much like the other veterans. Vossler said, "The first thing I remember walking down the steps of the plane was the feeling of the heat and humidity. And it was only two in the morning." In addition to the feeling of the weather was the smell of something else. The smell of burning shit. That smell cleared up his clogged head in a heartbeat. "God the place stunk," Vossler remembers.

Since he was still sick with pneumonia, Vossler had a few days of downtime to rest, build up some strength, and get healthy enough to be transferred. He was then moved to his company at Bearcat base. The sign entering the base had a painting of a bear that said, "Welcome to Bearcat." Vossler was home in Vietnam.

During his first few days in his new company, Vossler was sent to the supply room to have his equipment distributed to him. As they passed out his equipment Vossler noticed he was being given things that he didn't think he'd ever need while doing helicopter maintenance. An M16. A 45-caliber pistol. Ammunition. When he received these weapons of war, he said, "I thought I was getting a toolbox!"

He was supposed to fix helicopters, not shoot weapons. But in Vietnam, in the middle of a war, you never knew when the war would be thrust upon you and you'd need to protect yourself or the buddy next to you.

Greg Goble

There were a few other things that Greg Goble remembers vividly as he thinks back to his first impression of Vietnam. The first were the heat, humidity, and smell. When he got on the steps of the plane to descend into Vietnam, it was hot, it was humid, and it stunk like a swamp. The combination was almost sickening. But he also had an experience that didn't nauseate him like the weather and smell did, but rather made him a little nervous.

"At the bottom of the ramp," Goble remembers, "was a long line of GIs waiting to board the plane. Guys who were going home." These GIs had made it through their experiences during the war in Vietnam. Seasoned, battle-hardened troops. Most of them looked 10 years older than Goble but they were probably about the same age. Being in war can age a person rather quickly.

As he and the rest of the new troops descended the steps, Goble said, "We were replacements, not only for those injured or who did not survive, but for those guys standing in line who were going home after making it through their tour of 12 or more months." But then something rather depressing happened. "A few guys on the ground began to verbally harass us, calling us 'cherry boys' (a slang for new, inexperienced soldiers), telling us to make sure we ducked, and things like that." Goble further said, "I was not feeling too good hearing these guys intimidating us like that."

Someone said to the guy in front of Goble that he would not make it, and Goble said, "I vowed that if I was lucky enough to be boarding that Freedom Bird, I would never, never do the same thing!"

Ron McCarville

After infantry training at Camp Pendleton, Ron McCarville was sent to North Carolina for further training and then to Guantanamo Bay in Cuba. From approximately March to September McCarville was assigned to guard duty at Guantanamo Bay, and then he got orders that he was being rotated to Vietnam.

Before he left for Vietnam, McCarville went home on leave. He remembers when he got home for leave, most of his friends were gone. Some were in Vietnam, some were in other parts of the world serving in the military, and some were away at college. Since most of his friends were not home, he felt alone.

After his leave at home was over, his mom, his girlfriend, and a school teacher who was a friend of the family, drove McCarville to Visalia, which was the first stop on his way to Vietnam. The drive was a quiet one, but McCarville said, "I wanted to get it over with. I was ready to get on to Vietnam."

His flight to Vietnam was uneventful. He had been mentally planning for this trip since he was young and had decided that he wanted to enlist in the Marine Corps. He flew from Travis Air Force Base to Anchorage, Alaska, to Okinawa, and then to Vietnam. He remembers that the mood on the plane changed as they got closer to Vietnam. He said, "The closer we got to Vietnam, the quieter the plane became." The loud chatter and laughter were slowly being replaced with silence and reflection. Finally, they landed.

Like the other veterans, his first impression of the country was the heat, humidity, and smell. The place was miserable. And it really didn't change for the next eight months. But there was one other thing that made an impression on him after only a few days in the country.

When he got to Vietnam, the unit that he was assigned to was just coming back in from an operation. One of the guys in his unit said to him, "Everyone in your squad is probably going to get wounded." Not exactly the kind of things you want to hear when you are first introduced to your new unit after just a few days in the country. Was that guy telling the truth?

Well, McCarville would find out soon enough.

Todd Pixler

One of the first impressions Todd Pixler remembers having when he first got to Vietnam, was a sense of relief. A sense made possible

117

by a friend from Porterville High School.

Pixler said, "We had just gotten to Vietnam and me and some other guys were made to stand in line and were told that Sgt. Johnson would come out and give us our assignments." Not knowing who this Sgt. Johnson was, Pixler stood at attention in line waiting for the sergeant. Would this sergeant be a jerk looking to harass these unsuspecting green soldiers? Would this sergeant be in the mold of Ermey, the sadistic DI from the movie *Full Metal Jacket* who his friend Ron McCarville had as his DI at boot camp? Pixler was nervous, waiting in anticipation, and worrying about what he was going to be assigned to do.

Sgt. Johnson came out and started walking down the line and giving assignments to these new, scared soldiers who were fresh off the plane with no experience and a ton of uncertainty about being in Vietnam. Pixler said, "Sgt. Johnson came up to me, stared me in the face and said, 'I'll take this guy.'" In military fashion, Sgt. Johnson and Pixler had to maintain their composure while in line. Otherwise, they probably would have hugged each other or given each other high fives. Why? Because Sgt. Johnson was Bob Johnson, Pixler's high school classmate.

Pixler was able to stay with Johnson a couple of days and being with a friend in a country at war eight thousand miles from home, helped Pixler better handle the transition from home. Since Johnson had already seen the worst of what life was like in Vietnam from being wounded twice in battle, he gave Pixler some friendly advice. As Pixler explained, "Bob basically said, 'Don't worry about the heavy crap, just do your job and whatever happens will happen.'" In other words, Johnson was telling his friend to not spend a lot of time worrying about what might happen, just do your job.

Too bad everyone when they first arrived in Vietnam didn't have a friend to lean on the first few days like Pixler did. Especially, a friend from home.

Richard Walker

When Richard Walker was getting ready to fly to Vietnam, he wasn't particularly worried at the time. "I didn't worry about it like a lot of the other guys did, until...." His attitude changed when he saw something on the grounds of Vietnam. "When we landed and I saw all of the military stuff," he said, "I remember thinking to myself, 'This is real.'" And indeed, it was. He was in the very place that he thought he would avoid by joining the Navy.

Walker said, "One of the first things that impacted me was that I saw an instant difference between where I lived in Terra Bella as compared to these Vietnamese people." They were poor and lacking in any living comforts that Americans take for granted. "I felt sorry for the people," Walker said, "and I told myself then, 'I'll never complain about anything in my life again.'"

However, that caring attitude and feeling toward the poor Vietnamese changed later when Walker was in a fight for his life.

Don Dowling

Because of the specific day it was, when Don Dowling landed in Vietnam he should have been in a festive mood. He should have had a party to celebrate something important in his life. He should have been surrounded by family and friends. But he wasn't.

The military had timed Dowling's trip to Vietnam almost to the minute. Dowling said, "In order for combat soldiers to be sent to Vietnam, they were supposed to be 18 years old. But when my plane left the states for Vietnam, I was only 17." However, something happened to Dowling when he landed in Vietnam. "My plane landed in Vietnam on my 18th birthday."

Happy birthday. And, by the way, you are now old enough for combat.

Prior to leaving for Vietnam, Dowling received some words of wisdom and encouragement from his top sergeant. "Top asked me what I thought about going to Vietnam," Dowling said, "and I told him it scared the hell out of me." Dowling said that his sergeant gave him some suggestions, and talked with him about what to expect, what to do, what to watch out for, and that helped to release some of the tension Dowling was feeling about going to Vietnam. Dowling said, "Top also told me to watch the old guys who had been there for a while." And Dowling took his advice.

So, when he walked up the stairs and into the plane back in the states, he was not old enough yet to fight in combat. But when the plane landed and the doors opened, he was. Perfect timing.

Dan Boydstun

As with most of the veterans who remembered their first impression of Vietnam to be the heat, humidity, and smell, Boydstun had a similar recollection, but he also had a few other first impressions that were more serious. His first impression of Vietnam came just before he landed, just before he was able to open the door and feel the heat, humidity and smell that awful smell. His first impression came from the pilot over the plane's loudspeakers when he made the following announcement just before they were to land in Vietnam.

"There is activity on the runway. Everybody get in the crash position."

"Crash position?" Boydstun thought. When stewardesses on domestic flights give demonstrations about crash positions at the beginning of the flight, or how to handle a loss in cabin pressure, most passengers pay little attention. But not on this flight. Boydstun paid close attention and did what the pilot ordered them to do. "I got into the crash position, closed my eyes, and hoped for the best." Well, the best came because the plane landed.

And this was only Boydstun's second time he had been in an airplane.

As he was disembarking from the plane, Boydstun also witnessed something that bothered him. There was a group of GIs standing in line ready to get on the plane. Soldiers, Marines, airmen and sailors who were going home. Those who made it through their year in Vietnam and were about ready to get on the Freedom Bird and fly back to the world. Boydstun said, "Some of them looked like they had just gotten out of the bush." When the new group was walking past those who were going home, Boydstun said, "Those guys were shouting things at us that were not too encouraging like 'Make sure you duck,' that sort of thing. And it sure didn't make me feel very good."

At the temporary barracks he was first assigned to, Boydstun noticed the stacks of sandbags around the barracks and he found out that the area had been overrun by the Viet Cong the year before. When he learned this, he thought to himself, "This is serious."

So, Boydstun's first impression of Vietnam was a variety of feelings, senses, and smells. Crash position, heat, humidity, smell, taunting words, and learning that his area had been overrun by the Viet Cong a year earlier. Nothing like back home in Porterville.

Ron Crabtree

After Ron Crabtree graduated from high school, he began working in a variety of jobs looking for something to make a career out of. He even moved to Los Angeles for a little while in search of employment. Eventually, someone else found him a job. And that someone else was the military. Crabtree got drafted.

Crabtree went to boot camp at Ft. Lewis, Washington. Near the end of boot camp he found out what his MOS was going to be. Infantry. His first words that came to his mind when he found out he was going into the infantry were, "Oh, crap!"

He remained at Ft. Lewis for his infantry training and then came home for a 30-day leave before he was to fly to Vietnam. When he was home, most of his friends were not around. Some were serving in a variety of places in the military, while others were in college or working. When it was time to leave for Vietnam, and as he was boarding the plane, Crabtree said, "I was still the eternal optimist."

What did he mean by labeling himself as an eternal optimist?

Crabtree said, "I was thinking that maybe my plane will break down, they'll need to land, put me in a jeep, and send me back home." Well, his optimism was really only a fantasy, because the reality was that his plane never broke down. They never put him in a jeep, and they didn't send him back home, at least for another 12 months. He was going to Vietnam.

His flight took him from Washington to Japan, the Philippines, and then Vietnam. "We had a stopover in the Philippines," Crabtree said, "and man that place stunk. It was putrid." But how did the smell of Vietnam compare to the Philippines? "Vietnam smelled even worse than that," Crabtree said.

When he got to Vietnam, one of the first impressions he remembers was not just the smell. Although the place stunk worse than the Philippines. It was not the humidity. Even though the humidity was suffocating. His first impression was a question he remembers asking himself when the plane first landed.

"Where's my M16?"

Tony Forner

Dealing with the stress of going to Vietnam was a little easier for Tony Forner than it might have been for the other veterans, because he went with his high school friend, Vince Arcure. Forner said, "Arcure and I went to boot camp together, infantry training together, and flew to Vietnam together." Certainly, having a friend along for the ride made the trip easier, but once they arrived in Vietnam, their being together finally came to an end.

Forner remembers when the pilot came over the loudspeaker and said, "Welcome to Vietnam" and then it got really quiet. Few of the passengers were speaking and most had looks of concern and even fear on their faces. When they exited the plane and were on the ground of their new home, Forner said, "That was one hot freaking place, and it felt like we walked into an oven."

When they were making assignments to their respective companies, Forner and Arcure were split up because, as Forner said, "They did not want guys from the same hometown fighting in the same unit together." Even though they were hometown buddies who had been through boot camp and infantry training together, the separation was not really an emotional one. Forner said, "We figured we'd cross paths again sometime so we just basically said, 'See you later' and went off to our new companies."

They did, in fact, see each other again, but this time in Okinawa when Forner was there for additional training and Arcure was there after being injured and eventually being reassigned to Okinawa. Forner said, "It was in Okinawa where they took our M14 and gave us the worthless M16."

And Forner used that worthless weapon an awful lot during his remaining months in Vietnam.

Anonymous

Although one of the veterans had the similar first impressions of Vietnam being the heat, humidity and smell, the one thing that stands out in his memory was something different. For this story, he chose to remain anonymous, for obvious reasons.

He remembered that during some impromptu orientation for the new personnel in Vietnam, the sergeant speaking said something that was probably included in every orientation or mentioned in every conversation with those who were new to Vietnam. And it was something that he never forgot.

When talking about the local population, the sergeant said, "You've probably heard that *some* of the local girls around here have VD (venereal disease). Well, that's not true. They ALL have VD!" This veteran eventually tested that theory and found it to be true. He said that he got the clap so many times that he felt like he was being applauded for supporting the local commerce so much. You can understand why he chooses to remain anonymous.

His secret is good with me.

There was a unanimous first impression the veterans had about Vietnam - it was hot, it was humid, and it stunk. And this first impression became a daily reality during their 12 or so months in the country.

Once their plane landed, it did not take long for some of them to realize they were in a war zone. Some were under enemy attack almost the minute they got there, while others went out on patrol shortly after they landed. Their first impressions also included emotions of fear, worry, and stress. They often did not have lengthy orientations that gave them time to adjust to their new world, because many were thrust into the war without much transition time.

This was a far cry from being home in Porterville, cruising Main, partying, or watching a football game on Friday night. For some of them, the difference between being at home in Porterville and finding themselves on the battlefields of Vietnam was only a few days.

The next few months would be hell on earth.

Vietnam War and Wall Facts

The First Casualty [1]

The first soldier killed during what later became known as the American War in Vietnam was Air Force Technical Sergeant Richard Bernard Fitzgibbon, Jr. He was not killed, however, by enemy fire or in combat. Rather, he was murdered by another airman after an argument and died of his wounds on June 8, 1956.

At the time, the Department of Defense considered the official start of the war to be a few years after Fitzgibbon's death, but after some reconsiderations and family appeals his name was added to the Vietnam Memorial wall in 1999. Ironically, his son, Richard, was also killed in Vietnam on September 7, 1965.

8

The War in the Bush

"You don't go into battle to die for your country.
You go into battle to make the other bastard die for his country."

George Patton, Jr., 1941

IT WAS THE place in Vietnam that most wanted to avoid. Being there meant you were in the middle of the war and staring death in the face. Living there meant you were existing in primitive conditions, rarely bathing, sleeping on the ground, dealing with insects, leeches, parasites, and jungle rot. It was an awful place, a place that carried with it the daily stress and worry about whether or not you'll survive another day in it. What was this place called?

The bush.

In some places in the bush, or in the jungles of Vietnam, the foliage was so thick you could only see a few feet in front of you. Sometimes, the only way to walk through it was with a machete leading the way. And in the bush, if the enemy didn't attack that day, chances are the insects did. Lice in their hair, blood-sucking leeches stuck to their bodies, and large red ants that would clamp on the skin to where they were almost impossible to remove, and there were snakes, lizards, and rats.

For troops in the infantry, the bush is where they lived for about 300 days out of their one-year assignment in Vietnam. When the infantrymen would come out of the bush, they stunk, their clothes were rotting off, their hair was unkempt, faces were unshaven, their bodies were riddled with bites, scratches, and blisters, and they looked ten years older than they actually were.

Roland Hill, a helicopter crew member who was involved in many battles in the air, commented on his admiration and respect for the grunts in the field. As Hill mentioned, "While I was in a relatively safe place with a roof over my head, the infantrymen were living in terrible conditions." He mentioned how the infantrymen were under constant stress, facing the trauma of war, while battling not just the enemy, but also booby traps, illness, and infections. "I really admired those guys," Hill said.

The bush was a horrible place to live, yet some of the young men from Porterville High School called the bush their home.

Ron McCarville

"How can you not be affected by that?"

That was a question Ron McCarville asked several times during our interview as he recalled the ugliness of his experiences in Vietnam. He saw some of the worst while living in the bush, and anyone who saw what McCarville did would be affected by that.

McCarville remembered the first time he came close to a sniper's bullet. He was walking in the bush near another Marine, who was about 15 feet from him, when a shot rang out and the other guy got shot in the foot. McCarville remembered thinking, "Some guy out there is trying to kill us." They didn't see the sniper, nor could they tell where exactly the shot came from. So, what did they do? They hunkered down, waited a bit, and then kept on walking. "Even though there's someone out there trying to kill you," McCarville said, "you can't let it affect you. You've got to move on."

As a Marine in the infantry, McCarville experienced some of the most brutal aspects of the Vietnam War. He remembered an instance when he had to sleep at night next to a dead North Vietnamese soldier. When he was describing an intense fight they were in one time, I asked him how close he was to enemy soldiers during that battle. He looked around the house, pointed to a sofa in the other room which was a distance of about 15-20 feet, and said, "About from here to there."

He then described one day when he saw a stack of rifles, and next to the rifles was a stack of helmets. And next to the helmets was a stack of bodies. "How many bodies?" I asked. And he replied, "About a hundred." "Enemy soldiers?" I asked. "No," he said, "Americans." After taking some time to gain his composure, he asked, "How can you not be affected by that?"

At one point during our interview, McCarville said that he wanted me to see something. He got up out of his chair, walked into another room, and brought back something that looked like a red diploma cover I used to hand out to graduates during commencement at Porterville College. I opened the cover and noticed there was one document placed on the inside left cover, and another on the inside right cover. This is what the first document I read said:

"The United States of America. This is to certify that the President of the United States of America has awarded the BRONZE STAR MEDAL to Corporal Ronald E. McCarville, United States Marine Corps for heroic achievement on 27 May 1968."

The folder held the citation McCarville received for heroism in battle. The Bronze Star. Rather than summarizing what he did that day to earn the Bronze Star, the following is the language directly from the citation:

"For heroic achievement in connection with operations against the enemy in the Republic of Vietnam while serving as a Squad Leader with Company K, Third Battalion, Fifth Marines,

First Marine Division. On 27 May 1968, during Operation Allen Brook, elements of the Third Battalion became heavily engaged with a numerically superior North Vietnamese Army force entrenched in a village on Go Noi Island in Quang Nam Province. In the initial moments of the fire fight, Corporal McCarville's squad sustained two casualties and was pinned down by intense machine gun, mortar and B-40 rocket fire from nearby hostile positions. Disregarding his own safety, he directed accurate suppressive fire against the enemy as he boldly moved forward into the fire-swept area and assisted in recovering the two wounded men. Then, rallying his squad, he directed the delivery of a heavy volume of fire which killed three enemy soldiers who had advanced to within twenty meters of his position. Skillfully maneuvering his men to more advantageous positions, Corporal McCarville consolidated his position with the adjacent units on his flanks, halting the enemy's advance and accounting for two additional North Vietnamese soldiers killed. When his radio operator became a heat casualty, he carried his own radio and continued to move about the hazardous area adjusting artillery fire to within fifty meters of his position. His heroic actions and bold initiative inspired all who observed him and contributed significantly to the subsequent defeat of the enemy. Corporal McCarville's courage, aggressive leadership and selfless devotion to duty at great personal risk were in keeping with the highest traditions of the Marine Corps and of the United States Naval Service."

The citation was signed by H. W. Buse, Jr., Lieutenant General, U.S. Marine Corps, Commanding General, Fleet Marine Force, Pacific. This is certainly a vivid depiction of heroism. I'm sure even Drill Instructor Ermey would have been impressed with McCarville's actions that day.

You will also see in a following chapter, that one of the 40 names listed on the Vietnam Veterans Memorial at Veteran's Park is that of

Stephen Austin. Austin was killed on June 8, 1968 during Operation Allen Brook which, ironically, was the same operation during which McCarville received the Bronze Star for what he did about 12 days earlier.

Once Operation Allen Brook was over, McCarville walked on to the next battle. McCarville said, "We would have some sort of contact with the enemy about every four days or so." The contact could have been just a lone sniper trying to pick off an American, an ambush, or a larger battle lasting an hour or more.

McCarville mentioned that approximately 80% of his time while in Vietnam was spent in the bush. Walking, dealing with an ambush, and then walking again. Day after day after day. He remembers his clothes were filthy, with some of his clothes actually rotting off, and they smelled - bad. "The only time we got to bathe," McCarville said, "was when we were walking through rivers or maybe bomb craters that were filled with rainwater." But these so-called baths were nothing like lying in a bathtub back home, soaking in bubble bath, while listening to music. "You didn't stop to bathe," McCarville said, "you bathed as you walked through the water."

McCarville talked about some of the necessities of life, and how these were hard to come by in the bush. For example, as they drudged through the jungles while being enveloped with heat and humidity resulting in parched mouths and bodies needing replenishment, where did the water they needed come from? Well, canteens certainly weren't filled with cool water from the faucet of a kitchen sink. Rather, they were often filled with water from dirty and diseased waters found in rivers, canals, or bomb craters. As McCarville explained, "In order to make the water healthy enough to drink, you had to drop an iodine tablet into the canteen to kill the bacteria." Then, they added Kool Aid powder to make this putrid taste somewhat manageable. Oh, but no ice. The water they drank was as warm as the outside weather.

C-rations, or food in cans, were included among the 100-pound pack carried on their backs. McCarville had an interesting comment about C-rations when he said, "They were the one thing that the military couldn't screw up." Certainly, GIs couldn't carry enough food to last for their entire time in the bush, so helicopters would periodically fly over the soldiers in the bush to drop off food or other necessities. When asked if the helicopters dropping these necessities would give away their position, McCarville said, "The enemy knew where we were. Our location wasn't a mystery to them."

During the time he was in the bush, McCarville estimated he lost about 30 pounds.

McCarville said, "When you are in the bush for so long, it can start to work on your mind." Their contact with others is limited, and there is very little information shared with them about what is happening in the outside world. You're out humping the bush looking for the enemy. That's your life existence. One time when he was finally back at a rear base camp and going to take a shower, McCarville said, "When I went into the shower for the first time in a long time, I stood there and played with a light switch, turning it off and on. Then, I walked around the shower room turning on all of the shower heads." Things we take for granted, but things that are marvels or curiosities to those just out of the bush.

This was the life of a Marine Corps infantryman in Vietnam and McCarville was right in the middle of it. Horrendous living conditions. Death. Stench. Stress. Injury. Fear.

How can you not be affected by that?

Robert Johnson

Robert Johnson's first two weeks in Vietnam were spent in orientations and classes that trained them further in aspects of a jungle war with ambushes. He was then taken to his company. He might have expected some sort of gathering to welcome the new troops to the company. But that's not what he got.

When asked what he did when he got to his new company, Johnson said, "My first day with my new company we went on assault." He'd been in Vietnam for only two weeks, he had just joined his new company, and he was already going into the jungle. And not only did they go out on assault, but they also came under enemy fire.

Johnson remembers loading up into the helicopters, taking off and wondering what he was going to be faced with. "Since this was my first time out, I didn't really know what to expect," Johnson said. But he found out soon enough. Sometime later, the helicopters began to descend for the soldiers to disembark. "As soon as I got out of the helicopter and jumped onto the ground we came under enemy attack," Johnson remembers. Shots were being fired at them from the trees and bushes. Rockets and mortars were incoming. Soldiers were screaming and hollering to each other over the sounds of the battle.

Johnson was firing like crazy, unloading his M16 into the trees. But, as he said, "I couldn't see what I was shooting at." He knew where the enemy shots were coming from, but he couldn't see who was firing them. And not being able to see the enemy is part of the difficulty of jungle warfare. Johnson made sure he got out of the elephant grass that engulfed the area. He said, "They told us that the elephant grass could catch on fire if it was hit by tracers."

What he saw during the battle, what he heard, and what he felt, he said it "Scared the shit out of me!" The battle lasted about an hour and then it was over. Injuries and death lay all around him.

Only two weeks in Vietnam and he was already in a battle for his life. Only two weeks. And he had about 50 weeks left to go.

Johnson's life as an infantryman during the war in Vietnam was an existence few could imagine. He would be dropped off in the mountains and then would walk every day. Up and down hills, often passing dead Vietnamese soldiers they left lying on the ground. He walked through dense foliage, fighting insects, and dealing with ambushes from a hidden enemy. He said, "My first time out, I was in the field for about three months. Then we got three days off and then back out into the field again." During that time, Johnson said he didn't really shower or bathe for about six months. As Johnson admitted, "We couldn't tell who smelled. We all smelled bad."

Back in the late 1960s, when a guy turned 19 years old, he might have gotten an eight-track tape player for his birthday. Or maybe a tape of *The Doors* with their hit song, "Light My Fire." Or maybe he got a date and went to the Porter Theater to watch the movie "Cool Hand Luke," with the young actor, Paul Newman. Well, Johnson got none of those on his 19th birthday, but he did get something unique. Something none of his friends from Porterville High School got on their 19th birthday.

Johnson got shot.

On the last night of his 18th year of life, Johnson was asleep on his poncho liner on the ground as the Vietnamese were quietly moving in to set up an ambush for the following morning. Then, as the sun arose in the early morning hours over the canopy of the jungle, Johnson said, "Shit started flying everywhere. It was a freak show."

Mortars, rockets, and shots were incoming, and everyone was "shooting their asses off," as Johnson explained it. It was total chaos and confusion. As Johnson was fighting back in the middle of the battle, shooting his M16 towards the incoming rounds from the bushes and trees around him, a bullet from the enemy hit his body. "I got shot in the spine and the bullet went out my leg," Johnson said. "It hurt a lot at first, but then it didn't." He was too involved in the battle that was happening around him to notice the pain.

But being shot didn't stop Johnson. "I kept shooting. Crawling around the ground," he said, "I couldn't walk." After about 30 minutes in the battle, helicopter gunships came that provided the necessary firepower support that ended this battle in the Americans' favor. Johnson said, "Once the gunships came and the battle was over, they carried me, since I couldn't walk, and put me on board one of the helicopters and gave me some morphine." They took Johnson to a hospital for surgery where he spent the next week, and then to Okinawa where he spent the next four months recuperating from surgeries on his injured leg and spine.

While he was in the hospital in Okinawa, there was one place Johnson said he wanted to be. No, it wasn't back home in California.

It wasn't on the beaches of Hawaii on rest and recuperation (R and R). It wasn't a hotel somewhere where he could have a cold beer and take a shower. So, where did he want to be?

"I wanted to be back with my unit," Johnson said, "I felt guilty not being with them."

After his time in Okinawa was over, back with his unit is exactly where Johnson found himself. And on his second day back with his unit, he found himself in another battle with the enemy. Only the second day back. Then, approximately three months after returning to his unit from Okinawa, Johnson was wounded again.

"We were in Cambodia, and this time during a battle I received fragments from an explosion," Johnson said, "and that landed me back in the hospital for a month." But at the end of this battle, after he loaded onto the helicopter, Johnson noticed something that was almost unreal.

The helicopter pilot that was taking Johnson from the battlefield to the hospital was Geary Baxter, a Porterville High School friend of Johnson's. What an incredible and unique high school reunion. According to Johnson, Baxter later joined him in the hospital and brought along some whiskey. Like old times back in Porterville, they drank the whiskey and got drunk. In addition, however, Johnson said, "We both got chewed out because I was on morphine and wasn't supposed to be drinking whiskey."

A reunion like none other.

In addition to being an infantryman, one of Johnson's other volunteer assignments that often placed him in harm's way was that of a tunnel rat. The motto of the tunnel rats was a Latin phrase, "Non Gratus Anus Rodentum." Which meant, "Not worth a rat's ass."[1] But to me, these guys were worth a heck of a lot. Not many would volunteer to go down into tunnels looking for the enemy, but Johnson did.

The Vietnamese had developed an elaborate tunnel system that was used by the communists during the war. The tunnels often included storage rooms for weapons, supplies and food, offices, barracks, meeting rooms and space for soldiers to hide from the Americans.

It was the responsibility of the tunnel rats to find, search, clear, and destroy tunnel complexes. Obviously, the assignment was incredibly stressful.

The tunnel rats never really knew what was in the tunnel before they entered it. There could be no one, or there could be a significant number of the enemy with weapons at the ready. Whenever they would find the opening of a tunnel, Johnson said, "It was spooky. I was always nervous looking into the hole." And who could blame him? He didn't know what might be staring him in the face when he did. So, before he entered the hole, Johnson said, "I'd throw in a hand grenade to eliminate any enemy who might be near the tunnel's opening."

On numerous occasions, it happened that the toss of a grenade into the hole saved his life. "I'd often find dead or disoriented enemy soldiers in the tunnel when I went in to inspect it after throwing in the grenade," Johnson said. Knowing that there were enemy soldiers just a few feet away as Johnson approached the tunnel opening, the enemy would certainly have killed Johnson had he not tossed the grenade into the hole prior to entering the tunnel.

Most of the tunnel rats were smaller men who could fit easily into the tunnel, but Johnson was larger than many of the other tunnel rats. Therefore, he said, "I'd go into the ones I could fit into." One time, when they entered a tunnel they found something quite interesting.

A hospital.

And not just any hospital. It was an underground complex that included six floors of hallways, rooms, storage areas, and walkways. Johnson said, "They had been working on this hospital since when the French were there." Using their keen sense of their surroundings, Johnson said "We noticed a lot of rock in the river, rock that didn't match the river bottom it was lying in. This rock had obviously been taken out of the ground and dumped in the river." Seeing this, they knew a tunnel was nearby. They found it, and in they went.

Johnson also experienced something he never could have imagined would happen to him on the battlefields of Vietnam. He was on national television.

CBS was doing a commentary on race relations among the soldiers in Vietnam. Since Johnson's unit was ethnically diverse and the soldiers were known to have worked cohesively together, a CBS crew followed his unit around the jungles of Vietnam. "The guys who got interviewed the most," Johnson said, "were the ones from the South, like Arkansas or Alabama. Since I was from California, they weren't interested in interviewing me very much."

One time, with the CBS crew following, Johnson's unit came across a tunnel. When they did, Johnson went into action and down into the hole to investigate. And all this was being filmed by the CBS crew. When I interviewed Steve Durtsche, a friend of the veterans, he mentioned this television report and when he heard about it back then he said, "Everyone in Porterville was calling anyone they knew to tell them to watch Bob on television that night." Obviously, Johnson did not know it at the time but being on national television upset his dad.

Why?

Like what many GIs did in Vietnam so their parents wouldn't worry about their sons during the war, Johnson had not always been truthful with his parents when writing letters home. Johnson said, "When I wrote home to my parents, I'd usually tell them that everything was okay, and they had nothing to worry about. I never told them much about the war or what I was doing or experiencing." So, when his father saw Johnson on national television crawling into a hole, he realized that his son was in more danger than he had been letting on. "Dad got pretty pissed at me," Johnson said.

Vince Arcure

When Vince Arcure landed in Vietnam he stayed for about two weeks in the rear getting adjusted to his new life in Vietnam, being assigned his equipment, and then was sent to his new battalion. There were no more orientations when he first got to his new battalion. There was no welcome barbecue for the new guys, no easy assignments for the first few days until he got used to where he was at. Quite the contrary. In fact, Arcure said, "My first night with my new battalion I went out on patrol."

His first taste of war was later when a sniper tried to kill him as he was standing around with some of the other guys in his unit. "We heard a shot," Arcure said, "and a bullet went about three feet over my head and hit the tree behind me." After the shot hit the tree behind him, he and his buddies quickly looked around in the direction from where the shot came from. "We saw a guy running away, but he was too far away by that time to fire back at him," Arcure explained. "Even though I wanted to chase the bastard," Arcure said, "I couldn't. Because you might be running into an ambush."

When asked what his reaction was, and the reaction of the guys who were standing there with him, when the shot hit the tree behind them, Arcure said, "We all laughed." So, what in the world could they have laughed at, and he said, "Because the sniper was such a bad shot." Lucky for Arcure he was. But, eventually, other enemy with a slightly better aim would put their sights on Arcure.

This time, they wouldn't miss.

Approximately five months after Arcure arrived in Vietnam he was in a battle that nearly took his life. It happened on May 9, 1967 to be exact. This particular battle included Arcure's company, which was not at full strength at the time, but included 57 of his company's fellow Marines. At the end of the day, 30 of the 57 were killed, 15 were wounded, including Arcure, and only 12 came out of the battle that day with no injuries. Only 12.

The term "casualty rate" includes both those who were killed and those who were injured. With that, the casualty rate for Arcure's company on this day was 79%. That is staggering. Fifty-three percent (53%) of his company were killed, 26% were wounded, and 21% were not wounded. To underscore the significance of the casualty count, his company that day earned an unwanted distinction.

Arcure said, "This was the first time in Vietnam when there were more Americans killed than wounded during a battle." And he further said, "That was a big deal."

The battle took place in the mountain area near Khe Sanh. Like in so many battles in Vietnam, Arcure at one point could not see the enemy he was shooting at. He does remember, however, when he shot and killed one enemy who was going up a nearby knoll, and then silencing another enemy with a hand grenade that he tossed into the area where the enemy was approaching. But then it happened.

Arcure got shot. And not just once, but twice.

Arcure said, "The first time I got shot, I was shot in the head." In fact, the bullet hit his helmet on the one side, and then exited out the back leaving an entry and exit hole in his helmet. In addition, the bullet grazed the side of his head, leaving a flow of blood down his face, and eventual stitches required to close the wound. Since the bullet traveled through his helmet and across his head, shrapnel from his helmet was left in his head.

Explaining how it felt to be shot in the helmet, Arcure said, "It was like a baseball bat hit me on the side of the head and pushed me straight into the ground." Arcure does not remember if he was knocked out or for how long he might have been unconscious from the shot. But once he gained his senses again, and since he was out there basically alone, he thought he should try to get back to his squad. How did he get there? He crawled. And he crawled somewhere around 50 feet, keeping his body as close to the ground as he could.

Arcure remembered, "As I was crawling, bullets were hitting all around me, between my legs, arms, everywhere." Bullets peppering the ground, kicking up dust and dirt as they entered the ground next to him. All around his body, inches from being shot again. And then Arcure said something rather profound about the experience.

"When I was crawling," Arcure said, "it felt like someone was laying on top of me." It was almost like someone was protecting him. "Could it have been God?" he wondered. Maybe an angel or the spirit of someone else? He didn't know. But he made it back to his squad, nonetheless. As the battle continued, and as napalm was being dropped on the enemy, Arcure and another guy continued climbing up the hill to get to their objective. Then it happened again.

Arcure got shot again. This time, in his left hand.

This shot was Arcure's ticket out of Vietnam. It was a serious wound and he needed medical attention. He was eventually picked up by helicopter and taken to a field hospital. About an hour later he was flown to Da Nang, and then to Japan where he spent almost three months in recuperation after surgery to repair his hand. His time in the hospital in Japan was an eventful one, too.

During his stay in the hospital, one of Arcure's doctors was not particularly skilled or useful, and Arcure did not have much patience with his incompetency. In fact, Arcure ended up getting into a fight with the doctor. Responding to the incident with Arcure, the doctor threatened to put Arcure in the brig, which is the equivalent to a civilian jail. But that didn't happen since, Arcure said, "There was a policy that injured GIs could not be sent to the brig." Arcure was off the hook. The doctor, however, may not have been so lucky.

Arcure learned later that due to his incompetence, the doctor was eventually kicked out of the military.

When he healed from his injury, Arcure was not sent back to Vietnam but was reassigned to Okinawa where he was a base MP and worked in the R and R center. When he was sent home, his plane flew into March Air Force Base in San Bernardino where his parents picked him up. This time, his dad did not punch him, but bear hugged him, along with his mom, of course.

He spent the final four months of his military commitment at Camp Pendleton, still in the infantry but helping to train new Marines who were going to Vietnam. And these new recruits certainly had an experienced instructor.

As Arcure explained in his story above when he got shot in the head, the bullet passing through his helmet left shrapnel in his head. Due to the nature of the wound, when they stitched Arcure's head, the doctors decided to leave some shrapnel in his head because they were afraid that some particles may shatter and cause more problems.

Eventually, Arcure did something rather unique that most injured GIs would never do. He became his own doctor of sorts.

He said, "After about a year when I was at Camp Pendleton, they were operating on my left hand because it looked like a club. While I was in the hospital, the shrapnel that they left in my head started to work its way out." So what did Arcure do? He said, "I pulled it out myself." Since I have a hard time hearing, I had him repeat that again because I couldn't believe what I heard. And, yes, I was correct. He took the shrapnel out of his head himself.

First Lady Roosevelt would have been rolling in her grave if she heard that about our local Marine.

Tony Forner

As an infantryman in the Marine Corps, Tony Forner was involved in some of the most fierce and up-close battles in Vietnam. Reflecting back on his experience, especially the battles where many soldiers were either killed or wounded in action, he said, "Think about it. You have 18-year-old kids going through this. Only freaking teenagers." Eighteen years old and experiencing some of the most awful and horrendous things in the war.

After one of the battles where many were killed or injured and he wasn't, Forner thought to himself, "It wasn't my time. Could be the next time though." And that was the attitude he took. "Regardless of what happened, we had to keep going," Forner said. He continued, "Sometimes we would walk a few days and not have any contact with the enemy. But you knew it was coming. The enemy was out there either looking for us, too, or waiting until we found them."

After a while of listening to his myriad of fascinating stories, I put down my pen, quit taking notes, and just listened. I marveled at his memories of combat and the courage and strength he displayed on the battlefields to even survive such an experience. When sharing the stories of his experiences in Vietnam, Forner made a rather poignant statement.

"The names fade away but faces never do."

He still remembers the faces. After over 50 years since his time in Vietnam, it may be difficult to remember the names of those he served with, but he will never forget their faces. In fact, I found his memory of the events and the names of those involved to still be rather sharp.

Only about a couple of weeks after he landed in Vietnam, Forner was with his new unit doing perimeter duty and running patrols. He'd walk the bush looking for the enemy. Forner said, "Everything in Vietnam is a booby trap. The Vietnamese could make a booby trap out of everything." And several times he witnessed the devastating effects the booby traps and land mines had on the human body. Regarding the skill of the North Vietnamese Army (NVA), Forner said, "They could make bunkers that could survive a B-52 attack."

Contrary to how they are sometimes portrayed, Forner said the Vietnamese, and, especially, the NVA, were actually very good soldiers. "I had a lot of respect for the NVA," Forner said. And I'm sure the NVA had a lot of respect for Forner, too.

Forner eventually found himself patrolling the mountains around Khe Sanh, a location that would later become one of the deadliest battles during the Vietnam War. There was fierce fighting happening in and around these mountains. At one point as he was watching the helicopters working up in the mountains, he described the area when he said, "This place smelled like death." Forner said, "One day, as we were going up the mountain a group of Marines was coming down. Or what was left of them." Forner called them the "Walking Dead."

The "Walking Dead" was actually a nickname for the First Battalion, Ninth Marine Regiment. They were given this nickname because they suffered the highest killed in action rate and endured the longest sustained combat of any regiment during the Vietnam War.[2]

Forner explained, "Each company of Marines was assigned to take certain hills." But during one particular battle there was one thing that concerned Forner almost as much as the enemy in the area. His friend, Vince Arcure from Porterville High School, was in the area, too. And Forner found out that Arcure's unit had been hit hard.

In early May of 1967, when Forner was on patrol, one group of

Marines near him had been attacked and were being decimated by the NVA. "They lost around 30 guys that day, plus the wounded," Forner said. One of the reasons they had lost so many men was something the enemy often did during a battle that emphasized the ugliness of war. "They would go around and shoot any of the wounded they could," Forner said with a certain amount of understandable anger and bitterness in his voice.

"I knew Vince was there," Forner explained, "so, after the fighting was over, I went looking for him." When he got to where Arcure's unit had been, Forner saw numerous Marines who had been killed lying around. Forner said, "I saw one guy lying face down and it looked like Vince. I thought, 'Oh, crap, there's Vince.'" When he turned the body over, he realized it was not his friend, so Forner was obviously relieved. And he kept looking.

Forner said, "I went up to a guy and told him I was looking for Arcure. And he told me that the medevac came and took Arcure out." As Forner further explained, "My group walked out of the area, but Vince's group got out by helicopter." When asked why Arcure's group got out by helicopter while his group had to get out by walking, Forner said, "Vince's group got out by helicopter because there weren't that many of them left."

One noteworthy battle that Forner participated in was Operation Hickory.[3] The international agreements that often guided American policy in Vietnam stated that the Demilitarized Zone (DMZ) was a neutral area, in addition to Cambodia and Laos. Even though the Americans generally observed this neutrality, the North Vietnamese never really did. The NVA would often conduct operations outside of the DMZ and then use the DMZ as a safe haven for its troops when things got rough.

Due to the increase in enemy activity in the DMZ area, Washington finally approved an operation into the DMZ and Forner's company was part of that operation. In an effort to reduce NVA activity in the area, the Americans swept through the southern part of the DMZ clearing out the NVA. Forner said, "One time, while patrolling in the DMZ area, 200 rounds of artillery was fired in only about five minutes. That's a helluva lot of artillery." He explained one of the situations he found himself in by saying, "As I was in a sprint to get out of the area when we were under attack, a guy running behind me all of a sudden hit me in the back. He had been hit by shrapnel and the impact pushed him up against me." Forner said, "He was not killed, but he was paralyzed."

Forner also watched something he still can see today when he said, "I watched two guys running and they jumped into a fox hole to save themselves. But then two artillery rounds followed them into the foxhole. They were both killed instantly."

He also remembers a kid who was the polar opposite of the stereotype that people have about Marine Corps infantrymen in combat. "We had one kid who acted like he was lost all of the time," Forner said. He said the kid was very immature, but Forner also thought that maybe he had special needs. Regardless, Forner said, "This kid should never have been in combat." Then during an exchange with the enemy one day, the kid was shot along the stomach and began calling for his mom. He later went into shock and died.

During that same battle, Forner remembered a machine gunner who "was shot in the forehead but he survived." Forner learned later that to repair his wound they had to put a metal plate in his forehead. "You just never know what injury will kill you," Forner said. One was shot along the stomach and died, while the other was shot in the forehead and lived.

In a period of only ten days during Operation Hickory, from May 18 to May 28, 1967, around 150 Marines were killed during the fighting. Although the operation did reduce the activity of the NVA in the area at the time, in about a year or so after the conclusion of Operation Hickory and the withdrawal or reduction of American forces, the NVA was back in full force in the area.[4]

When reflecting back on his time as a Marine Corps infantryman in the Vietnam War, Forner said, "After you have been in the bush for a while and engaging the enemy, you get a certain 'combat high and low.'" He explained what that meant. "When the bullets are firing and the mortars and rockets are incoming, you get a certain adrenaline high." He further explained, "But when the bullets stop firing, there's a low. Almost like boredom. When the battle is over you have to clean up the mess, which means walking around picking up body parts. An arm here, a leg there. That's the low, the boredom." He summarized it by saying, "People who have never been in combat can't understand the feeling."

And, finally, there was one thing that Forner said he could never forget about his experiences during the war in Vietnam. The smell of burning flesh. "That smell has never gone away," Forner said, "I can still smell it 50 years later." He was saying that as he was shaking his head and looking down.

John Alba

John Alba's first few days in Vietnam were spent in an orientation where they were told about what to expect in Vietnam, rules and regulations, and other things regarding the country. Prior to finally getting to his new unit, Alba's group had a stop off at a place they called Wonder Beach. "It was almost like a mini vacation," Alba said, "because we could body surf, swim, or just lay around the beach and drink beer." But once he got to his new unit, the vacation ended, and it was now time for serious business. For most of the next 12 months of his tour, Alba spent it riding a tank in the bushes of Vietnam.

Alba was assigned to an armored tank unit. At the beginning of his assignment, he drove the tank for the tank commander. Then later, he became the tank commander himself. Most of his time was spent in the bush, fighting against the invisible enemy, using the strength and power of his tanks to search and destroy the enemy and its resources.

In addition to looking for the enemy during their patrols, Alba's unit would often come across villages that had been evacuated. Even though no one may have been occupying the huts and shacks that were scattered about within the villages at the time, these villages were often used by the enemy to hide or store weapons and food for their fight against the Americans. Since these villages could be used again by the enemy, Alba's unit was responsible for eliminating them. "We couldn't let the enemy use these villages, so we would flatten them." And then Alba said, "We'd light them on fire and burn them."

While on patrol, Alba said, "One of our biggest worries was land mines." In addition to land mines, "We always worried about ambush," Alba said. "When we'd drive through elephant grass, the grass was so high that it almost hid the tanks," he explained. And that left them ripe for an ambush. "Although it never happened to our tanks," Alba said, "we had heard of the enemy actually running out of the grass, up the tank, drop a grenade inside the tank, and then run off back into the elephant grass. So we were always on the lookout for that."

When he explained a particular ambush one day, Alba mentioned that the NVA fired a white phosphorous rocket-propelled grenade (RPG) into one of the tanks in his column. White phosphorus had the nickname of "WP" or "Willie Pete." As Alba explained white phosphorous, "You can't put it out. Once it starts burning, it continues to burn." As he further explained, "The only way you can put it out is to smother it, so it loses oxygen." You can't put out the phosphorous fire with water, only by oxygen deprivation.

During this particular ambush, Alba said, "A white phosphorous RPG entered one of the tanks behind me, basically burning a small hole into the tank." As Alba said, "When that happens, everyone inside the tank is burned or suffocates." When the RPG was fired into the tank, Alba said, "Our medic was able to crawl out, but he was being burned by the white phosphorous. They tried to smother it out, but it was too late. The medic died, as did everyone else inside the tank." When he finished telling about the medic, Alba looked the other way and shook his head. The memory obviously still lingering in his mind.

During his tour in Vietnam, Alba's unit lost four tanks due to enemy attack and ambush. And one time, their worry about land mines became a reality and ended up with Alba receiving a Purple Heart. In fact, Alba received two Purple Hearts during his service in Vietnam.

"The first Purple Heart I got was when I got hit by shrapnel when an incoming shell hit our area," Alba said. He was out of action for about a week recuperating from his injury, but then, only 11 days later, he received his second Purple Heart. Alba explained, "As we were on a patrol, the tank I was riding in hit a mine and blew off the side of the tank." And not only did it blow off the side of the tank, Alba said, "It also sent me sailing into the river." Again, he was injured, but this second injury resulted in something that still bothers him today.

When he was injured the second time, another soldier had to take his place on his tank. And during a subsequent patrol, while Alba was recuperating back at the base and his substitute was riding for him in his tank, they got ambushed. During the ambush, the person who took Alba's place on the tank was killed, shot in the head. And something about that ambush bothered him even more many years later.

"The mother of the guy who got killed contacted me years after the war to find out how her son got killed. She was looking for answers about her son's death," Alba said. And who could blame her? Like what many other mothers so desperately wanted who lost a son in Vietnam, this mother wanted some closure, too. But Alba explained, "The hard part in talking with her about what happened was that I couldn't tell her that her son got killed subbing for me." As he got emotional telling the story, Alba looked down and said, "That's bothered me for a long time. Still does."

Finally, after an almost daily routine of searching, destroying, and fighting against enemy ambushes and attacks, his time in Vietnam was coming to a close. "When I had one week left in my tour," Alba said, "they took me off the tank and kept me on base." During that last week, he pulled some guard duty and prepared for his trip home, including getting five medical shots in one day.

Looking back on his time in Vietnam, Alba said, "The first 30 days and the last 30 days were the scariest for me." He explained that the first 30 days he was still new and scared not knowing what to expect.

On the other hand, the last 30 days he was scared because he had heard of soldiers dying just before they were to go home and he was hoping that wouldn't happen to him, too. And that scared him.

Don Dowling

The interview with Don Dowling about his experiences in Vietnam and elsewhere during his 23-year career in the military, especially the time when he was in Special Forces in Vietnam, was a walk through a kind of life people only see in movies. He was in demolition, Special Forces, infantry, airborne, reconnaissance, and a variety of other assignments. "I did a lot of things," Dowling said. And he certainly did.

He talked about amazing challenges, harrowing experiences, life and death situations, and the emotions of war and life in the military. During our conversation I made a comment about the number of medals he must have won during such a long career. Regarding his medals, he said, "Medals mean nothing to me. A cup of coffee costs the same downtown if I had a chest full of medals or not. Besides, I was just doing my job."

And he did his job very well.

One experience he talked about was when he was assigned to a demolition team in Vietnam. His team would go out on search and destroy missions and, Dowling said, "Whatever needed to be blown up, we did." One day his team received word that a C-130 plane had crashed. The plane carried equipment, supplies, and sensitive material, and Dowling's unit was assigned the responsibility to find the plane and destroy any sensitive information, equipment, or material. Dowling said, "We didn't want the NVA to have and use anything on the plane." To get to the downed aircraft, it took about two days of hiking through the jungle to find the C-130. And what they found was awful.

"When we got to the plane," Dowling said, "the pilot was still sitting in his seat. He had been burned to death." But then something happened that he can still see today. "When one of the guys touched the pilot's body to try and move it, his whole body fell apart. It just crumbled." Dowling further said, "There were seven members in that crew. The ones in the front of the plane burned to death, the ones in the back died from the concussion and heat of the crash." When he finished the story he just looked away in reflection and shook his head. It was obvious from the expression on Dowling's face that it was a sight he will never forget.

In order that the equipment on the plane could not be disassembled and used by the enemy, Dowling's unit made sure that wouldn't happen. "We burned what we could and blew up everything else," Dowling said.

Reflecting back on the many ambushes and battles that he was part of, Dowling said that something happened during one particular battle that he never saw again in Vietnam. During this time, a report came in that they located a "brigade of bad guys" as he called them, and his group was assigned to go out and get them. The brigade was guarding a radio relay site and this site was of strategic importance to the NVA.

When the Americans got to the location of the enemy, Dowling said, "We walked straight into an ambush." Dowling estimated the Americans were outnumbered as much as 8:1. In addition to the one brigade, there was another brigade on its way to the area. And what still bothers Dowling today, he said, "Our leaders knew there were two brigades of NVA in the area, not just the one. But they told us there was only one."

At approximately 9:00 a.m., Dowling said, "We got hit hard and 32 Americans were killed almost immediately." During the battle, Dowling said, "One of my engineers went out to help guys who were injured, even though he was not a medic, but he was killed." There was death and injury all around. At some point, medevac helicopters came in to pick up the dead and wounded Americans, and that's when Dowling saw something happen that he never saw in Vietnam again.

Dowling said, "It was the only time I saw the war stop."

As the helicopters were flying into the area and descending onto the hot landing zone to pick up the dead and injured Americans, Dowling said, "The NVA stopped shooting. For a brief time, the war stopped." They weren't shooting. They weren't firing mortars. They weren't tossing grenades. "They waited until the choppers picked up the dead and wounded and lifted off again. And when the choppers were above the trees, they started shooting again." Dowling said, "It was like they respected our dead soldiers and allowed our medevac choppers to get them off of the battlefield."

Later though, Dowling said that never happened again because, "The NVA finally realized that the choppers were not always just picking up our dead and wounded. They were delivering supplies and ammunition, too." So, the NVA never stopped shooting again. But, at least, on one brief occasion, the war stopped for Dowling and his fellow Americans who were in a fight of their lives.

During intense battles when the helicopters or airplanes are called in for assistance, Dowling said, "There's nothing more lovely than the sight of an F4 Phantom jet coming in low dropping napalm." The sight of an F4 was a welcomed sight to the Americans who may be in serious trouble and needed support to survive. But an F4 and its cascading napalm bombs are certainly not a welcome sight to an enemy that will soon be decimated by the aerial response.

Dowling told of a time when he was doing reconnaissance and located the NVA moving equipment through the jungle. They immediately called in air strikes to destroy the convoy of enemy vehicles. But when the equipment was hit by the American aircraft, Dowling said something else happened. "When the airstrikes came, the NVA knew we were out there. They knew someone must have seen them," Dowling said, "and they came looking for us."

Dowling and his group of three others did the only thing they could do to avoid being captured by the enemy. They ran. And it wasn't just a short run around the block. They ran for three days. Dowling said, "I was pretty scared. As we were running from them, they were shooting at us." It wasn't just NVA soldiers chasing them either. Dogs were, too. "As we were running," Dowling explained, "we dropped pepper and any kind of powder or chemicals we had that might get the dogs off our trail."

Finally, an American helicopter found the location of Dowling and his group. Hovering over the area, the helicopter dropped down ropes to the soldiers, and they hooked themselves onto a STABO rig. STABO stands for Stabilized Body, which is a harness used for extracting soldiers by helicopter. Once they were hooked up to the STABO, the helicopter lifted them up over the canopy of the jungle and flew them out of the area. Dowling explained, "We were hanging about 120 feet below the helicopter as it flew off. And we were being shot at from below." Dowling said he was thinking one thing as they were flying off, "Get me the hell out of here." It wasn't just a short ride by any means. They flew for about 45 minutes, hanging from ropes below a helicopter. Not your typical leisurely drive you might take on a Sunday in Porterville.

One time, the need for a cup of coffee almost cost Dowling his life.

Ben Het was a Special Forces camp that came under siege on June 23, 1969. Three thousand North Vietnamese troops cut off the camp using mortar and artillery rounds. At the time, only about 250 American troops and 450 South Vietnam Montagnard tribesmen defended the camp.[5] They were in serious trouble, and heavily outmanned. As Dowling explained, "The place was getting hammered. So my group was called in to assist."

The location of the base was only about six miles from the junction of the borders of Laos, Cambodia, and South Vietnam. So, the base was of strategic importance to the Americans. Dowling said that when he got to Ben Het, "We were greeted with 100 mortar rounds." After about a week of intense fighting and heavy bombardments from B52 strikes, the siege was over. But something happened during the battle that showed Dowling how lucky he really was.

During a slight lull in the aerial bombardment, Dowling went into the mess hall to get a cup of coffee. "Just when I went in there," Dowling said, "an 82-mm mortar round came through the roof and landed on the coffee." When it came through the roof, Dowling hit the floor. "I didn't even have time to pray," Dowling admitted. Luckily, the mortar did not explode. The mortar may not have exploded but something else did. Dowling said, "The coffee pot exploded." When that happened, Dowling said he thought to himself, "Gosh, a guy can't even get a cup of coffee around here."

Ron Crabtree

When Ron Crabtree's plane landed in Vietnam, he knew he was in a war, and he wanted his M16 as soon as he could get it. After a week of orientation and getting adjusted to his new life in Vietnam, Crabtree was sent to his new unit. A unit that spent a lot of time getting its feet wet.

You see, Crabtree spent most of the next six months wading through rice patties searching for the enemy. For a while at least, his daily schedule was almost routine. "Every morning we would be taken out by chopper a couple of miles," Crabtree explained, "dropped off in a rice patty, search for the enemy, and then be picked up the next day."

Sometimes, just being dropped off in the rice patties was a harrowing experience by itself. "You really didn't know how deep the rice patty is until you were dropped into it." Crabtree said. "It might be shallow or deep. You never knew. You hoped it was shallow, so you didn't sink."

The encounters with the enemy that Crabtree experienced the most that resulted in death or injury were not as much from the bullets of an enemy rifle. Rather, the deadly encounters he faced the most were from something the enemy hid, sometimes hidden months before, that were now exacting their vengeance against the Americans.

Booby traps.

"We encountered a lot of booby traps in the rice patties," Crabtree said, "and they were pretty devastating." Most of the guys who tripped a booby trapped were killed instantly, as well as anyone standing next to him. Crabtree said, "A booby trap would often kill about three or four of those who were standing near the guy who tripped it." For those who weren't killed, Crabtree had a hard time explaining what happened to them, and I didn't ask him. I didn't need to. I could tell by the expression on his face that it was pretty devastating.

Crabtree said they experienced about two booby traps a week. In addition, Crabtree said, "I lost two of my best buddies who got blown up together by a booby trap." Because of that incident Crabtree explained, "I didn't make any close friends after that." And in a nod of respect to the Vietnamese, he said, "Those guys were masters at booby traps."

Crabtree explained what happened when a booby trapped was tripped. "The trip wires were often placed on the berms of the rice patties," Crabtree said, "and that is where the Americans walked in order to get through the rice patties." Whenever they would encounter the enemy within the rice patties, "We'd throw a concussion grenade into the water," Crabtree said, "hoping to kill any enemy who might be hiding under water." But Crabtree said he noticed something interesting most of the time when they threw concussion grenades in the water.

"Fish would float to the top of the water, but usually not a Vietnamese," Crabtree said. Somehow, they got away through other means. "They probably escaped into a tunnel," Crabtree assumed. Crabtree could determine whether or not the Vietnamese working in the rice patties were the enemy by their reaction when the booby trap was tripped when he said, "If they ran, they were the enemy. If they didn't run, they were okay." And if they ran, they became targets themselves.

In addition to wading through the rice patties, Crabtree's patrols often took him through many river crossings as well. During one particular river crossing, Crabtree almost lost his life. But not by a booby trap or a bullet from an enemy rifle.

One time when crossing a river by rope, he was about chest-deep in water, hanging onto the rope, pulling himself across the river while carrying a heavy pack of equipment on his back. "As I was crossing the river on the rope," Crabtree explained, "I was holding onto the rope and my rifle. When I tried to switch hands, I missed the rope and fell off." And since he had so much weight on his back, Crabtree said, "I started to sink." Terrified, Crabtree was struggling to get his head above the water. He was drowning.

He went up and down three times gasping for air, and Crabtree said about the experience, "You think of crazy things when you think you are going to die." And when asked what he thought about as he was drowning he said, "I was wondering what kind of flowers I wanted at my funeral." Luckily, he didn't need to worry about flowers at his funeral because on his fourth time back up someone nearby saw what was happening and was able to pull Crabtree out.

"I don't really remember who pulled me out," Crabtree said, "but whoever did saved my life." Crabtree was rattled from the experience, gasping for air, and shaking from almost drowning, but he was alive. What his fellow GI did was the kind of brotherhood that was often found in Vietnam. Brothers saving brothers.

Crabtree mentioned a time when the new year was almost upon them and he was reflecting back on the year that was coming to a close. He was thinking about all of the death and horrors of war that he experienced during the past year, and on January 1st he said in a silent conversation with God, "Lord, please make this next year a little easier than the last one." And in an interesting sort of way, the Lord answered his prayer.

One time, Crabtree and some of his friends went to a place that was off limits to have a few beers. When it was found out they had been to a restricted place, Crabtree and his group were threatened with discipline, including being busted down in rank and even facing a court-martial. But something happened right after that incident that was totally unexpected.

"I was on the chopper pad waiting to be taken out to our next mission," Crabtree said, "but I was pulled out." Crabtree wondered "What's going on?" Come to find out, instead of being court-martialed or busted in rank, Crabtree was being promoted and transferred to a new, safer unit. How did that happen? Obviously, someone made a mistake in processing but, regardless, Crabtree benefitted from this clerical error. When one of his superiors found out that Crabtree was being transferred and promoted he asked, "Damn, Crabtree, is your father a United States Senator or something?"

And Crabtree proudly replied with a big smile on his face, "No, sir, my daddy is a cotton picker from Woodville, California!"

Crabtree was transferred to Saigon and assigned to an MP unit. He was not an MP, but an infantryman attached to an MP unit. His new duty included going out at night to inspect around ships looking for enemy infiltrators, guarding warehouses where ammunition and equipment was stored, and other duties related to inspection and MP support. Sure, this new duty was still dangerous, but nothing like dodging booby traps in the rice patties.

The Lord certainly answered Crabtree's prayer to his satisfaction. I asked Crabtree if he thanked the Lord for answering his prayer in such a way and he said, "You bet I did, numerous times."

Felix Hernandez

When his plane landed in Vietnam and the door opened, and as he stood on the top of the stairs before descending down to the tarmac, Felix Hernandez first thought to himself, "Oh my God, what is that smell?" Well, that smell was Vietnam, and Vietnam was his home for the next year.

Although his MOS was in armor, Hernandez was assigned to an artillery unit. He spent the next 10 months of his life in the middle of rice patties with a group of soldiers that included six artillery pieces and support personnel to total about 100 or so men. When describing where his unit was located, Hernandez said, "Everything was out in the open. We had no protection. We were like sitting ducks." So, Hernandez and the other men tried to do something to provide some level of protection. "We filled boxes with mud," Hernandez said, "and built a wall that way." Certainly, the mud-packed wall did not provide enough protection, but it provided some. At least more than what they had before.

"Where we were located," Hernandez said, "there was fire constantly. Our artillery pieces could hit a target from about 14 miles. And if the target was over 14 miles, we had to move to get closer." When they had to move closer, they would often take two trucks, each dragging an artillery piece, and each truck mounted with a 51-caliber for fire support. "When we'd get incoming fire from the trees, we'd open up on the trees and just shred them," Hernandez said. "Sometimes we didn't know if we got them or not." But by the looks of the trees, or what was left of them, they got them.

Hernandez received two pieces of advice that he used throughout his time in Vietnam. The first was, "When you hear a gun go off, duck." And the other was, "When there is incoming, put your head down and don't look up until it's over." Two pieces of advice he used quite often while in the bush of Vietnam. Hernandez also tried to pass these helpful hints to his fellow soldiers, especially the new guys. One time Hernandez told a guy, "Never expose yourself." But the guy didn't listen to him. "He did what he wasn't supposed to do, he exposed himself." And what happened to him? "He got shot."

Hernandez said someone asked him one time how many people he might have killed in Vietnam. His reply was, "Artillery pieces don't tell you how many you killed."

When describing something about life in Vietnam, what Hernandez described showed the challenges our GIs faced when fighting an enemy they often could not see and one they could not trust. About the locals who sometimes worked on the American bases doing things such as laundry, cleaning, and other menial duties, Hernandez described them as "Vietnamese by day, Viet Cong by night." Another Vietnam War veteran said something similar when he described some of the locals as "Friends during the day, enemies during the night." The locals who worked on the bases were friendly with the Americans during the day, but when night came and they left the base, they became our enemies again.

Hernandez described an incident when one of the local girls came to his camp to work, but she really was there for a different reason. Hernandez noticed her doing something that caught his eye. "I could tell by the way she was walking that she was pacing off feet to find out where to fire the next day." What a challenging place to live when you can't even trust the person working next to you. Is that person a friend or is that person an enemy? The American GIs never really knew for sure.

Hernandez explained a time when he felt some satisfaction for what they were doing in Vietnam.

"We got a report that some of our guys were pinned down in the bush and we went to help them," Hernandez explained. "We got about as close as we could get, set up, and then began to fire." When the back and forth firing finally stopped, and the Americans were in control, Hernandez said, "These green guys started coming out of the trees." Those green guys were Americans. They had been saved by Hernandez's group.

"When they came out of the trees," Hernandez said, "they said things like, 'What took you so long?' and 'Thanks for coming.'" But then one also said, "Damn, you guys got your shells kind of close to us a few times." However, they were saved, and Hernandez said this about the experience, "It felt good to help them. We saved their lives." And he should feel good. Because without the assistance of Hernandez and his group of artillery soldiers, those grunts probably would have been killed.

As he was sharing his experiences about his time in Vietnam, Hernandez said, "I had action the whole time I was in Vietnam, but nothing like this." And that 'this' he was referring to was the Tet Offensive that began on January 30, 1968 and lasted through September 23, 1968. As mentioned previously, the Viet Cong broke the Tet Lunar Year ceasefire and launched a massive assault against American and South Vietnamese bases throughout the country. It was the turning point that changed the perception of the American public back home. And Hernandez was right in the middle of it. There were significant casualties on both the American and Vietnamese sides.

At one point during the night, a friend of his who was working the radar said he wanted to show Hernandez something on the radar. Hernandez said, "It looked like a swarm of bees on the radar coming in." And what was that swarm? The Viet Cong. From the sight on the screen, it was obvious that his area was going to be attacked and attacked hard. Explaining how he felt looking at the screen and realizing a massive attack was imminent, Hernandez said, "The hair on the back of my neck stood up, and I thought to myself, 'Is this going to be it?'"

Hernandez equated the attack by the Viet Cong on his base during the Tet Offensive to the Japanese kamikaze pilots during WWII when he said, "They were like kamikaze pilots coming in. They just kept coming and coming and coming." All night long there was shooting, mortars, and artillery pieces being fired at the attacking swarm.

During the Vietnam War, the success or failure of a battle was determined by body count. The number killed was often the barometer used to measure the success of the operation. Well, on this night, if body count determined the success of an operation, then Hernandez and his group had a successful evening. But he said this about the body count, "We didn't even count the Viet Cong casualties." And "Why not?" I asked. Hernandez replied, "There were too many."

Hernandez received a Purple Heart from being wounded during the Tet Offensive. "I got shrapnel in my neck," Hernandez explained, "and some of it is still inside me." They didn't take all of the shrapnel out of his neck, but, as Hernandez said, "What's still in me doesn't bother me." But what remains of the shrapnel is a reminder, nonetheless.

As mentioned earlier, Hernandez said he did not experience anything like this in Vietnam again. He was in constant fire during this time in Vietnam, and participated in some deadly battles, but the Tet Offensive was the worst he experienced. After the Tet Offensive was over, he certainly wondered about what his remaining time in Vietnam would be like. And he had a reason to.

The Tet Offensive happened when Hernandez had only been there for 10 days.

As a grunt would walk through the jungles of Vietnam, he never knew if he was in the gunsights of an enemy soldier resting his finger against the trigger ready to squeeze it. Attacks came when they were least expected and came during the day or night. The attack could just be one shot from an unseen sniper who runs off back into the dense jungle, or battles lasting several hours.

The grunts were often supported by men riding in tanks close to the action or providing artillery support from miles away. They were also supported by those in Special Forces whose missions are often classified and unnoticed. Helicopters brought them in and took them out and the chopper pilots risked their lives to support the grunts in the bushes.

The American soldiers and Marines in the bush often fought an enemy they could not see. Many times, the only enemy they could see were muzzle flashes coming from the trees. And there really were no frontlines in the war in Vietnam. Rather, the lines were all around them. A 360-degree war. An attack could come from the front, the rear, left side, or right. It didn't matter. And sometimes, the attack came from more than one side.

The NVA or the Viet Cong weren't the only enemy the American GIs had to face while in the bush. Insects, lizards, snakes, leeches, ants, mines, suffocating humidity, infections, malaria, lack of drinkable water, and swollen feet, were often foes that the grunts battled while simultaneously fighting the enemy.

They saw death, and they smelled death. They saw injuries and bodies ravaged by a mine, mortar, bullets or shrapnel. They witnessed minds being shattered from the inability to handle any more stress, anxiety, or fear. They walked through jungles riddled with booby traps and hidden wires if touched would mean death or profound injury. They saw it all. They experienced it all.

As McCarville asked, "How can you not be affected by that?"

Vietnam War and Wall Facts

The Last to Leave [6]

The person who was selected to be the last American combat soldier to leave Vietnam was Master Sgt. Max Beilke. He was at the end of the line of combat soldiers walking up the ramp into a C-130 plane to leave Vietnam on March 29, 1973.

He survived two wars, Korea and Vietnam, but did not survive the War on Terror. He was killed on September 11, 2001, when one of the highjacked planes crashed into the Pentagon where he was working as a civilian employee.

9

The War in the Air

*"If you're in trouble anywhere in the world,
an airplane can fly over and drop you flowers;
a helicopter can land and save your life."*

Igor Sikorsky

IROQUOIS "HUEY", HUEYCOBRA, SeaCobra, Seasprite, Sea King, Jolly Green Giant, Cayuse "Loach," Sioux, Chickasaw, Shawnee, Raven, Choctaw, Mojave, Huskie, Sea Knight, Chinook, Sea Stallion, Super Jolly Green Giant, Sky Crane, Kiowa.

These are certainly odd names. But what are they names of? Are these names of horses who have won the Kentucky Derby? Are these cities in the southwestern region of the United States? Could these possibly be names of sea creatures found in the waters of the Pacific Ocean off the coast of California? No, these are names of the workhorses of the Vietnam War.

Helicopters.

The list above seems like a confusing set of names, but some veterans from Porterville High School can probably still recite the names, design number, and mission code of each of these helicopters almost verbatim. These veterans flew the choppers, fixed them, or fought on them.

Helicopters in the Vietnam War provided a wide variety of service and support to the troops in the jungles. Medevac, removing injured soldiers from the battlefield; as gunships, providing cover for the troops fighting the enemy below; troop insertion or removal, to bring in additional troops to help improve the chances of success in the battle, or to bring back those who might have been killed or injured; re-supply, to bring in ammunition, food, clothing, or anything the troops needed.

And to many Vietnam War veterans, they can still hear the "thwap thwap thwap thwap" sound the Huey chopper blades make as it is going into or leaving a landing zone. Sometimes that sound brought fear, or sometimes that sound brought comfort. Regardless, it's a sound that many who served in the jungles of Vietnam can still hear today.

Roland Hill

As a helicopter crew chief, Roland Hill was considered a "flying crew member" monitoring instruments, being responsible for loading equipment, and tying down supplies such as gas, water, food, and ammunition. He said his job and the responsibilities of his Chinook helicopter were like being the "Fedex of Vietnam."

After a while, flying on the Chinook and delivering supplies became repetitive and boring. Not as boring as his Anthropology class at Porterville College, but boring, nonetheless. "I really wanted something different," Hill said. He learned of a position that had become available to fly on the battalion helicopter, which was a Huey. If he got the job, this new assignment would take him right into the middle of the war. That's what he wanted, and that's what he got, because he was accepted for the new assignment. Now, his job was no longer routine, no longer safe, and certainly no longer boring.

As Hill explained, "We had recently been converted to a 'firefly' model UH-1, which was a retrofit configuration with a large spotlight added to the left side of the helicopter and a twin M60 armament system added just forward of the light." And as Hill further described the helicopter, "The system was designed and purposed to illuminate the target at night while simultaneously delivering right at 1,200 rounds a minute rate of fire from the M60s. And the right side of the aircraft maintained the typical single M60 machine gun system."

So, in order for the helicopter to be operational at night, it had a spotlight to illuminate the targets below. A spotlight. Certainly, the enemy didn't want to be seen at night, so the spotlight was one of their preferred targets to eliminate in order to reduce the chance of being seen at night. But where the light came from, so did the bullets.

The firefly had a minimum of five air crewman on board, including a pilot, co-pilot, one person to operate the spotlight, one to operate the twin M60 system, and one to operate the single M60 gun on the opposite side of the helicopter. "However," Hill said, "most of our flights had six air crewmen on board. The additional crewman would assist in the loading of the weapons systems and rotate through the gun and light positions during long duration assignments."

August 11, 1969, started out for Hill like any other day in the life of an Army helicopter crew chief. He conducted the regular maintenance duties on his helicopter making sure it was operational and airworthy for whatever was in store for it and the crew that night.

"We left the cozy confines of Phu Loi a little after sunset," Hill said, "and headed for our 'AO' (area of operation). After being airborne for a short while, we received directions to assist some grunts who were out on a night patrol, that were meeting heavy enemy fire." The grunts had been ambushed by a sizable group of Viet Cong and they were getting hit hard with a significant number of casualties. Hill said that once they got to their destination and spotted the strobe signal from the grunts, "We engaged the spotlight and began firing on the enemy position."

As he continued to explain the battle, Hill said "While we were continuing our aerial support we received word from the patrol leader that one of the grunts was seriously hurt and they felt that he would not survive the delay until the medevac could arrive." Hill's crew was asked if they would consider picking up this wounded soldier and transport him to the evac. Although that sounded like a rather basic or reasonable request, it was nothing like that.

Hill said, "The reality of that request was that we would have to make a night landing in a hot LZ (landing zone), having unknown vegetation hazards, exit the aircraft and assist loading the wounded GI onto the ship, reboard, and take off, all under heavy enemy fire." There was a quick crew discussion about the request, and everyone was asked if they wanted to take the chance. "The decision to assist in favor of the medevac was unanimous," Hill said, "So down we went."

When the helicopter touched down, Hill and a fellow crew member immediately exited the helicopter while under enemy fire. They ran to assist the other grunts who were carrying the wounded soldier, loaded him into the helicopter, re-boarded, and gave the signal that they were clear to take off. Hill said, "We immediately returned to our gun positions and delivered return fire while we lifted off and flew away from the fire zone." They successfully flew the wounded soldier to the nearest evac. On a side note, Hill never found out if that soldier lived or died. But if he lived, he has Hill and the other crew members to thank for saving his life.

As he explained what it was like to be under fire that night, Hill said, "Gun fire, while wearing flight helmets and earplugs, combined with the chopper noises, all makes for a surreal detached effect as everything is muffled." He further explained that night, "The presence of tracers flying everywhere all around us made it very evident that this was serious shit and was a strong inducement to hurry like you've never hurried before."

And after all of that, you'd think they'd regroup and take a break or a short rest. But not Hill's crew. "We returned back to the same location to continue providing aerial gun support until Charlie had enough." And, eventually, Charlie did have enough.

While inspecting the helicopter the next day, it was obvious that it had received considerable fire damage from the night before and, Hill said, "We were just very fortunate and blessed to have not sustained any fatal strikes to the ship or crew." Due to his heroic involvement during the rescue mission, Hill was awarded the Air Medal for Heroism. The following are some of the comments that were made on the medal's citation explaining Hill's and his crew's action during the mission:

> "These men distinguished themselves by exceptionally valorous actions...Although under intense automatic weapons fire they provided valuable direction to the pilot that allowed effective suppressive fire to be brought upon the enemy positions and allowed the pilot to make a blacked out approach to evacuate a wounded patrol member. They leaped from the aircraft and assisted in loading the wounded soldier. After reaching the nearest medical facility and discharging the passenger they volunteered to return...although the aircraft had been damaged by enemy fire and prolonged flight was hazardous. Returning to the scene of action, they continued on station until the enemy had withdrawn..."

Job well done.

As Hill further described nighttime missions such as the one where his crew rescued the injured soldier, he said, "With the mortars, bullets, and tracers being fired from below, along with the gunships firing from above using the light of his helicopter's spotlights, the whole place is sometimes much like a 4th of July display."

One time, during the confusion of battle, he witnessed two American gunships collide and exploded in the air, killing the crews. "I'll never forget that sight," Hill said, as the emotions of that memory were evident on his face. And as he was speaking about the incident, he shook his head and looked away. Hill then commented, "The pilots of helicopters were the cream of the crop in the military." Brave men, doing a difficult job under enormous stress, being fired at from below by rifles and mortars. And, Hill said, "Many of those pilots were only 20 years old."

Later, his crew won a citation for their work and heroism during the longest battle he was part of while in Vietnam. Hill explained, "When I was at the base camp, we got word over the radio that a group of our soldiers were getting their asses kicked. So, we loaded up the Huey and went out to help." Back and forth his helicopter went, providing fire support, delivering ammunition, or picking up dead or injured soldiers. Anything they could do to help. This battle was different than other battles he had been involved in because it did not last for 30 minutes, or an hour. Describing the battle, Hill said, "This one lasted for five hours." Five hours.

He was not ashamed to admit that he was scared during this battle. Hill remembered hearing from someone once a description of what being scared in combat is really like. The description is graphic, but it certainly explained the feeling like no other explanation could. He said during that battle his "asshole got so tight that you couldn't pound a needle into it with a sledgehammer!" No better description of being scared could be said so eloquently. Graphic, yes. To the point, certainly.

The stress during that battle was enormous. The crew was exhausted. His helicopter was riddled with bullets. But they kept going back. And back. And back. Until the battle was over. Five hours later. And Hill commented, "Try to sleep after that." For their part in this battle, Hill and his crew were awarded the "Army Commendation Medal for Heroism." The crew certainly deserved the citation they received. And they deserved some rest. But did they get any? Not really.

Since life on a helicopter crew like Hill's was a stressful and arduous experience, he said, "Humor is a good thing for treating tension and angst." And there certainly was a lot of tension and angst in Vietnam, especially in a unit like Hill's. He remembered one time how his first sergeant helped to reduce the tension by doing something that their commanding officer (CO) did not find particularly amusing. At least not initially.

Describing the incident, Hill said, "The first sergeant submitted a bereavement leave request to his CO, while we were in Nam, stating that his uncle had died. Well, his 'uncle' was Ho Chi Minh, leader of the North Vietnamese, who was not-so-affectionately referred to as 'Uncle Ho.'" When hearing about what his first sergeant did, Hill said, "Man, we laughed so hard. But the CO didn't initially think it was very funny." However, Hill said that later on, the CO would come around to anyone who was willing to listen and tell them about the crazy first sergeant who requested leave from a war zone so he could attend his uncle's funeral. Uncle Ho.

Obviously, another way to deal with the stress and anxiety is with rest and recuperation. Most of us would think that after battles such as Hill's five-hour battle that the crew would be given a few days off. Maybe take some time off to relax, have a few beers, play a little poker. Or head into the local village looking for a companion to catch a venereal disease from. But not this crew. Not in Vietnam. Hill said, "We went out every night. Every night. Sometimes taking a day off during the week." But for the most part, this was a daily or nightly routine.

"And I flew right up until the day I was to leave Vietnam," Hill said.

Joe Souza

When Joe Souza first enlisted in the Army in 1960, Vietnam was not on the minds of most people back then. In the early 60s, the United States was involved in Vietnam more on an advisory basis, and the Americans had not yet been directly or openly involved in a combat role. Souza was an advisor, assisting the South Vietnamese to learn how to use military equipment and other operational aspects within the military.

"One of the first things I remember about Vietnam when I got off the plane the first time," Souza said, "was the smell of fish." Yes, it was hot, and it was humid, but it was the smell of fish that he remembers most. Later, the smell of fish didn't impress the new soldiers as much as the smell of human excrement that was being burned in 55-gallon drums. As an advisor, Souza wore civilian not military clothes, so he didn't look like a typical GI in green fatigues. "The only fighting I saw during my first tour," Souza said, "was between the Catholics and Buddhists." But all that later changed.

After the assassination of South Vietnamese President Diem in 1963, just a few weeks prior to the assassination of President Kennedy, the situation in Vietnam became noticeably serious. Souza remembers, "After Diem was assassinated, we were placed on 'red alert' and the advisors were provided ammunition, M16s, and other combat-related gear." He further explained, "Those who were not already qualified were required to get qualified in shooting rifles and machine guns." This was not what an advisor was supposed to be worried about. Little did Souza know at the time, but the advisors would soon be supplemented with combat troops, and our involvement in Vietnam would change substantially.

But Souza's time in the Army was coming to an end, and he was discharged in 1964. After coming back home and going back to work, he thought more about what he wanted to do in life and decided, "I wanted to make the military my career," Souza said. So, he reenlisted in 1967. "Even though I had already gone through one tour," Souza said, "they still made me do basic training all over again, stupid." After basic training at Ft. Polk, Louisiana, he went to various flight training schools in the South to become a helicopter pilot.

Upon completion of flight training, Souza said, "There were 11 in my group waiting for our assignment. Eight of us went to Korea, and three of us went to Vietnam." Souza was one of those three. When he got to Vietnam, Souza did not have much time to get adjusted to his new assignment in Vietnam. When asked how soon he saw combat after arriving in Vietnam, Souza said, "The first day."

As a helicopter pilot during the Vietnam War, Souza's job was to transport whatever was necessary to the troops in the field and elsewhere. Water, food, ammunition, other troops, whatever. If the troops needed it, he would bring it to them. And the return trips would sometimes include bringing the dead and wounded troops back to basecamp. His helicopter was also equipped with two M60 machine guns with gunners at the ready in case of enemy fire.

Souza said, "The most difficult missions for me were those conducted at night." During the day, he said, "You couldn't see the bullets coming so you didn't really know what you were flying into." Souza said, "I could feel the bullets hitting his helicopter, I could hear them, but I couldn't see them." At night, however, the enemy would fire with tracer bullets. And tracer bullets can be seen from a long way away. So, Souza explained, "When I was flying into an area at night that was under attack, I could see the bullets coming at me. The sight of the bullets coming at me brought a different feeling to the battle."

His daily routine was rather consistent. Wake up at four in the morning for breakfast, attend a briefing at five, load up his helicopter, and then head out. He would usually spend seven to eight hours a day flying missions, and then return for a debriefing in the evening. Dinner after that, and then hit the sack. Wake up at four and start all over again. Every day. "We hardly ever had a day off," Souza said. He remembers an incident when a friend of his in another chopper crashed and all those on board were killed, including his friend. "That's something I'll never forget," Souza said.

His mission one day started out like any other mission. But it certainly didn't end that way.

On this day, Souza was observing and communicating on the radio, while the other crewman was flying the helicopter. One of their assigned missions at the end of that day was to transport a colonel to another location. As they were flying, a radio operator told them that they were flying into a monsoon. "Since there was a monsoon in the area, we were given alternative coordinates to follow." As they were advised, they adjusted their route, but, Souza said, "Before long, I got shot."

Souza explained, "It wasn't a large scale enemy attack, but rather one random shot through the bottom of the helicopter." As he further explained, "The bullet ripped through the floor of the copter, up between my legs, and through the lower part of my jaw." Part of his jaw and many of his bottom teeth were ripped out. The inside of the cockpit was sprayed in his blood, bone, and teeth. If the bullet would have entered the cockpit an inch or so closer to his groin, he would have been killed.

The pilot began hollering a distress call into the radio assuming there may have been significant damage to the helicopter and that Souza's injury was more serious. But Souza reassured the pilot that he was fine, and the pilot eventually landed the helicopter. Souza was able to walk out of the helicopter on his own, and they placed him on a stretcher. Upon examining his injury, it was noticed that in addition to the damage to his jaw and teeth, his tongue had been cut in half and the bullet was still lodged in the roof of his mouth. Regarding his split tongue, "They told me it was a muscle that would heal itself," which it eventually did. And what happened to the bullet?

"I still have it," Souza said.

Souza was taken to a hospital where, he said, "I was told later that I spent nine hours on the operating table in surgery." That injury, he said, was his "ticket out of Vietnam." After many months of surgery, recovery, and reconsideration of making the Army his career, he was discharged in 1971.

Looking back on his time in the military, even with his near-death experience, Souza said "I'd do it all over again."

Geary Baxter

"Boy, I really like talking with him." That was what Melvin Braziel said to me and my brother, John, as we were driving back from Kingsburg one day. The "him" that Braziel was referring to was Geary Baxter.

After my initial interview with Baxter, I had some follow-up questions for him and wanted to review the information I had to double-check the accuracy of my notes from our first meeting. So, we met with Baxter at a restaurant in Kingsburg and this second meeting was actually much like the first.

When speaking about his time in Vietnam as a helicopter pilot, Baxter spoke with detail and precision. He took us through a lesson in aerodynamics, hydraulics, mechanics, lift, and drift. He talked about how to maneuver the chopper into a landing zone so as not to land on dead soldiers, or how to play "Russian Roulette" with mortars while timing their explosions in order to make a landing. He was smart, confident, but not cocky. He had a sense of humor, but his experiences in Vietnam were no laughing matter. Just by listening to him you could tell he was an excellent pilot. He was among the best of the best. And it showed.

Baxter was a member of the Ghost Riders, an elite helicopter unit of the 101st Airborne Division. The unit had a reputation that if the situation was bad and our guys needed help, the Ghost Riders were called. And Baxter was there to receive those dangerous calls along with the other pilots and crews of the Ghost Riders.

"We provided anything the troops needed. Food, water, supplies, ammunition or replacements," Baxter said. "Each helicopter carried a crew of four, including yourself. And I eventually became the aircraft commander in charge of the crew." Each member of the crew had a nickname, and they often didn't even know the real names of the various crew members. Baxter's nickname was 'Bixby.' Baxter said, "They said I looked like the actor, Bill Bixby, on the show, *My Favorite Martian.*"

A few times, Baxter even had assignments such as spraying the jungle with Agent Orange, a defoliant used to destroy plant and jungle foliage in order to deprive the enemy of concealment. The problem with Agent Orange is that it has now been proven to cause cancer and other health ailments in those who may have been in contact with it. And Baxter was certainly in contact with Agent Orange.

"We'd spray with boom sprayers," Baxter said, "and we would often have to spray the area three times in order to kill the triple canopy jungle to see the ground." Baxter said, "At the time, I thought it was just a defoliant like when spraying cotton fields." But this was much more serious, and deadly.

While spraying the chemical, Baxter said, "The chemical mist would sometimes swirl around inside the helicopter so we would put our helmet visors down to keep the aerosol spray out of our eyes. And since the chemical would leak on the floor of the helicopter the souls of our boots would be stained." He further explained, "When we went back to the base we had to use engine fuel to clean up the chemical." When looking back on the experience, Baxter said, "I was so fortunate I didn't get cancer or some other illness."

Yes, he was very fortunate.

An interesting story about one of Baxter's harrowing experiences was highlighted in a History Channel documentary titled, *Operation Reunion*. The documentary focused on a battle near Firebase Ripcord in Vietnam on July 21, 1970 that Baxter was involved in, and the reunions that the helicopter crews from the Ghost Riders have every two years. Baxter shared with me the DVD of the documentary and explained to me more about the incident. An incredibly fascinating story.

This particular program highlighted Warrant Officer Larry Kern, a helicopter pilot with the Ghost Riders, and his crew, during the battle near Firebase Ripcord. And one of the 20 pilots in 10 helicopters who flew with Kern that day was Baxter. The battle near Firebase Ripcord became one of the deadliest battles during the Vietnam War.

Firebase Ripcord was known to be an area that was almost always under attack, and if you flew into the area you could expect to be shot at. As Baxter said in the documentary, "If you had to go to Ripcord that day, you were stressed a little. It was very isolated." He further explained, "We'd put them (soldiers or Marines) in there by helicopter and the only way for us to get them out was by helicopter." Eventually, on July 23rd, the command determined that the area was no longer defensible, so the decision was made to withdraw.

As Baxter explained the incident, "On July 21st, two days before the extraction of all troops from Firebase Ripcord, the Americans inserted a company of soldiers at the bottom of a ridge near Firebase Ripcord. Their mission was to recon the area and to be picked up that evening at the top of the ridge." But something went terribly wrong. "The company unknowingly walked into an unknown VC stronghold and were greatly outnumbered," Baxter explained. The American soldiers were being decimated by the North Vietnamese and needed to be extracted immediately.

Baxter and his fellow Ghost Rider pilots and crews went into action. Ten helicopter crews were sent to rescue the company.

During the battle near Firebase Ripcord, Kern, Baxter, and eight other pilots flew into the area to extract our soldiers. Baxter said, "It was horrific for the fellows on the ground. So you just did your best to get in and get out." There was almost continuous fire being directed at the troops. And not only was this fire directed at the troops on the ground, it was also directed at Baxter and his Ghost Riders.

When the choppers would fly into a battle, their order in line is called "chalk." Chalk one means you are the first in line, chalk two the second in line, etc. Baxter was originally scheduled for this mission to be chalk four and Kern chalk two. But prior to the start of the mission, Kern wanted to trade his order with Baxter, and Baxter agreed. So now, Baxter was chalk two and Kern chalk four.

When flying into the landing zone that day, chalk one and two, Baxter's chopper, came through fairly unscathed, chalk three took some hits, and chalk four, Kern's chopper was shot down. Remember, chalk four was initially Baxter's position, until they traded. Looking back on that, Baxter said, "After that, we never traded assigned positions again."

As explained in the documentary, when Kern was trying to land to pick up troops, he got delayed slightly from another helicopter that was overloaded with troops and had not yet left. During the brief delay, his helicopter got hit by an RPG and his gunner was shot.

When his helicopter was hit and his gunner shot, Kern began to fly out of the area. However, he was told on the radio that he was on fire and should return to the landing zone. There was no way he was going to make it without returning to the landing zone. Flames and smoke were coming out of the back of his helicopter and they were in serious trouble.

When Baxter heard on the radio that Kern's helicopter was on fire and having difficulty maneuvering, Baxter said, "I knew everyone on that helicopter, and I knew they were going down. Deep down inside you're saying a prayer for them, hoping they're going to make it out of there." And Baxter thought, "God, you hope they make it." As Kern was descending into the landing zone his helicopter crashed, pinning his injured gunner under the helicopter.

The last time Kern saw his gunner, he was on a stretcher and being loaded onto a helicopter for evacuation. He was seriously hurt, but Kern didn't know what happened to him. Since he was the pilot of the helicopter, Kern lived with guilt for many years because he felt responsible for his crew. As the years passed after the Vietnam War, Kern needed closure. He needed to find out about his gunner. Was he alive? Did he make it home? Was he okay? Finally, after hiring a private investigator to search for his former gunner, he was found.

And he was okay, too.

Baxter mentioned that later the same day, he was given a mission to resupply Firebase Ripcord with small arms ammo and retrieve some wounded soldiers. About the mission, Baxter said, "It took several attempts to land due to heavy mortar fire and 50-caliber antiaircraft fire." After he was finally able to land, a mortar landed near him. As he explained it, "When the mortar exploded, it felt like a shovel full of dirt hit me in the head."

Fortunately, the only chopper that was lost on that particular day was Kern's. But during the total siege at Firebase Ripcord, Baxter said, "The Ghost Riders started out with 20 assigned choppers. But after the worst two weeks in July, there were only four or five choppers left that could fly. The rest were out of commission." Only four or five left that could fly. That was it.

As Baxter explained, "The military didn't want the media to cover the battle because of their fear of getting the same bad press that followed the battle at Hamburger Hill." So at the time, most outside of the military didn't know about the battle at Ripcord. The public did not learn until much later about the 139 Americans that were killed during the four-and-a-half month siege at Ripcord, or the 75 Americans who were killed from July 1st to July 23rd, or that the brother of Chuck Norris, movie and television actor, was killed in the battle.[1]

Through the continuous hale of artillery, mortars, and bullets, Baxter survived. Yes, many were killed, but many more American soldiers and Marines survived, too, because of the heroism and bravery of Baxter and his fellow helicopter pilots and crews.

Baxter mentioned that even before this particular day, if you flew into Firebase Ripcord you could almost be guaranteed you'd be shot at. So I asked Baxter how many times he flew into and out of Firebase Ripcord during the few months of the siege. He thought for a minute and said, "More times than I care to remember."

Baxter and his fellow Ghost Riders have regular reunions where they get together, share stories, lean on each other, and experience the comradery they had while back in the Vietnam War. These reunions are certainly social times, and maybe a little therapeutic, too.

One time during our first interview he said, "What kept me going during the Vietnam War was that there were American GIs out there. Whatever they needed, we were ready to bring it to them." And Baxter got a little emotional when speaking of the combat troops he often brought out to the battle fields, when he said, "My heart would bleed for them. We dropped them into hell, and I hoped they were still there when we came back for them."

He had a hard time finishing that last sentence.

Since the fight in Vietnam was in dense jungles, mountains, rivers, and rice patties, being able to drive a truck or ambulance out to the wounded soldiers would be difficult or almost impossible. Especially if the wounded soldier was seriously injured and in need of immediate medical care.

Regardless of its name, the helicopters and their crews were an indispensable part of the Vietnam War. Bringing in more troops, extracting wounded or dead soldiers, delivering supplies, providing cover for the troops below. And many times, doing all of that under enemy fire.

These choppers and their crews did it all.

Often, the choppers would be flying into a hornet's nest of activity, braving a cascade of bullets being fired at them from below. Dodging shells, mortars, and tracer bullets. Risky landings in hot LZs, the possibility of getting tangled in the vegetation below, and being easy targets of the enemy while descending or ascending from the battlefield.

Without the dedication of the chopper pilots and their crews, the chances for success on the ground would have been significantly diminished. On the battlefield, the code of the military is to leave no soldier behind. And with the service of the helicopters during the war in Vietnam, that code was met, time and time again – thanks to the brave and courageous pilots and their crews.

Vietnam War and Wall Facts

The Highest Per Capita Killed [2]

By the end of the Vietnam War, it was determined that Beallsville, Ohio had the highest per capita number of soldiers killed during the war. Beallsville had a population of 475 and six (6) of her sons were killed.

10

The War on the Rivers

"In war the heroes outnumber the soldiers ten to one."

H.L. Mencken

MILES AND MILES of rivers wind their way through the dense, tropical foliage and landscapes of Vietnam. In places where the jungles have not been affected by napalm, Agent Orange, bomb craters, or bulldozers, the area is actually a beautiful cascade of trees, lush plants, and thick ground covers.

But for those American soldiers and sailors serving on the waters of Vietnam, admiring the beauty of the rivers and jungles through which they passed was overshadowed by keeping a keen eye out for the enemy who lurked within the jungle, or those who rode upon the waters.

In order for the Americans to restrict the enemy's use of the rivers to transport troops or bring them supplies and ammunition, certain vessels were used by the Army and Navy. Commonly called "the brown water Navy," small vessels called Patrol Boat River (PBRs) would wander through the rivers looking for vessels the enemy may have been using to transport troops or supplies. Their responsibility was to stop the boats, or sampans, and inspect them for enemy troops or ammunition they may have been concealing.

Another craft, the Armored Troop Carrier (ATC), would not only search suspected boats as did the PBRs, but they also had the additional responsibility to transport troops deep into the jungles. The trips along the waters for the crews of the PBRs and ATCs were certainly no vacation cruise. Rather, these trips often brought to the riders of these vessels the horrors of war.

Chuck Migalski

After making the decision to go to Vietnam instead of being court-martialed, Migalski was sent to Vallejo, California, to be trained on the ATC. As noted above, these vessels would transport troops, in addition to ammunition, equipment and supplies to the GIs in the jungles. Migalski said, "The ATC carried a crew of seven and was only 55 feet long and 18 feet wide." A far smaller vessel than what he was used to on the USS Bauer.

An ATC was designed and equipped for close-up fighting along the banks of the Vietnam rivers. It carried weapons such as a cannon, grenade launchers, and machine guns, in addition to any personal weapons the soldiers had such as pistols, rifles, and hand grenades. The ATC was also equipped to carry a 40-man infantry platoon and it became the workhorse of the war on the rivers.

Since it was the workhorse during the war, duty on an ATC was dangerous, as Migalski would soon find out.

When Migalski got to Vietnam, he would become part of the joint Army-Navy Mobile Riverine Force. The Army used the Navy's ATCs to transport its troops and supplies throughout the waterways of the Mekong Delta. Since the Viet Cong operated on the rivers daily, this sometimes led to close engagements with the enemy. The Viet Cong would use sampans, which were small boats, to transport weapons and food to the enemy forces. What they were transporting to their troops was often hidden within the sampans. When his boat would spot a sampan, Migalski's said, "We would stop the sampans and inspect them for anything they might have been taking to the enemy." He went on to say, "We almost always found weapons and rice." These weapons would either be confiscated or dumped in the river.

When he first arrived at his base camp after his arrival to Vietnam, Migalski's ATC was being loaded and prepared for a trip out into the rivers to transport combat troops into the jungle. The routine was to load up the boats, spend the next two weeks on the river transporting troops, weapons, and materials, inspecting sampans, and then back to the base camp to be loaded and prepared for the next trip. What was also routine, however, was something far more serious.

After only four days in Vietnam, Migalski said his ship "caught some shit." In other words, it came under enemy attack. As his ATC was cruising through the river on its way into the jungle shots rang out from the riverbanks, mortars were fired at the boat, and rockets were incoming. He grabbed a weapon and fired back. During his first attack, "I was too busy to be scared," Migalski said. He was fighting for his life and the life of his fellow GIs. He didn't have time to be scared. After the attack was over with, he had time to think about what just happened, and to realize how close he was to being injured or killed. "That's when I got scared," he said.

Coming under attack during the day along the riverbanks meant Migalski would fire back without a visible target, not knowing were the shots were coming from. His vessel came under attack both day and night, with around 90% of the attacks coming at night. Although they usually got hit hardest during the night, Migalski said, "At least at night, you could see the muzzle flashes from the enemy rifles, so you knew where to direct your shots."

The rivers they traveled were sometimes a half-mile or wider or narrow enough to where, as Migalski explained, "Someone could toss a grenade into the ship from the banks of the river." And as they traveled along the riverbanks, anyone seen with a weapon would become a target. You would sleep when you could because you never knew when the next attack would occur. At least two men always had to be awake, one to drive the ATC and the other to watch.

Coming under enemy attack became rather routine. Migalski explained, "We came under enemy fire around six days out of seven." Read that again - six days out of seven. Daily stress. Daily worry. Daily anxiety wondering when the next attack would happen, knowing that it was inevitable that it would.

When thinking back to his experience, Migalski mentioned that two of his best friends on the ATC were killed. As he remembered them, his voice began to trail off, he puffed harder on his cigarette, and the painful emotions from that memory were evident on his face. Staring down and shaking his head, he said, "I think about those guys all the time."

Thanksgiving Day is a national holiday that usually includes travel to see parents, children, or other members of the family. The dining room table is full of turkey, gravy, stuffing, and rolls. The television is playing a National Football League game while the over-stuffed men in the family sit around the television drinking beer and cussing the referees. People are celebrating the holiday, laughing, talking, and sharing stories. But Thanksgiving Day in 1968 was nothing for Chuck Migalski to celebrate.

On that day, Migalski earned a Purple Heart.

He was injured in an attack, suffering shrapnel wounds from a rocket that hit his ATC while it was under attack. "That was a hell of a way to celebrate Thanksgiving," Migalski said. Since his injuries were not serious enough to require hospitalization or being taken off his ship, he was fortunate that he survived the attack and to stay with his crew. But then it happened again.

Two weeks later, he earned another Purple Heart. Again, suffering wounds from when his ATC was attacked from the riverbanks by the invisible enemy. And if that was not enough, it happened again a couple of months later. "My third injury landed me in the hospital where I spent four days and then was sent to Okinawa for two weeks." Normally, when a GI receives three Purple Hearts he is immediately discharged. "My third Purple Heart was my ticket out of Vietnam," Migalski said, "but I felt like I was letting my buddies down by being sent home before my full tour of duty was over with."

Three Purple Hearts. Incredible.

Migalski's ATC often transported some other living creatures along with the troops. These creatures he transported were troops, too, but not human troops. They were dogs.

Dogs are the unknown soldiers that served in Vietnam and saved thousands of lives during the war. Most people do not even know that dogs were used in Vietnam. Nor do they know the impact the dogs had on the soldiers they served alongside with.

Dogs have a superior ability to hear, see, and smell. They can detect the scent of people or objects such as equipment, land mines, booby traps, tunnels, and ammunition. During patrols in the jungle, or walking sentry duty around a compound, the soldiers' ability to hear, see, or smell was often limited or impaired. Since dogs have keen and profound senses, they were able to detect trouble ahead that humans could not.

Although impossible to determine accurately, some have estimated the number of lives saved from the service of dogs in Vietnam to be around 10,000.[1] So, without the assistance of dogs during the war, the names on the Vietnam War Memorial Wall in Washington, D.C., could have been around 68,000 names rather than 58,000.

Migalski remembers most of the dogs were either German Shepherds or Doberman Pinchers. These dogs were not only trained, but they were mean. When back at the base camp, Migalski saw what damage these dogs could inflict. Describing the effects of injury the dogs inflicted upon the enemy, Migalski said, "The dogs shredded them to pieces."

Richard Walker

As Richard Walker said, "When I enlisted in the Navy, I never dreamed I'd be in a boat on the waters of Vietnam." But he was. After arriving in Vietnam, Walker was assigned to a PBR. As he explained, "The PBR was a boat that was made specifically for the Vietnam War, and our main goal was to try and disrupt the flow of weapons from one side of the river to the other." An additional responsibility of the PBR was to insert and extract Navy SEAL teams.

PBR's were found patrolling in the Mekong Delta, Rung Sat Special Zone, and the Saigon River. As Walker explained, "The PBR was only about 30 feet long and 11 feet wide and carried a crew of four." Not a very large craft. But it was fortified with mounted machine guns, grenade launchers, in addition to carrying rifles, handguns, shotguns, and hand grenades. The boat itself was designed for rapid acceleration and enhanced maneuverability in order to speed out of difficult situations.

When on the rivers, Walker's boat would pull up next to other Vietnamese boats or sampans to inspect them for weapons they may be carrying. "If we were ever fired upon by a boat in the water," Walker said, "we could shoot back. But if we pulled up next to a boat and it disobeyed our orders and took off, we had to get permission to fire on them."

Walker's PBR would be on patrol for four to five days and then return to the barge where they lived when not patrolling. On November 27, 1967, Walker's outlook on the Vietnamese people and his life in general changed when he stared down death in the belly of his boat.

One night while they were docked alongside the barge and most everyone was sleeping, the Viet Cong swam up underneath the barge and attached explosive devices. A short while later, they detonated the explosives. "I heard a loud explosion and got knocked out of my bed. I wondered 'What in the hell is going on?,'" he explained. Water was rapidly coming into the area where the men were sleeping so Walker and the others scrambled for safety. But by the time Walker was able to react, he could not walk or run out of the area, he had to swim. The water rapidly was filling up the sleeping compartment and the bottom sections of the boat.

Walker remembers that a couple of the crewmen were trapped

inside. "They were screaming for help," Walker said, "but they couldn't be reached." When asked what happened to them, he said with obvious pain on his face and looking down, "They died." And they weren't the only ones.

Ten (10) died that night on the barge, and two were friends of Walker's from his PBR. Struggling to further describe the experience, Walker went on to explain that one of his fellow crewmen that night was badly burned from the explosion. "I remember seeing him lying on the table and they were pulling the burned skin off his body. And he was screaming." He later died, too.

When remembering that experience, Walker said, "It was the first time I saw the human equation in war. I'll never forget it." He further stated, "That was the day my feeling sorry for these people changed. I wasn't sorry for them anymore."

Walker had sustained serious smoke inhalation and was awarded the Purple Heart. When he was in the hospital, the staff asked Walker if he'd like them to notify his parents that he was in the hospital and recuperating from his injury. Walker appreciated that gesture and agreed to that request, but he also assumed they would notify his parents with a phone call or a telegram. But that's not exactly what happened.

Yes, they notified them by telegram, but they also notified them another way.

Two military officers went to Walker's house to notify his parents of their son's injury. But what were his parents to think when they saw the officers pull up to their house? "When dad saw the car pull up with two officers in it, he thought they were there to notify him that I had died from my injuries," Walker said. What a whirlwind of emotions his father must have felt. In just a matter of moments, thinking that your son was dead to finding out he was alive.

Seniors in high school during the 1960s often had a choice to make regarding their military service. Should they enlist or take their chances on being drafted? If they enlisted, they could choose the Navy or Air Force and, hopefully, avoid being sent to Vietnam. If they took their chances on being drafted, they would be drafted into the Marine Corps or the Army, usually guaranteeing them a front seat to the war. For many of those who chose the former option, they enlisted in the Navy to avoid the possibility of going to Vietnam. They assumed their time in the military would be spent on the waters of the world, sailing through seas off the coasts of countries far away.

However, being in the Navy was not a guaranteed pass at avoiding service in Vietnam. In fact, being in the Navy put some from Porterville High School in the middle of the country, traveling through the myriad of rivers looking for enemy soldiers or defending themselves against an enemy lurking along the banks of the rivers.

The war on the river waters of Vietnam brought the ugliness, terror, and stress of battle onto the decks of the vessels on which the sailors traveled. Their responsibilities included transporting troops deep into the jungle, restricting the flow of enemy weapons, or inspecting boats or sampans that may be delivering troops or ammunition to the enemy. And this duty often placed them in the middle of battles in which they were injured and some of their friends killed.

This was not the Navy they expected when they enlisted.

Vietnam War and Wall Facts

The High School with the Most Killed [2]

64 soldiers who attended Thomas Edison High School in Philadelphia were killed during the Vietnam War.

11

The War on the Roads

"People tell me I saved hundreds and hundreds of people. But I have to tell you: It's not the people you saved that you remember. It's the ones you couldn't save."

Navy SEAL Chris Kyle, *American Sniper*

BEING A TRUCK driver in the Vietnam War might seem like a job that required little knowledge or skill and was basically free from the stress and worry of being in combat. While navigating the roads of Vietnam, a truck driver could harken back to the good 'ol days in Porterville driving around the countryside with his girlfriend, hoping to run out of gas so he'd have an excuse to pull over and make out. Cruising down a road in Vietnam with the windows down, hair blowing in the wind, puffing on a Marlboro cigarette while listening to the Beach Boys on an 8-track tape player. Not too bad of duty.

But this was no Saturday afternoon cruise through Porterville. This was Vietnam. And this was war.

Certainly, mounting an M60 machine gun on a jeep at the front and rear of the convoy meant trouble could occur at any time. Needing to sweep the roads looking for mines before starting out on the drive was a sign that the flat road could turn into a deep crater in an instant. Having a few MPs escorting the convoy showed that this drive was a serious one.

The roads these convoys traveled on were often ripe for an ambush. There were tight, hairpin turns, steep and slow terrain, and narrow trails. Since speed was one of the best means of defense against an attack, the roads were often not conducive to this line of defense.

Attacks on a convoy were often brief with the attackers hoping to knock out a few vehicles. Some of their primary targets were the vehicles carrying ammunition and fuel. Then, shortly after the attack was engaged, the attackers would slip back into the jungle waiting for the next convoy to pass them by. Surely, these drives were no picnic.

Todd Pixler

As part of his transportation MOS, Todd Pixler's job was to transport troop reinforcements, supplies, ammunition or anything else the troops needed in the jungle. This was after the Tet Offensive, and "Everyone was still on edge and expecting anything," Pixler said. Rather than driving as far away from the action as possible, Pixler volunteered to stay with the soldiers and drive supplies out to them directly to where they were fighting. He would often follow a jeep to the fire base, sometimes carrying 10 soldiers in the back. Often, the roads were very rough and bumpy. "Because the drive was so bumpy, I had to periodically look in the back and take inventory to make sure no one fell out," Pixler said.

He often drove through what was once thick foliage but now was decimated due to defoliants and bulldozers. When he was driving his truck out in the jungle, Pixler said, "I always had a soldier with me riding shotgun and holding a weapon." Since he never knew when or if his truck might come under attack having someone riding with him that was armed was a necessity. He also mentioned that the roads were sometimes mined, and a truck hitting a mine would have a devastating effect. Probably death, certainly injury. "I would always drive around anything in the road that was sticking out from the ground. I was never confident it was just a bump or debris, when it could have been a land mine buried in the road," Pixler said. So better to be safe than sorry. He drove around it.

One of the items he enjoyed taking out to the troops was ice cream. These soldiers had been in the jungle for months, eating nothing but C-rations, which was basically food out of a can. So, ice cream to them was a delicacy that most of us take for granted. "Sometimes," Pixler said, "the ice cream was soft or even melted by the time it got to the troops, but that didn't bother them at all." Pixler said, "I still remember the look on these soldiers' faces when they got to eat ice cream after spending months in the jungle."

Hard, soft, or melted, it all tasted great to them.

Since he volunteered to drive his supply truck out closer to the action, Pixler's truck came under sniper fire a few times, but nothing too serious at the beginning. He remembers on his trips back and forth from the fire base to the main base, Pixler would often drive by trucks and other vehicles that had been blown up and lying disabled on the side of the road. He was hoping, praying and crossing his fingers that his truck would never be in that same position someday. Because if it was, that would mean he was probably killed or seriously injured.

Then one day, he was faced with the possibility of death.

When he was with the troops at their fire base, shots started being fired from the trees into their location. They were under attack. Pixler said that "Shots were being fired and mortars began hitting around us, and everyone was scrambling." When this happened, Pixler remembers jumping out of his truck to take cover. Tracers were coming in and bouncing around, while shots were being fired in both directions. It was crazy. Pixler was a truck driver, not a combat soldier. He wasn't supposed to be in this kind of craziness.

For about 30 minutes utter chaos filled the air and ground around him, but then came the helicopters. "During the attack," Pixler said, "a Huey gunship was hovering over my head firing rounds into the trees." The power of the weapons on the Huey firing the rounds was so strong, he said that it "caused the Huey to back up in the air." The sounds, the hollering, the fear. "Scared the crap out of me," Pixler said.

This was far different than running track against a competitor at Occidental or beating recruits in Pugil stick training at boot camp. This was serious. The war was right in his lap and soldiers were fighting, being injured, and dying all around him. And then something happened that he still can't fully explain.

"My mind shut down," Pixler said. "I didn't remember anything that happened after that."

He doesn't remember when the firing stopped. He doesn't remember the trip back to the main base taking dead or wounded soldiers. He doesn't remember loading up any equipment. He doesn't remember who rode shot gun with him, or if anyone rode with him at all. He just doesn't remember. Certainly, the stress of what happened caused his mind to blot out his memory of the experience. But he survived, regardless if he remembers what happened or not.

Pixler talked about another time when our soldiers were sent into Cambodia to confront the enemy. He said, "A report came in that our soldiers were getting our asses kicked." In Pixler's mind, "Cambodia was their country, so sending in troops to fight there was stupid." But he still volunteered to drive to the fire base to take in the supplies, food, and other equipment. Since the soldiers needed it, he was willing to risk what it took to get it to them. What he found there was horrendous - death, injury and destruction.

On the return trip, he hauled back a dozen or so soldiers that had been killed, many from booby traps. When he was loading the body bags onto his truck, he remembers thinking "There's a person in that bag." And that's something he's never forgotten.

He and others in his unit were eventually awarded the Bronze Star for bravery in action.

Greg Goble

The first time Greg Goble faced enemy fire was when the jeep he was riding in, along with other military vehicles, came under attack. He heard shots being fired and then, close to his jeep, he could hear the sounds of the bullets hitting his jeep and the environment around him. People were running for cover. "Me and my friend Craig, jumped off the jeep and took cover behind a pile of logs," Goble said. And the sound continued.

Thud! Thud! Thud! Thud! Thud! In rapid succession.

The VC had set up a small ambush. "The bullets were hitting just on the other side of the stack of tree wood we were huddled behind," Goble explained, "and only a few feet of wood separated us from the bullets." A few feet and a pile of wood were the difference between life and death and he was in a battle for his life.

Goble couldn't stick his head over the top of the wood pile to take aim at those who were shooting at him or he would have been killed for sure. So, he did the only thing he could do. "Craig and I stuck the heavy M14 rifle out around the side of the pile of wood and just started shooting back," he said. Shooting indiscriminately. Emptying his magazine at an enemy he could not see. Finally, the battle was over. "I'm sure we did not hit anyone," Goble said, 'but at least we could tell the other guys we shot our weapons and save a little face."

"I was not scared during the shooting," Goble said, "because I was too busy reacting to what was happening around me. But once it was over, then I got scared." Thinking back on the experience, he said, "Those damn logs saved my life."

When most people think of MPs in Vietnam, they often assume the MPs stayed on the post for gate duty, traffic control, or as a guard at Long Bien Jail (LBJ). But Goble's company was comprised of combat MPs. With that, Goble's role as an MP in Vietnam was often much more dangerous.

Goble referred me to the website of the 720th Military Police Battalion Reunion Association that describes convoys and the role of the MPs in protecting those convoys.[1] On the website there were two quotes that emphasized the hazardous conditions those in convoys often found themselves.

The first quote was from former SFC Richard L. Dehart, B Company, 720th MP Battalion, 1967-68 when he said, "Establishing a routine in the field will get you killed quicker than anything else."

The second quote was from CPL Thomas T. Watson, from the same battalion and company, when he said, "In a guerilla war with no front lines, the enemy hides and observes what you do and capitalizes on your weaknesses. With limited resources, the guerilla fighter strikes only when he believes it is to his advantage, when and where he can inflict the most damage and casualties…With this kind of approach to war, the daily convoy supply runs that were always routine, exposed, slow and cumbersome, became one of his favorite targets of opportunity. Unfortunately for the truckers and MPs who had to work the convoy runs, there was no way to eliminate the predictability they presented…"

In other words, convoys were not an evening stroll through the countryside of Vietnam. These drives were serious, and often costly and deadly.

A war could not be successfully fought without ammunition and supplies. And in order to get these needed materials to the troops in the jungle, it was necessary for truck convoys to deliver the material to the surrounding bases. Truck convoys were an absolute necessity to the American war effort. However, these convoys could not have been successful in their efforts without the MPs who guarded them.

As the convoys moved tons of ammunition, supplies, and materials, they were long, slow, and vulnerable to an attack. Traveling the roads was often hazardous, so the MPs would escort these convoys to make sure they got to their destination. Prior to moving the convoys, the roads were often swept for mines. Goble said, "I started off as a driver which I became skilled at missing potholes and never venturing even a little off the road avoiding possible road mines planted by the Viet Cong."

As an MP assigned to escort convoys, Goble said, "It was the responsibility of the MPs to protect the equipment and truckers who drove the vehicles." Goble said he still marvels at the thought that 18-year-old MPs were responsible for millions of dollars of equipment in addition to protecting the soldiers who drove the trucks. As Goble said, "These MPs were only teenagers and responsible for all of that? That's a heavy responsibility to place on a young guy like that."

Goble explained, "Some convoys included up to 40 trucks and the trip could take two to four days to complete, depending on the conditions of the roads." Sometimes, they didn't stop for night and always slept inside the rig. Since the rig was loud, hard, and extremely uncomfortable, bouncing over cracks, holes and bumps in the road, Goble said, "A good night or day's sleep was almost impossible."

Sometimes the convoys would pass through villages where there was evidence of a recent firefight between the Viet Cong and the ARVN, the South Vietnamese who fought with the Americans. Goble said, "If the VC won the firefight, there would be stacks of dead bodies of men, women, and children with body parts stuck in various places and signs telling this is what happened to American lovers." Oh, the horrors of war.

Since the MPs were responsible to repel attacks by the enemy, the jeeps and vehicles the MPs traveled in were modified and equipped with machine guns and other weapons to provide any fire support that may be necessary to defend themselves from an enemy attack. One of the vehicles the MPs used on convoys was the V-100 Commando. Goble said, "I always wished I could have dragged Main Street in Porterville with it." As Goble described the vehicle, "The V-100 was amphibious, had big tires instead of tracks, and was equipped with a wench to pull trucks that hit a road mine or were hit with an RPG." When a vehicle was disabled, the road needed to be cleared so the convoy could keep moving. "The Viet Cong certainly wanted the supplies being carried by the Americans to support them in their own war efforts," Goble explained. Because of that, the threat of ambush was always there.

But there was one instance which happened that still has a

profound impact on Goble. And it really had nothing to do with his role as an MP protecting a convoy.

One day while waiting for the trucks to unload before heading back to Long Bien, Goble said, "One of my buddies comes in and says, 'Hey, Goble, did you say you were from Pootersville?'" Back in the 60s, Porterville was known as a small, rural, farming town, and people would sometimes call Porterville a derogatory name such as 'Hooterville' or some other name. So when his friend asked that question, Goble sternly corrected him and said, "No, Porterville!" And then his friend said something that still bothers Goble to this day.

"Shit," his friend said, "one of the guys said there is a kid from that town in one of the body bags in the truck."

Thinking back to that instance, Goble said, "There is no way to explain the emotional bomb that hit me. Here I am, thousands of miles away from home and here is someone from my town in a body bag. No one knows except me. I broke down."

What Ron McCarville said in a previous chapter certainly fits here with Goble's reaction to finding out someone from Porterville was in one of the body bags in the truck: "How can you not be affected by that?"

In Vietnam, no job was safe. Driving a truck or some other type of transport vehicle might have seemed like easy duty, but not in Vietnam. Many of the convoys were attacked by the NVA or Viet Cong leaving drivers, riders, or escorts with injury or death. There was stress, anxiety, and fear around every hairpin turn in the road.

Soldiers, airmen, and Marines in the jungles, or sailors on the rivers, could not carry a rifle, load their weapons with ammunition, eat food, be cared for with medical supplies, get mail from home, or whatever, without the persons behind the scenes who delivered those needed materials to the troops. Those behind the scenes that made sure the troops had what they needed in the jungles of the Vietnam War were often the truckers of convoys and the MPs who protected them. The cargo the convoys were carrying were supplies the Americans needed in their war effort. The Viet Cong and North Vietnamese wanted these supplies, too. Or, at least, they didn't want us to have them.

You never knew when an attack would come, and that uncertainty made the trips along the roads all the more hazardous, challenging, and stressful.

Vietnam War and Wall Facts

The Last Pilot Killed [2]

The last pilot killed in the Vietnam war was Air Force helicopter pilot Second Lieutenant Richard Vandegeer. He was killed
when his helicopter crashed during the Mayaguez incident on
May 15, 1975. The Mayaguez incident is considered the last
combat action of the Vietnam War.

12

The War on the Bases

"Son, if the Marines thought you needed a wife,
we would have issued you one."

Gen. Lewis B. "Chesty" Puller,
responding to a Marine's request to be married.

DURING THE MOVIE, *The Wizard of Oz*, Dorothy was talking to her dog and said, "Someplace where there isn't any trouble. Do you suppose there is such a place, Toto?" Well, if Dorothy was asking that about Vietnam during the war, the answer to her question would be, "No!"

No place was safe during the Vietnam War. Sure, some bases were safer than others, but there was trouble everywhere. Even at your base, which was your home in Vietnam. Being home on your base in Vietnam was not necessarily a safe place, or a haven from the horrors of war. You would think that the bases were built in areas far away from the enemy. A place where you could sleep undisturbed, walk leisurely to the PX without any concern to buy some clothes, play catch on the baseball field with friends, or just snooze under the shade of a tree. The bases may have been built initially in places thought to be far from the enemy, but the enemy eventually closed in.

Rather than catching baseballs with friends, the GIs on base were often "catching shit" as mortars were incoming, and people were jumping into bunkers in mad scrambles for their lives. Dreams at night were often interrupted with shouts for help. The silence of the evening was often broken by the explosions of rockets. Hootches became craters. And life became death.

Jim Rouch

The United States Naval Construction Battalions have the nickname "Seabees" which is a heterograph of the first initials "C" and "B" from the words Construction and Battalion. Seabees are part of the Navy, and during the Vietnam War their responsibility was construction and focused on such things as surveying, building facilities, roads, bridges, runways. They provided valuable support to the troops in building roads and facilities for them, and also to the pilots of planes and helicopters who needed someplace to land their aircraft.

Sometimes, these responsibilities were completed far away from the battlefield. Other times, they were completed right in the middle of combat.

Jim Rouch was a Seabee, whose MOS was in heavy equipment. After he completed his training at Port Hueneme Navy base in Ventura, California, Rouch found himself on a plane ride to Vietnam. Certainly, with an MOS such as his, being placed in a combat situation would probably be nothing he would have to worry about. But this was the Vietnam War, and no MOS was immune from the possibility of combat.

After he first landed in Da Nang, Rouch went by boat to his base at Dong Ha. During the ride through the river, he said, "I was scared to death." Often looking over the edge of the boat to see if there were enemy out there. The boat ride to Dong Ha took about 24 hours. Twenty-four hours of being scared to death, not knowing what may be lurking on the banks of the river as he peeked over the edge of the boat.

One of his initial assignments was to build a base at a five-acre spot. They had to build housing for eight companies or one battalion. The buildings were quick, plywood and metal units Rouch called "glorified tents." But anything better than a tent or sleeping on the ground was a luxury to the troops in the field. Rouch was in a group of about 35 other Seabees that eventually was sent to a place called Khe Sanh.

Little did he know at the time, but Rouch was being sent to a place that would become one of the Vietnam War's most infamous sieges, and one of the deadliest and costliest battles of the entire war.

As Rouch explained the territory, "The Khe Sanh base was on a plateau that was a few miles away from the Ho Chi Minh Trail, and just over the ridge from the base was the Demilitarized Zone and beyond that, North Vietnam." Obviously, he was close to the North Vietnamese soldiers and the area was of strategic importance to them, and to the United States.

When he got to Khe Sanh one of his first assignments was repairing the runways for the planes to land to deliver supplies and additional troop reinforcements. When the large planes landed, Rouch said, "Their heavy weight would tear up the runways." Due to their size, and the condition of the ground, Rouch explained, "It was difficult to get and keep a good base on the runway."

At one point, Rouch began to notice that there was a gradual increase in the number of troops, in addition to supplies, ammunition, and weaponry being flown into the base. "We could tell something was happening, but no one was telling us anything," Rouch said. One of the Marines who recently came to Khe Sanh commented to Rouch, "There is a lot going on out there." Still, there was no communication from anyone as to what was going on. Marine patrols went out around the base and began making more contact with the enemy and they could tell that the enemy was planning something big.

Then, in the early morning on Sunday, January 21, 1968, it happened.

Approximately 20,000 North Vietnamese troops began a series of attacks and surrounded the Khe Sanh base that held approximately 5,500 Marines and support personnel, including Rouch.[1] "Mortars, rockets, and artillery shells were being fired into the base. Everyone was ducking for cover," Rouch said. There really was no place safe to hide, but everyone was jumping into bunkers or trenches, behind vehicles or equipment for cover.

The ammunition dump was hit that erupted in a number of ear-piercing explosions. The smell of gasoline and smoke filled the air. The mess hall was destroyed, fuel storage areas were set on fire, the commanding officer's quarters were hit, and several helicopters and other pieces of equipment were blown up or rendered unusable. People were being killed and injured. It was hell.

The only road up to the plateau, Route 9, had been cut off, so, Rouch said, "The only way the base could be reinforced or be provided with supplies was by air." The planes that flew into Khe Sanh came under heavy fire when they approached the air strip as well as when they landed and took off again. Rouch said, "I still remember watching a Marine C-130 plane that was landing take a direct hit from a North Vietnamese rocket." He said, "The plane exploded in a giant fireball and everyone on board was killed." As he became emotional telling the story, Rouch said, "They were all incinerated." That was one of the disturbing images of Khe Sanh that Rouch will never forget.

He talked about another time when an Air Force C-130 was coming in for a landing but missed the runway and crashed. There was no definite reason given for why the plane missed the runway, possibly from pilot error. Rouch mentioned, "We tried to go out and help the guys but were ordered not to." And why not? "They said the plane was carrying ammunition," Rouch said, "and they were afraid the ammunition might explode. So we had to stay back. And that was hard."

Rouch said, "During the siege, there was never really much of a break from the attacks." Day after day. Night after night. Incoming artillery, mortars, explosions, death, and injury for over two months straight. "I was scared all the time," Rouch said, "and no place was safe. You never knew when or where the next rocket would hit."

One time, Rouch mentioned, "As me and another guy were out stealing some food from the compound, an explosion hit just a few feet from me and tossed me up into some Constantine wire." He survived, but if the rocket would have hit a couple of feet closer to him, he would have been killed. He did, however, suffer permanent hearing damage from the explosion. When asked why he was stealing food, Rouch said, "The amount of food they gave us was equal to only about two meals a day in C-rations. We were hungry and wanted more to eat." And who could blame them? Looking back on the physical affect the war had on his body, Rouch said, "I lost 30 pounds during my first tour."

There was one word that produced immediate fear in Rouch and the others who were being faced with the daily attacks from the enemy. And that word was, "incoming." When someone yelled "incoming" that meant a shell was on its way into the compound. And when you heard the word, Rouch said, "You immediately dropped what you were doing and jumped into a bunker." As Rouch explained, "When you heard a mortar or rocket fired, or when you heard someone yell 'incoming,' you only had a few seconds before it exploded. So, you scrambled for your life." He also mentioned, "It was very intense during mortar attacks because you were hoping that a shell did not hit where you had taken shelter." Rouch was lucky, but many weren't.

When there was a let up in the shelling, Rouch and the other Seabees went to work repairing the damage. Then, another attack would occur, and more damage was inflicted. More repairs done, and then more attacks followed. This became a daily routine. Rouch said, "The B-52s would bomb around Khe Sanh during the night, and the North Vietnamese would shell the base during the day." Every day, every night, for two-and-a-half months. You couldn't sleep. Even though this was life for over two months, Rouch said, "It was never something you got used to." The fear of being killed or injured was always there.

Finally, on April 8th, after 77 days of intense bombing and shelling on both sides, the North Vietnamese attack was repelled, Route 9 was reopened and the siege was over. The United States held the base, but at a terrible cost. Two hundred and seventy-four (274) Americans were killed, and approximately 2,500 Americans were injured. The number of North Vietnamese soldiers killed was estimated to be around 10,000-15,000.[2]

Then on July 5th, only about three months after the siege had ended, the Americans destroyed and abandoned the base. After all of that injury, destruction and death, we left. Rouch had actually left Khe Sanh before the end of the siege but when he later found out the Americans were abandoning the base after so many were killed or injured defending it, he said his first thought was, "What the hell is this all about?" When describing his feelings about the Americans leaving the base, Rouch said, "I was hurt. In fact, I was in shock."

When looking back on his service during the war, Rouch extended a compliment and word of gratitude to the military doctors and the jobs they did. Rouch said, "These doctors spent years in college and had medical practices back home. Then they enlist and were taken from their families." And instead of living in their houses with four bedrooms, a two-car garage, and a swimming pool, Rouch said, "They're living in tents along with the rest of us." Rouch further explained, "These guys did a sometimes impossible job trying the save GIs who were severely injured." One instance he remembered was when a Marine who was fighting in the area around Khe Sanh was injured, and they medevac'd him to Khe Sanh. What was particularly dangerous about his injury was that it could have subsequently injured and killed multiple others as well. Rouch said, "He had a mortar round lodged in his body that didn't go off." So, the operation to dislodge the mortar was a delicate one because one mistake by the doctors could cost the life of the GI, the doctors working on him, the nurses who were assisting, and any medical support staff in the area. Due to the skill of the doctor, the mortar round was dislodged without further injury.

There was something that Rouch saw one time that could have eventually changed the outcome of the war. "We were at a location about seven or eight miles south of the DMZ," Rouch said, "and there were tanks, trucks, equipment and vehicles as far as the eye could see. I had never seen such a huge amount of vehicles before. No one had either." And what was the purpose of this incredible mass of equipment?

"Our military leaders were considering invading North Vietnam," Rouch said.

Russell Vossler

"Is today the day?"

That's a question we've all asked ourselves at one time or another. "Is today the day my boyfriend will ask me to marry him?" "Is today the day that I'll finally buy that new car I've been wanting?" "Is today the day that I find out about my promotion request?"

For about a year, Russell Vossler asked that same question every single morning when he woke up. But his question didn't relate to wedding proposals, car purchases, or job promotions. His question related to his life.

"Is today the day that I'll be killed?"

Every morning Vossler asked that question. Why? Because Vossler was in Vietnam and it seemed like every day there was another mortar attack on his base. Another injury. Another death. He had been lucky, but he felt his luck was going to run out. Vossler said, "I always had a feeling that I wouldn't make it out of Vietnam alive." And, the stress of wondering what the answer to his question would eventually be, took an emotional toll on him - big time.

Death didn't always come to just those in combat. One of the first guys Vossler made friends with at his base called Bearcat was a blonde-haired, dark-tanned guy from Southern California named Larry. "Larry had been in Vietnam for a while and he helped me with my equipment and getting adjusted to Vietnam," Vossler said. In a very short period of time, Vossler grew to like Larry. "He quickly became my best friend in Vietnam," Vossler said.

Vossler first met Larry a few days before Christmas. Larry had recently received some Christmas presents and goodies from home that he shared with Vossler. Since Vossler had only been in Vietnam a short period of time, he had not yet received any mail from home. Larry made Vossler's transition to Vietnam and Bearcat an easier one, and Vossler liked his new friend.

But then tragedy struck.

Only about 10 days after meeting his new friend, Larry was killed in a helicopter crash. Vossler explained, "A helicopter pilot was screwing around, hit some telephone wires, flipped over and exploded. Four were killed, including Larry." Vossler had lost his uncle that he admired in a traffic accident. He lost a high school friend who was killed in Vietnam. And now he lost his new best friend in Vietnam in a helicopter crash. After that, Vossler said, "I did not want to get close to anyone again in Vietnam." That was his defense mechanism to avoid further pain. And, in fact, the same defense mechanism that many GIs took during the war.

During one routine day, Vossler thought that the answer to his question, "Is today the day?" was going to be answered.

"Early morning, around 2:00 a.m.," Vossler said, "I heard this god-awful sound and it blew out the end of the hootch we were sleeping in. We were hearing shots fired so we immediately hauled ass out to the bunker." He said that while they were in the bunker he saw silhouettes of guys running across the company area and then the guys dropped. Someone had killed them. Vossler said, "I was thinking to myself, 'What the hell is going on?' and everyone was freaking out."

He realized then that the Viet Cong had infiltrated the area. Vossler said, "My heart was in my throat. I was having trouble breathing, and I remember I immediately started praying." During his prayers under the chaos of the situation, Vossler said, "I was making all the promises in the world to God." And who could blame him?

Vossler remembered, "After we were first hit with a mortar attack, hit the floor and ran out to the bunker, I was looking for the sergeant that was in the same hootch." Vossler then explained how he and another guy couldn't find the sergeant, so they both went back to the hootch again looking for him. This time, they found him. Vossler said, "The sergeant was underneath one of the bunks in a state of shock. Me and the other guy picked him up and we part carried him and part dragged him outside. The sergeant was our go-to guy in this type of situation, but he definitely was not functioning this time."

As the battle continued, Vossler said that someone with some sort of authority came to where he and other guys were at and said that they were looking for guys to go out to the perimeter. The guy said, "The VC are coming over on this one side." Vossler said to everyone there, "I don't know about you guys, but I'm volunteering." He said he thought to himself, "At least on the perimeter I would know who the bad guys were." During the chaos of the battle, Vossler said, "Some of our guys were killed by friendly fire, and that was just devastating for me." He further said, "It was bad enough to have to fight the VC, but to worry about your own guys shooting you really messed with my head."

Finally, that battle was over, but there was still no lasting peace. They just waited in nervous anticipation for the next attack. "After getting hit that first night," Vossler said, "we got hit approximately every two hours on the hour for about two weeks." This time period was the anniversary of the Tet Offensive, and, Vossler said, "The constant mortar attacks really worked on everybody's nerves."

And remember, Vossler was a helicopter mechanic not an infantryman.

Regardless of the ongoing attacks, "The mission still had to be done," Vossler explained, "The equipment had to be fixed, and you couldn't just stop." He further said, "Everybody was on edge and the short-timers were basically living in the bunker. They would hardly leave even when it was their time to pull duty. They'd get someone else to cover for them so they could stay in the bunker."

One day, as Vossler was on top of a chopper making some repairs, and the sun having just gone down, their area began to get mortared again. Vossler said, "I jumped off the chopper and started running to the main bunker." That was certainly the right thing to do, but he said, "As I was running to the bunker I started getting shot at by our own guys." He said, "I thought everyone knew where I was at, but they thought I was the VC." Fortunately, their shots missed hitting him and he found protection behind a cement wall. He stayed there, hunkered down, until it was safe to come out.

Thinking back on his combat experiences, Vossler said, "Since you never knew when you'd be attacked or killed, you just lived for the moment. If they get me, they get me. You just get to the point where you accept that."

Vossler was always under the fear and stress that his area could be mortared at any time. Night attacks were worse because you couldn't see what was out there. In addition, Vossler said, "The only way to have a good night's sleep was through utter exhaustion." And the worry didn't end when the mortars did, because "You were always tired, and on edge," Vossler said, "and worrying about the next attack." Day after day after day.

Brian Rattigan

Brian Rattigan described his combat experience as passive, meaning that his experiences were more with mortar and rocket shelling than in active infantry combat in the bush. In fact, active combat experience was what he expected to find when he got to Vietnam. While stationed with the 82nd Airborne Division, Ratting served as a fire team leader, infantry weapons specialist and instructor in the Division's air cavalry troop. He also graduated from the Third Army NCO Academy. Thus, Rattigan said, "I expected to be sent to an airborne infantry unit when I arrived in Vietnam, so I was completely surprised and disappointed when I was not assigned to an airborne infantry unit." Instead, Rattigan was assigned to an assault helicopter company in a combat aviation battalion in II Corps – Central Highlands where he served as a helicopter gunship weapons specialist NCO.

What Rattigan found in his assignment he described as "significant periods of boredom in relative comfortable living conditions as compared to arduous and dangerous combat infantry duty." When his battalion camp was sometimes shelled, he said, "I didn't feel in any manner unnerved by the shelling when the rounds were not hitting in my vicinity." But it was a whole different story when the shelling was closer to where he was located.

As Rattigan said, "There were incidents of momentary stark terror when mortars and rockets would impact the company hootch area at night." These attacks generally occurred around one to four in the morning, a time when almost everyone was asleep, except the helicopter gunship alert crew and the GIs on guard duty in the perimeter bunkers. When explaining what it was like during a mortar attack that was up-close and at night, he said, "Being pelted with debris and feeling the swoosh of heat from shell explosions while trying to outrace incoming rounds to get to the bunker in one piece was the ultimate rude awakening."

Rattigan described a time when he was frightened during a nighttime mortar attack and berating himself for not having his weapon with him. During the attack, he took cover behind a revetment/wall that was being hit on the other side by small arms fire. He said, "The entire bunker line opened up, so we assumed that the VC/NVA were probing the camp perimeter. My primary concern was lacking a weapon to defend myself should enemy sappers penetrate the camp's perimeter." He further explained his feelings during mortar attacks when he said, "In addition to at times being frightening, mortar and rocket attacks provoked a sense of helplessness. There was nothing to do to fight back. Just run for a bunker, which would not survive a direct rocket hit."

To be honest with you, I found nothing passive about Rattigan's explanation of his experiences in Vietnam and, specifically, during mortar attacks. From the perspective of someone who has never experienced combat before, his descriptions of the experiences he had in Vietnam seemed rather active to me.

Roger Gibson

After basic training, Roger Gibson completed his AIT at Lackland Air Force base in Texas to be trained in Air Force Police, specifically, K-9 training. In other words, he was trained to work with dogs.

Prior to being sent in Vietnam, Gibson was stationed in South Korea. Obviously, there was no war going on in the Korean peninsula at that time, but the threat of a North Korean invasion or attack was always there. And the South Korean and American forces needed to be on alert twenty-four hours a day in preparation for this possibility.

As a trained dog handler, Gibson's primary responsibility involved patrolling the perimeter of the base where he was stationed with his dog. One day while walking the perimeter of a bomb site, his dog alerted him to a potential problem. Gibson informed his superiors of his dog's alert signals, and they began searching the area looking for what might have resulted in Gibson's dog signaling about a potential threat in the area. And then they found it.

In the shallow waters just off the beach, they found a small, disabled submarine. "Seeing that submarine scared the hell out of me," Gibson said, "because I was afraid it was going to blow up." When they opened the hatch to the submarine, they found inside four dead North Korean soldiers. Apparently, the dead soldiers were patrolling off the coast, spying on the South Korean and American military, and then somehow they died from asphyxiation.

Fortunately, the Americans and South Koreans were in no danger this time. But had the submarine been carrying weapons or, especially, nuclear weapons, those on the base would have been in serious trouble. But thanks to the alertness of Gibson's dog, trouble would have been avoided, and lives would have been saved.

Gibson later received orders to Vietnam. While in Vietnam, Gibson was assigned to a dog named Trudy. Like most canine handlers and their dogs, Roger and Trudy became inseparable. They worked together, trained together, and understood each other very much. This bond between Trudy and Gibson was a special relationship, but it was a common bond that a handler and his dog developed in the jungles of Vietnam.

One night, Trudy saved Gibson's life, and the lives of others.

Trudy and Gibson were walking the perimeter of the base during the early morning hours. The sky was dark, humidity was in the air, and a quietness surrounded the compound. "As we were walking, there was nothing that suspected me that there would be any problems," Gibson said, "until Trudy reacted."

As they were walking, Trudy stopped, sat back on her legs with the front paws raised. Gibson's first thought was, "Oh, no. Not tonight!" Knowing this was a sign to alert Gibson there was a problem in the area, "I immediately phoned to headquarters to advise them of Trudy's reaction," Gibson said, "and alerted them to a major problem in the area."

Knowing anything could happen at any moment, rather than running into the nearest bunker with Trudy to take cover, Gibson took cover behind an ATV. When asked why he didn't run into a bunker, Gibson said, "There were often snakes in the bunkers. And I hate snakes." Trudy was right. There certainly was trouble in the area, and the trouble was enemy insurgents trying to enter the compound through the perimeter.

Mortars started falling from the sky, shots were being fired in both directions, men were scrambling to get into position to defend themselves. "Thanks to Trudy," Gibson said, "we had enough lead time to be ready for an attack." And Gibson was able to find safe harbor from the attack because Trudy alerted him in time for him to react. "Without the assistance from Trudy," Gibson said, "we would have been in serious trouble."

Because of this early warning from Trudy, the military personnel at the base were provided time to prepare and subsequently repel the attack. And Gibson is alive today because of the skill, dedication, and love of his dog. Gibson said rather sadly, "I don't know for sure what happened to Trudy after the Vietnam War had ended." He heard that she might have died from a disease that was contagious and prevalent in dogs. If Trudy died in Vietnam, she was not alone.

There were between three to four thousand trained dogs that served in Vietnam. They were commonly called "war dogs" but their correct title was "military working dogs." In essence, these dogs were soldiers, too. Like the GI that was assigned an identification number, dogs had "brand numbers" that were tattooed inside the left ear. Sadly, only about 200 of them returned home when the war was over. During their service in the war, some died from disease, others died due to exposure of the weather or environment, while approximately 300 were killed in action.[3]

After the war, dogs were classified as surplus equipment and left behind when the Americans left Vietnam. In addition, since there was a fear of disease that these dogs could bring home with them from Vietnam, it was determined the risk was too great. So, they were left behind. Some were given to the South Vietnam military to be used in the continuing war. Others died, while most were probably euthanatized.[4]

No one knows for sure what happened to the dogs after the Americans left. One can only hope for the best since this group of soldiers were so effective in battle, saving countless lives in the process. Regardless of the manner of their death, they were outstanding soldiers during their life in the Vietnam War. And trainers and handlers like Gibson should be proud of the work they and their dogs accomplished.

Don Wolfram

When Don Wolfram arrived in Vietnam, he spent about three days in a temporary location until he was sent out to his assigned base. As a Seabee, his unit's main responsibility was to assist the Air Force in keeping their runways operational. When he got to his unit, Wolfram was given a quick orientation on what to do if there is an enemy attack. Wolfram was basically told, "If you hear something, jump into a bunker." When he was told this, Wolfram thought, "And I have a year more left to do here!" Then, two days after he arrived at his unit, he got his first real taste of what life during the Vietnam War was going to be like.

The runway was attacked by enemy rockets. And Wolfram did what he was supposed to do. He jumped into a bunker.

Once the attack was over with, Wolfram and his fellow Seabees went out to repair the damage to the runway. "Other buildings could have been destroyed or damaged by the attacks," Wolfram said, "but the runways were our first priority to repair." He continued, "We experienced rocket attacks about four to five times a month. Sometimes, more. The enemy would mainly attack at night, and they would focus their attacks on the runways."

The rockets would come in at night, and the Seabees would repair the runways during the day. Wolfram said, "We worked 12-hour shifts. Twelve hours on, 12 hours off." He remembers the hardest time working during the war in Vietnam was in October of 1969. During that month alone, it rained 70 inches. Seventy inches. To put that in perspective, the yearly average of rainfall in Terra Bella, California where Wolfram was raised, is 10 inches per year. So, what Wolfram experienced in October of 1969 was seven years' worth of Terra Bella rain in just one month. "Try building something in those conditions," Wolfram said, "We were walking around knee-deep in water and mud."

But those conditions didn't stop Wolfram and the Seabees from doing their job.

Back home in Porterville, these men lived in houses where the doors were locked at night, alarms were set, garage doors closed, and the place secured. But in their homes in Vietnam, their hootches, there really was nothing that could be done to make it safe and secure from the enemy that lurked outside the gates. Sure, piles of sandbags stacked around their hootch helped, but nothing was safe from the direct hit of a mortar.

No place was safe, and every place was a target. You just never knew when or where the next attack would happen. With that, troops could only sleep through sheer exhaustion and they were always on edge regardless of the circumstances.

The siege at Khe Sanh, mortar attacks, rockets launched, friendly fire deaths, plane explosions, Viet Cong crossing the perimeter, guard dogs signaling an attack was imminent, sergeants folding under the pressure - death, injury, diving into bunkers, destruction. And all this happened at home. On their base. In their hootches. These men from Porterville High School suffered through horrific experiences that the enemy brought to the doormats of their homes.

So, no, Dorothy, in Vietnam during the war, there was no place where there wasn't any trouble.

Vietnam War and Wall Facts

The First Soldier Killed in Combat [5]

Specialist 4 James Davis was the first fatality during combat when he was killed on December 22, 1961.

13

In Support of the Troops

*"Some people live an entire lifetime and wonder
if they have ever made a difference in the world,
but the Marines don't have that problem."*

Ronald Reagan

WHEN PEOPLE THINK of Vietnam War veterans, or any war veteran for that matter, they generally think in terms of a combat veteran. Someone who fought in the jungles or on the streets, someone who rode in tanks or fired artillery, someone who was often placed in harm's way that could result in injury or death.

But the majority of assignments during the Vietnam War were in non-combat responsibilities. Sure, as you saw in the previous stories, those who went into branches of service like the Navy or Air Force or had an MOS that had a higher probability of not being in combat, found themselves in combat situations anyway. But the war could not be fought without those who provided support to the soldiers or to the war effort in a non-combat role.

Medics, nurses, doctors, clerks, mechanics, electricians, construction, supply, plumbers, cooks, technology, satellites, radar, and communication. The list goes on. Without these positions providing support for the troops in the bush, on the waters, or in the air, the success of our GIs would have been almost impossible.

Alfred Alba

There were no front lines in the Vietnam War. The war was all around you. Battles were often small ambushes, booby traps were everywhere, and the fights were often unpredictable. There was often no hospitals nearby to treat the wounded in Vietnam, because you never really knew where the fighting would come from. And in order to best administer aide to those who were injured, the response to the injury needed to be fast. The longer the wait, the less of the chance of survival.

The major method during the Vietnam War to speed up the time medical assistance could be administered was through the use of the medevac helicopter. The primary helicopter used to extract the wounded or dead on medevac missions was the Huey. Since the fighting in Vietnam was in dense jungles, mountains, rivers, and rice patties, being able to drive a truck or ambulance out to the wounded troops would be difficult or almost impossible. But with the skill of the Huey pilot, the medevac helicopter could maneuver into almost any terrain.

From a medical perspective, it was estimated that the most optimal time in which to treat a wounded GI before he went into shock or cardiac arrest was no more six hours after injury. During the Vietnam War, medevac helicopters could often deliver the wounded to a hospital within thirty-five to forty minutes. As a comparison, during the Korean War, the average medical evacuation time was about four to six hours. The speed and efficiency of the medevac process in Vietnam, including its pilots, crews, and communication capabilities saved countless lives.[1]

And one of those who served as a crew chief on a medevac

helicopter was Alfred Alba.

"Our mission was fairly simple," Alba said, "We went out to pick up the dead or injured. Simple as that." Actually, these missions weren't that simple. These missions were not just a helicopter ride, but rather often a ride into a war with bullets, rockets, and mortars being fired throughout the area as the helicopter was descending to do its job. "We'd often be hit by enemy fire," Alba said, "I was lucky I was never hit, but our helicopter often was." His helicopter was never shot down, but it did experience damage from the battles they flew into and out of.

And it wasn't just American soldiers or Marines they picked up. "Sometimes," Alba said, "we'd pick up Vietnamese children who had been injured." Kids who were hurt in the crossfire between two enemies. Kids who were living in a war as children their age in the United States are playing on school playgrounds or in the peace of their backyards at home.

Alba said, "We flew missions almost every day, 12 to 14 hours a day. Almost non-stop." Every few weeks they'd get a day off, but with troops being injured or killed every day, there was little time to relax. "We couldn't stop what we were doing," Alba said, "because how else could the injured GIs get back without us there to pick them up?"

Alba's day was almost routine. Wake up early for breakfast, check the helicopter to make sure it was ready, and then head out. But what they often found was not routine. "One of the members of our crew was a medic," Alba said, "so he could assist the wounded on the flight back to the hospital." Describing when they got to the landing zone to pick up the dead and wounded, Alba said, "Depending on the situation on the ground, we'd be there maybe 10 minutes at the most. Quickly load up the injured or dead. And get out as fast as we could."

Then they would head back to the base, unload the wounded or dead troops, wash out the floor of the helicopter that was often covered in blood, and then head back out. That was the routine, back and forth all day.

When landing, Alba said, "We would get the injured first. The faster we could get them treatment, the better their chances of survival." The maximum number of troops a medevac could carry was eight. "Any more than that," Alba explained, "and the chopper couldn't lift off." But they never carried the dead with the wounded. Alba said, "We'd fly two or three medevacs on a mission at a time. One would pick up the injured, and the other would pick up the dead." As Alba further explained, "We never carried the injured and dead in the same chopper because you didn't want an injured GI lying next to a dead buddy."

When asked about his feelings of loading up body bags onto his helicopter knowing there were dead soldiers or Marines inside, Alba sort of corrected me. He explained, "Some of the time, they weren't in body bags. They were put in body bags after we dropped them off at the base. There was often not much time to put them in body bags while they were still fighting and we were coming in to pick them up."

As his dad said, "It's a job." But Alba's work on the medevac helicopter was more than just a job. It was a lifesaving effort that allowed many of our wounded Marines and soldiers in the jungle to survive and be able to return to their families back home.

Dan Boydstun

Obviously, the greatest tragedy of war is death. During the Vietnam War, over 58,000 Americans lost their lives. When they were killed in action or died later due to injuries suffered on the battlefield, their bodies were processed through the mortuaries in Vietnam. This process included the identification of the bodies, being embalmed or appropriately processed, and then safeguarded until they could be shipped home. An awful and depressing assignment.

According to Bill Ellerman, an instructor at the Joint Mortuary Affairs Center in Fort Lee, Virginia, the process that eventually brings the deceased soldier home is, "...one of the most important missions during war." He continues, "There is no better way to honor the fallen then to return them back to their home."[2]

Dan Boydstun was an integral part of this important mission.

During the bulk of the Vietnam War, there were two main mortuaries that handled the physical processing of the GIs who had been killed in action or died later due to their injuries. One mortuary was in Da Nang, and the other in Tan Son Nhut near Saigon. Boydstun was stationed at the Air Force base in Da Nang.

After the bodies went through the morgue where they were identified and processed for the trip home, the bodies were placed in metal containers. Since these metal caskets included American GIs who paid the ultimate price with their life, there was a deep and profound respect for the process of returning their bodies back home. Inside each of these caskets was more than just another GI killed on the battlefields of Vietnam. Inside was a son, a brother, a nephew, a father, or a friend. The one life that was in that metal container represented multitudes of people back home who were now mourning the loss of the person inside that casket.

Once the bodies were processed, the caskets were then delivered to where Boydstun worked, and he had the responsibility for the final processing of the casket for departure back home. "There was a packet on the front of the casket that included information about the individual inside," said Boydstun. "As we waited for loading the caskets onto a plane, we'd put the caskets in an air conditioned room that usually handled about 20 caskets," Boydstun said. He also said, "I can never remember the room ever being empty."

One thing Boydstun remembered is something he did not see. "I never saw any caskets with American flags on them," Boydstun said. "You'd see that in the movies, but not in real life." Actually, during the Vietnam War, the bodies or the remains of those killed were transported without a ceremony. No fanfare or brief service with a priest saying words over the casket of the person killed in action as it was being loaded onto the plane. None of the caskets were draped with a flag and no officer or military personnel escorted the casket home. Sometimes, another family member who was serving in Vietnam at the time may have escorted the body of a relative home, but not very often. However, the Air Force did have a policy that the caskets were loaded onto the plane headfirst and were loaded in such as way as to be the last cargo that may have to be jettisoned in case of a plane going down.

The number of caskets Boydstun processed each day was kept confidential. Boydstun said, "We didn't want the count to get out. The number was kept secret." Not only was the number kept secret from the Americans because such a number could be demoralizing to the troops, Boydstun said, "We didn't want the enemy to know either."

Boydstun said the caskets would be there for no more than two days, because they wanted to send the bodies home as soon as possible. As he remembers looking at the caskets in the air conditioned room, stacked no more than three caskets high, and as he remembers putting these caskets on pallets, strapping them down, and then loading them onto a plane, he said, "You know there's a body in each of those caskets. It was hard knowing that. But you had to do it."

Sometimes the bodies would arrive to Boydstun in body bags, and not in caskets. "For those," Boydstun said, "we placed them on top of the caskets."

The activity of caskets being brought in for final processing for the flight home, placing the caskets on wooden pallets, and then loading them onto a plane, went on 24 hours a day, seven days a week. Flight in, process and load, flight out. All day, every day.

Boydstun further explained that when the caskets were sent home, they were either sent to Travis Air Force Base in California, or to Dover in Delaware. "Depending on where the deceased GI's hometown was determined which location he was sent," Boydstun said. "Those whose hometown was closest to California were sent there, while those whose hometown was closest to Delaware were sent to Dover."

When Boydstun's tour in Vietnam was over, he was then sent to Travis Air Force Base until his discharge. And what did he do at Travis? Basically the same thing he did in Vietnam, but in reverse. This time, he unloaded the caskets from the planes rather than load them. "Each day after we unloaded the caskets," Boydstun said, "the Oakland mortuary would pick them up. Usually picking up around 10 or so every day."

So for almost two straight years while in the Army, Boydstun loaded and unloaded caskets of Americans who had been killed in Vietnam. As Boydstun mentioned earlier, someone had to do the assignment. But as depressing as the assignment was, Boydstun was an integral part of one of the most important missions during the Vietnam war – returning the deceased back home.

John Schultz

John Schultz enlisted in the Navy after graduating from Porterville High School in 1966. Like other high school graduates during the Vietnam War, one of the reasons he enlisted in the Navy was to avoid the possibility, or probability, of being sent to Vietnam. But he got to Vietnam eventually, even though it was about 200 yards off its shore.

The war was almost at its height when he graduated from high school and some of the young men he went to high school with were beginning to return from Vietnam with horror stories, injuries, and some of them being killed. So, the choices for Schultz were to volunteer in the Navy or be drafted into the Army or Marines. Schultz chose the Navy.

Keep in mind, however, that enlistment in the Navy or Air Force did not guarantee your survival or avoidance of involvement in the war in some capacity. Many men from these branches of service lost their lives during the war. But enlisting in the Navy or Air Force was a way to serve one's country while, hopefully, reducing the chances of being directly involved in the war itself.

Schultz spent most of his tour either in Hawaii or on the USS Nicholas, a destroyer that was approximately 40 feet wide and 375 feet long. When out at sea, his ship would travel for a month or so while never seeing land. But they soon found land, and that land was Vietnam.

The Nicholas provided gunfire support off the coast of Vietnam during combat missions in the Mekong Delta region as well as near the DMZ. Often, the Nicholas was anchored only a couple hundred yards off the coast, firing its shells into the various locations where support was called for. Sometimes, Schultz said, "The crew would sit back and watch the fireworks while the coast was being shelled." The sky surrounding the Nicholas at night would often light up and the ship would be illuminated as shells were being fired into the coast. Luckily, they never faced any retaliatory enemy strikes.

Years after the war, Schultz was researching the times when the Nicholas provided artillery support for the troops. He found out that one time his ship was providing fire into an area of Vietnam where his friend from Porterville High School, Vince Arcure, was fighting with his Marine unit. About this same time, Arcure had been injured. When Schultz realized that Arcure was injured during this same time and in the same location, Schultz worried that maybe the shells from his ship injured his good friend from Porterville. He thought, "Crap, I think we shot Vince." But not to worry, Arcure was injured at another time. Schultz was off the hook.

In addition to her service in the Vietnam area, the Nicholas participated in the capsule recovery operations for the Apollo 7, 8 and 9 missions that were practicing for the moon landing.

The war in Vietnam was not the only place in the world at that time where U.S. military involvement was necessary. Another place was North Korea. In January of 1968, the USS Pueblo was intercepted by North Korean patrol boats as it was conducting routine surveillance off the North Korean coastline. The North Koreans claimed that the Pueblo was within the territorial waters of their country. After a brief confrontation, the Pueblo was boarded, and the crew was taken prisoner.[3]

In response to this incident, President Johnson ordered a military buildup near North Korea. The Nicholas, three other destroyers, and an aircraft carrier were sent to North Korea. As Schultz said, "We traveled up and down the coastline as a show of force to the North Korean government." This was happening at the same time as the Tet Offensive back in Vietnam. About 11 months later, the crew of the Pueblo was released.

Another time when the Nicholas was in the middle of an ocean during a torrential storm, Schultz received a message that he was to go up on the bridge to see the captain. "Since I was new on the ship, I didn't even know how to get there," Schultz said. "And what did the captain want to see me for?" Schultz thought. He finally made it to the bridge, and what the captain wanted to tell him was nothing Schultz wanted to hear.

Schultz's father had died of a heart attack, in the early morning the day after Christmas.

Plans were being made with the Red Cross to get Schultz back home for his father's funeral. The first step was to get him off the Nicholas and to an aircraft carrier to fly him home. But there was a problem. A storm was raging and the only way to get Schultz to the aircraft carrier was by helicopter. And the only way to get Schultz onto the helicopter was by a harness and rope that pulled Schultz off the deck of the ship and into the helicopter. "I thought I was going to die," Schultz explained, "so I held on and was scared to death." After a few tries, he made it onto the helicopter and eventually to the aircraft carrier.

Due to the raging storm, Schultz had to spend three days on the aircraft carrier waiting for the storm to die down. Back home, plans were being made for his father's funeral and the day of the funeral was fast approaching. Finally, the storm dissipated enough that he could fly off, and that trip was an experience in and of itself.

"They put me on a plane with a bunch of mail," Schultz said, "and when the plane took off I thought it was going to crash." As Schultz explained, "They shot the plane off the carrier using a catapult, and when the plane got to the end of the ship and was now airborne, I thought I was going to die." And why? "Because when the plane left the ship, I was expecting it to go up, but it went down." But that was normal. Planes like that take a slight dip down before they begin to ascend. Schultz was safe and on his way home.

"I got home only a few minutes before the funeral," Schultz explained, "and I was worried I was going to miss it." He put in for a hardship discharge, but it was denied. Once the funeral was over, it was back to the Nicholas.

Schultz remembered one day he woke up in his bedroom at home and could smell his mom's bacon frying on the frying pan. He could hear the crackling of the grease, and his mom milling around in her kitchen preparing his breakfast. The smell and sounds of his mom's breakfast preparations brought a smile to his face and a peaceful feeling in his heart. There was no better place to be than home, and his mom's bacon smelled better than any he would get from a Navy chow line.

But then something happened.

Schultz rolled over, hit the bunk next to him, and woke up. He was having a dream, and what ended up to be a real depressing dream. Because he was not at home, he was in the middle of the Pacific Ocean on the Nicholas, thousands of miles from his mom's kitchen in Terra Bella, California.

Louis Gurrola

The coordination and management of supplies is one of the most important, yet often unnoticed, aspects of military planning and execution. In order to survive, soldiers must have food, water, medicine, weapons, ammunition, and related equipment. In order for the troops to have what they need on the battlefields, there needs to be a planned and coordinated means of transporting these necessities to them.

Military leaders throughout time have often recognized the importance of maintaining a supply line to keep their troops equipped. Legendary German Field Marshal Erwin Rommel is credited with saying, "The battle is fought and decided by the quartermasters before the shooting begins."[4] Okay, I don't necessarily rely on the opinions of losers, but he has a point.

Louis Gurrola's work was in supply. Loading and unloading vehicles. Cataloging and distributing needed materials to the base camps for transfer to the troops in the field. Providing support personnel with the essentials of their jobs. His work may not have placed him directly in harm's way, but a war could not be fought without the equipment, supplies, and ammunition needed to do so.

Gurrola's worked touched everyone in Vietnam, regardless of their MOS or the location of their base camp, because, as he explained, "Everyone needed some sort of supplies." It was a difficult job, and an important one, too, that often goes unnoticed when discussing the Vietnam War.

He wasn't immune from the threat of war either. "I had to pull my share of the load and walk guard duty at night," Gurrola said. He carried his M16 and a pack full of ammunition as he walked the perimeter on guard duty. Almost no MOS was immune from guard duty or a soldier finding himself in the middle of the war regardless of job or location.

As Gurrola walked, "I often wondered what was out there in the dark," he said but, thankfully, he never found the enemy. Or, the enemy never found him. But one night, however, Gurrola's camp certainly felt like the enemy had found them.

Gurrola remembers one time, "The quiet night was suddenly broken by shots being fired and everyone was scrambling for safety." Gurrola explained that soldiers were diving for cover, jumping into bunkers, or running to grab their weapons. They were under enemy attack. Or so they thought.

One of the soldiers walking guard duty around the perimeter of the base heard a sound in the dark and noticed the enemy was coming up the hill. He began to fire shots at the enemy while everyone else was running for their weapons wanting to shoot back or diving for the safety of cover.

The firing stopped. The enemy had been killed. The attack had been repelled. But upon closer inspection, however, they realized that it wasn't enemy soldiers coming up the hill after all. The security of the compound had not really been threatened. In fact, there was no enemy. It was something else.

A huge, ugly, wild boar.

Gurrola said, "The base was jumping because one scared soldier shot a big, fat pig." Sure, the soldier was embarrassed for creating such a stir against a fat, four-legged enemy, but better to be safe than sorry in a war zone.

The soldiers in the bush, or those riding on river boats or flying in helicopters, would not have been able to do their jobs without the skill of those soldiers behind the scenes providing support for the war effort. In fact, the successful completion of any MOS could not be possible without the work of those who provided the support necessary for them to do their jobs. When a vehicle breaks down, who fixes it? A mechanic. When communication with superiors is not working, who makes the link? A satellite or radar technician. If you're hungry, who feeds you? A cook. If you want to be discharged, who completes your paperwork? A clerk.

These individuals deserve the recognition like all war veterans receive. And they have stories, too. They were assigned for their specific MOS because of their knowledge and skill in performing whatever it was they were assigned to. And they often became the unsung heroes of the war effort.

Vietnam War and Wall Facts

Bombing During the Vietnam War [5]

By the time the Vietnam War ended, it was estimated that over 7 million tons of bombs had been dropped in Vietnam, Cambodia, and Laos. This number was more than twice the number of bombs that were dropped on Europe and Asia during WWII.

Around Vietnam....

Bob Johnson and Todd Pixler in Vietnam and together again 50 years later.

Roland Hill receiving medals of valor.

Pat Higgins' friend Steve Durtsche looking at Pat's memorabilia.

Local children begging for C-rations and riding in vehicle –
compliments of Greg Goble.

Brian Rattigan at his base in Vietnam.

Richard Walker's PBR beached and in for repairs.

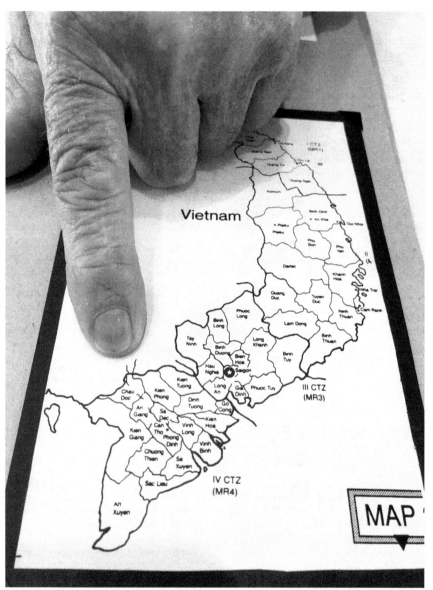

Richard Walker pointing to map where he worked the rivers in Vietnam.

Dan Boydstun at his base in Vietnam.

Geary Baxter and his crew.

The Ghost Riders – compliments of Geary Baxter.

Greg Goble in the driver's seat.

Alfred Alba and friend at their base in Vietnam.

John Schultz and shell casings aboard the USS Nicholas after shelling Vietnam.

ODA-3. (Halo-Training)

Don Dowling practice jump – second from bottom.

Handgrip of Ron McCarville's rifle shot off during combat.

Porterville College Veterans Club circa early 1970s.

14

Oddities of the Vietnam Experience

"People that spend time in a foxhole – they're never going to find that relationship again...veterans have a special brotherhood."

Sylvester Stallone

*****WARNING*****
Some words or descriptions may be considered offensive

WHAT STALLONE SAYS above is true. However, while living in Vietnam during the war, the Marines, soldiers, sailors, and airmen also experienced a special brotherhood through experiences they shared outside of the foxhole, too. What they shared with their fellow GIs in Vietnam were things that brought them closer together in unimaginable ways. Sometimes, in almost disgusting ways.

As the veterans explained their living conditions to me during our conversations, it was obvious that the GIs lived in a way that no one would have thought of back in Porterville. And, probably, no one back in Porterville would have tried if given the opportunity. But for those living in Vietnam during the war, they had no choice. These were part of their lives, like them or not.

The following are some of the oddities of the Vietnam experience that many non-Vietnam War veterans have not heard of before. Some of the oddities are absolutely gross and disgusting. Although the thought of toning down their descriptions would seem appropriate for this book, doing so would dilute our understanding of the experiences of the Vietnam veterans. I'm sorry if anyone is offended by these descriptions, but this was their life.

This is how they lived. Therefore, we should not hide behind a curtain of political correctness but rather tell it like it is. If you might be offended by graphic descriptions, skip to the next chapter.

Oddity #1

If you ever watch the comedy show MASH on television, the cast will frequently mention something about the latrines. Every now and then, some mention would be made, or a scene would be shown, of some poor GIs having to dig the hole in which the soldiers were to defecate into. In one episode as a new latrine was being dug, a joke was made to make the hole on the one side of the latrine deeper because that was where Major Frank Burns usually sat.

A latrine in Vietnam was not necessarily an oddity. Previous wars have included latrines on the military bases. But the latrines in Vietnam were not at all designed as those pictured on MASH. No holes were dug underneath the latrines in Vietnam. But something was used in place of the holes. And that's Oddity #1.

55-gallon drums cut in half
In Vietnam, most latrines did not consist of a sturdy, well-built facility covering holes dug deep into the ground with a cushioned toilet seat on top of the hole in which GIs did their deed. Rather, the

latrine was often a shabby enclosure concealing 55-gallon drums that had been cut in half, with a board or bench lying across the drums with holes cut out directly above the drums. Sometimes the holes had toilet seats attached, and sometimes the holes were just holes in the wood, nothing else for comfortable sitting.

In order to prepare the contents of the drums for future disposal, diesel was mixed into the drums. The smell of the diesel combined with the smell of the human contents did not lend itself to a relaxing experience, pondering the state of affairs while reading the paper and doing your deed.

The 55-gallon drums that had been cut in half served as rudimentary septic tanks. Just like in regular septic systems that homeowners use, once the tank is filled it needs to be pumped out. But in Vietnam, there was no local septic company that could be called, so the military devised a different way to eliminate the matter in the drums. And the manner in which the waste was eliminated is rather unique, and disgusting.

Oddity #2

Louis Gurrola's responsibilities in supply were often done without much fanfare or anyone even noticing. But one time, it was what Gurrola was not doing that got noticed by one of his superiors. During a normal, tedious day in Vietnam Gurrola's sergeant felt that he was not moving quick enough, so, Gurrola said, "He assigned me to one of the worst details in Vietnam."

Military personnel who have been through basic training, AIT, or at their regular duty stations, are certainly aware of the variety of details they may be assigned to because of slacking off, not following orders, or just being at the wrong place at the wrong time when a superior was looking for someone to do something menial. There are two basic and very common details most in the military have been exposed to, but there is one detail that only Vietnam veterans, like Gurrola, had the unfortunate opportunity to experience.

The first common detail is Kitchen Police or Kitchen Patrol, commonly called by its acronym "KP." This is a detail that includes washing dishes, peeling potatoes, mopping floors, and cleaning up the kitchen after breakfast, lunch, or dinner. Anything the cooks wanted the GIs to do, normally things they didn't want to do themselves, was given to someone who had been assigned KP duty.

The second common detail is called "policing the area." Policing means to walk around the compound looking for cigarette butts, pieces of trash that may have been dropped on the ground or blown into the compound, or anything relating to cleaning up the area. So, KP and policing are common to those in the military, regardless of their branch of service. But there was one detail that was only common to Vietnam veterans. And this detail was the most gross, the most sickening, and the most disgusting assignment imaginable.

Rather than sugar-coat the name, I'm going to call the oddity by the name the veterans I interviewed used, and several of them spoke about this sordid detail. It's part of the Vietnam War experience. The name itself might be offensive, but the actual detail is even worse. And that is Oddity #2.

The shit burning detail

The name is a concise description of what you did. Simple as that. No further explanation on the expected outcome of the detail is really necessary. But how did someone, like Gurrola, do this gross detail? It was not rocket science, and really took little to no training to figure out.

Once the drums were full, they would be pulled out of the latrine by the GI assigned to this detail, and new drums replaced. Then, the filled drums would be pulled to an area about 15 feet or so away from the latrine. Diesel was then poured into the drums, and the persons on detail would stir the diesel into the drum with a pole or long stick. He would then get some toilet paper, or some other flammable material, light it on fire, and then poke it into the drum's contents. Hopefully, the contents would light on fire.

Once the burning began, the poor GI would make sure he wasn't downwind of the smoke because the smell would permeate his clothes, hair, and skin. Often, everyone in camp could tell who the unlucky suckers were that got assigned to this detail that day because they smelled like shit. Literally.

It was a disgusting assignment, and sometimes locals were hired to complete that gross responsibility. But at other times, GIs like Gurrola would be tagged for this unpleasant experience. Gurrola certainly learned from his mistake. He said, "I never slacked off again."

Oddity #3

Placed in strategic locations around the base were vertical tubes sticking out of the ground, buried about 2/3 of the way into the ground. Some tubes were made out of pipes, some out of used shell casings, or some out of empty tubes that had been used to carry some sort of equipment. Some of the tubes had limited privacy built around them, while others were out in the open. What were these strange tubes sticking out of the ground? Oddity #3.

Piss tubes

As you can tell by their name, piss tubes were used to urinate into. When I asked Brian Rattigan why they didn't just urinate in the latrine, and he said, "The smell and stench in the latrines was often too overwhelming to be standing in just to urinate." Okay, we get the point.

In addition, some GIs even had piss cans inside their tents. Sometimes, the piss tubes had boxes built up or pallets standing up around them to provide some sort of privacy. But many of them were out in the wide open.

Piss tubes were part of the décor of the Vietnam landscapes back in the 60s, but you certainly wouldn't find one around Porterville.

Oddity #4

As was mentioned by most of the veterans regarding their first impressions of Vietnam, the weather there was hot, humid, and sticky. It didn't matter if it was early in the morning or late at night, it didn't matter if it was winter, summer, fall, or spring. It was hot. It was humid. And it was sticky.

Weather like that certainly takes a toll on the human body, especially the mouth and throat. Humid and hot weather usually means parched and dry mouths. Thirsty GIs. Bodies that sweat need water to replenish the system. Since deep wells with clear, clean ground water were not available in Vietnam, where did the GIs get their water to drink? That's Oddity #4.

Lyster bags (or also spelled, lister bags)

The lyster bag was a 36-gallon capacity canvas bag that held water to drink, water for cooking, or other purposes. The bags were hung on an improvised tri-pod with water faucets or spickets at the bottom of the bag. The bags were filled with water and then iodine was added to sterilize and purify the water. And it was from these bags that GIs often filled their canteens.

Lyster bags were actually used from WWI through the Vietnam War, but their use was discontinued after the war in Vietnam. Since then, other modern methods of purifying water were developed. In addition, packaged water or water in plastic bottles were introduced as better ways to provide water to the troops in the jungles.[1]

Some of Roland Hill's impressions of Vietnam that he remembered included these bags and the taste of water. Describing the water from a lyster bag, Hill said, "The water was hot and tasted like a rubber hose."

While in the field, the GIs would drop iodine tablets into the water they gathered from rivers, streams, or bomb craters after a rain in an effort to kill the bacteria that may have been in the water. If you want to get a similar taste of the water in Vietnam during the war, dip a glass into a chlorinated swimming pool. Let it sit in the hot sun for a while. Now, drink that and see how much you like it.

Since the water tasted so bad, some GIs improvised to make the water taste better. Feeling sorry for her brother, John Alba's sister used to send him Kool Aid powder. So, John would drop a packet of Kool Aid into his water to take away the bad taste. Sure, the Kool Aid wasn't cool, but it tasted better than warm, chlorinated water from a rubber hose.

Oddity #5

Every place in America has a trash dump somewhere. Oftentimes, waste disposal trucks pull up in front of houses on their scheduled day of disposal that week, grab onto the trash can placed on the side of the road with a mechanical arm, lift it off the ground, and dump the contents into the back of the truck. The can is set back onto the ground and the truck proceeds to the next house. Very routine, very orderly.

The trucker then drives to the local dump site, dumps its contents, while a bulldozer buries and compacts the trash. The whole effort is fairly sterile. No hands actually touched the trash, and no one is allowed to rummage through the dump site.

In Vietnam, the process for disposing of trash on military bases was fairly simple. Trucks filled with garbage would find a ravine, dry riverbank, or some other open location, and simply dump the garbage into it. Or, holes were dug on bases, trash was dumped into them, and contents then compacted by large bulldozers. Although this may sound similar to how trash is disposed of in the United States, there was one major difference. And that is Oddity #5.

Impoverished Vietnamese families eating the trash

The disparity of wealth between an American GI and that of a local Vietnamese farmer was significant. For most Americans, the salary of a GI has always been terribly low, but to a Vietnamese local, the GI was considered rich. So, Americans would often discard things that the Vietnamese would consider valuable. As the saying goes, "One man's trash is another man's treasure." And this certainly was an appropriate description of the Vietnam experience.

To many of the local Vietnamese, the dump site of the Americans provided them with sustenance they could not otherwise afford. The trash discarded included food that had been scraped off the plates of the Americans. This leftover food was fought for in a struggle to be eaten. Many times, the food was already covered in flies, but that did not stop the locals. Sometimes, flies were eaten, too.

The families that were scavenging through the trash were sometimes in danger. The trash they rummaged through could also include broken glass, nails, jagged edges of metal, or chemicals. In many cases, the MPs would not allow locals to rummage through the trash on a base dump site. But some were compassionate enough to look the other way, for a while at least.

Dan Boydstun also mentioned that many of the so-called homes the Vietnamese lived in were shacks often made out of cardboard boxes that had been thrown away by the Americans. Anything they could find that was tossed out by the Americans was often fashioned together into a makeshift shelter.

American trash was often their treasure.

Oddity #6

When you are in the military, you learn almost like a second language during the tours of your duty. Words or sayings that only another GI would understand. In similar fashion, Vietnam War veterans had their own language from that experience. And this is Oddity #6.

Vietnam War-related words and acronyms

Listed below are a few of the names and acronyms that the American GIs used during the war. See how many of them you know. The descriptions of these words and acronyms are in the glossary at the back of the book. Interestingly enough, everyone of these words or acronyms was said at some point during my interviews with the veterans.

AO	ARVN
Beaucoup	Boot
Charlie	Cherry
DMZ	Dust off
ETS	Freedom bird
Friendly fire	Gook
Grunt	Huey
Hot LZ	Jungle rot
Hump	M60
LZ	NVA
Pop smoke	PTSD
Rack	RPG
Sampan	Sapper
Tet	the World

How did you do?

Fifty-five gallon barrels filled with human excrement. GIs ordered to burn the contents. Water that was hot and tasted like rubber hoses. Outdoor tubes in which GIs urinated. Food scraps that were fought over and eaten by hungry locals. A language of acronyms and words that very few understand. These oddities were part of the lives of the Porterville High School veterans who served in Vietnam during the war. A big part of their lives. A sometimes disgustingly big part of their lives.

Some of this section may have grossed you out, but to truly understand what these guys went through during the war requires at least a rudimentary understanding of what their life was like outside of their assigned responsibilities. Yes, these oddities may have been some of the more disgusting aspects of life in Vietnam, but these were part of their lives. We can't deny that.

Certainly, the life of a GI during the Vietnam War was not a conventional life by any means. Actually, life during any war brings with it certain oddities. Since these oddities were part of their experiences in Vietnam, we can't disregard them as meaningless, or avoid mentioning them out of fear of offense. These oddities are important because they are part of their history. And, in a way, they are part of our history, too.

Vietnam War and Wall Facts

The Marines of Morenci [2]

On Independence Day in 1966, nine close friends and graduates of Morenci High School in the Arizona copper town of Morenci, population 5,058, enlisted as a group in the Marine Corps. Only 3 returned home.

15

In Memory of Our Fallen Heroes

"Our flag does not fly because the wind moves it. It flies with the last breath of each soldier who died protecting it."

Unknown

THE CRUELEST ASPECT of war is death. With that, this chapter will begin with the names of those who died in Vietnam that are listed on the monument at Veterans Park in Porterville across from Monache High School. The original title of this chapter was simply "In Memory." But I changed the title after hearing a comment during my interview with Chuck Migalski.

During his time in Vietnam, Migalski was injured three times, receiving three Purple Hearts. When he returned home, Vietnam was not discussed in his house. He didn't want to talk about the horrendous experiences he faced during the war. But one day, several years after his return from the Vietnam War, his granddaughter came up to him and asked, "Pa Pa. Were you a hero in Vietnam?"

And her grandfather answered, "No, all the heroes' names are on the Wall."

I was touched by what Migalski told his granddaughter, so I changed the title of this chapter to properly recognize these men as heroes. Please take a moment to reflect on the names of each of our heroes, and the casualty information that follows this list.

The order of information below is by rank, name, age, and branch of service.

Our Fallen Heroes

CPL Stephen E. Austin 21 USMC

CPL Roy V. Berry 20 USMC

CWO Rudy Bijl 30 USA

SP4 Phillip W. Bridges 23 USA

CMDR Rodney B. Carter 40 USN

PFC Dennis F. Ellis 20 USMC

SSGT Donald T. Erickson 32 USA

PFC Timothy D. Ewing 21 USA

PFC Timothy F. Fewell 21 USA

CPL Juan A. Garza 20 USA

SGT Daniel E. Goldsmith 20 USA

SP4 Larry G. Higginbotham 21 USA

CPL Patrick A. Higgins 20 USA

SP4 Fredrick A. Hitson 21 USA

PFC Clifford A. Jones 18 USMC

CAPT Terry L. Ketter 25 USA

CPL John S. Lewis 21 USA

SGT Joseph A. Lewis JR. 22 USA

PVT Ronald J. Medlin 17 USA

SP4 Joe L. Meek 19 USA

SP4 Tommy R. Mezzles 23 USA

CPL Roger C. Mitchell 20 USA

CWO Phillip S. Mohnike 22 USA

PFC Larry J. Moore 19 USA

SP5 Phillip A. Ogas 22 USA

SP4 Robert L. Pearson 19 USA

SP5 Eugene Petty 22 USA

PFC Ronnie L. Phelps 19 USA

SP4 Pat E. Phillips 19 USA

PFC Jewell L. Rainwater 19 USA

SGT Henry R. Reyes 22 USA

CPL Rudolph Rodriguez 28 USA

AA Ronald D. Shockley 20 USN

SSGT Albert R. Taylor 28 USMC

CPL Eddie D. Turner 26 USA

PFC Wayne D. Wagner 18 USMC

SP4 Jerry Lee Walker 28 USA

CWO James E. Watson 32 USA

SP4 Floyd D. Wimer 20 USA

PFC George H. Winkempleck 20 USA

Ledger of ranks and branches of service

Ranks: PVT – Private; PFC – Private First Class; CPL – Corporal; SGT – Sergeant; SSGT – Staff Sergeant; SP4, SP5 – Specialist; CWO – Chief Warrant Officer; CAPT – Captain; CMDR – Commander; AA - Airman Apprentice

Branches of Service: USA – Army USMC – Marine Corps   USN – Navy

The Timeline of Our Fallen Heroes[1]

1965

September 18	Specialist Joe Meek
November 6	Corporal Rudolph Rodriguez

1966

August 2	Staff Sergeant Donald Erickson
October 26	Commander Rodney Carter
December 17	Private First Class Timothy Ewing

1967

January 5	Private First Class Roger Mitchell
February 25	Chief Warrant Officer James Watson
February 28	Specialist Tommy Mezzles
March 6	Private First Class Wayne Wagner
March 11	Specialist Frederick Hitson
May 3	Private First Class Clifford Jones
May 13	Private First Class Ronnie Phelps
May 14	Specialist Pat Phillips
September 12	Specialist Eugene Petty
October 10	Private First Class George Winkempleck
October 23	Private First Class Eddie Turner
November 30	Specialist Phillip Ogas

1968

February 18	Corporal Roy Berry Jr.
March 13	Private First Class Larry Moore
April 2	Private First Class Jewel Rainwater
May 10	Private First Class Patrick Higgins
May 26	Specialist Daniel Goldsmith
June 8	Corporal Stephen Austin
June 18	Staff Sergeant Albert Taylor
August 24	Airman Apprentice Ronald Shockley

1969

March 1	Specialist Larry Higginbotham
March 11	Sergeant Joseph Lewis
March 19	Private First Class Dennis Ellis
April 27	Chief Warrant Officer Phillip Mohnike
June 7	Private First Class John Lewis
June 15	Sergeant Henry Reyes

1970

January 27	Sergeant Floyd Wimer
February 25	Specialist Robert Pearson
May 10	Captain Terry Lee Ketter
June 9	Private First Class Timothy Fewell
June 26	Corporal John Garza

1971

June 3	Specialist Phillip Bridges
November 4	Specialist Jerry Walker

The virtualwall.org website did not have information on Rudy Bijl or Ronald Medlin.

Casualty Summary of Our Fallen Heroes[2]

Average Age at Loss	22
Bodies Recovered	100%

Casualty Type	Number	Percent of Total
Hostile, died outright	28	74%
Non-hostile, died of other causes	4	11%
Hostile, died of wounds	2	5%
Hostile, died while missing	2	5%
Non-hostile, died while missing	2	5%

Casualty Reason

Ground casualty	32	83%
Casualty at sea	2	5%
Helicopter – pilot	1	3%
Helicopter – crew	1	3%
Fixed wing - pilot	1	3%
Fixed wing – non-crew	1	3%

Casualty Detail

Gun or small arms fire	11	29%
Multiple fragmentation wounds	7	18%
Other explosive device	6	16%
Air loss or crash over land	4	10%
Misadventure (friendly fire)	3	8%
Vehicle loss or crash	2	5%
Drowned or suffocated	2	5%
Artillery, rocket, or mortar	1	3%
Homicide	1	3%
Other causes (undefined)	1	3%

The casualty information above comes from the virtualwall.org website. It must be noted that casualty information on two of the forty names – Rudy Bijl and Ronald Medlin – was not found on the website. Therefore, the information above is based on 38 names.

Twenty-four years ago, on Thursday, April 27, 1995, Susan Sward, staff writer for the San Francisco Gate, submitted an article titled "After Vietnam: 20 years of sorrow, immeasurable losses, Porterville still struggling with the legacy of war sacrifices."[3] The more I read the article, and the more I thought about it, the more I realized that I couldn't paraphrase it. I couldn't cut and paste it. The article needs to be read in its entirety. Therefore, I received permission from the author of the article and through the copyright clearance process to print the article here in its entirety.

The article is quite moving.

Sward's article focuses specifically on the families and friends of those who died in Vietnam that were from the Porterville area and it tells their story. When we focus on the names of those who died, we must also remember those who lived. The mothers, fathers, brothers, sisters, children. They need to be remembered, too. Their story needs to be told, too.

Many of the family members, especially the parents, may no longer be living, but this article takes you back in time so that you can hear their story, feel their pain, and experience their emotions. If you've read it before, you should read it again. If you've never read the article, here it is.

On the edge of Veterans Park, the forest green Medevac helicopter hovers above Earth – forever frozen atop an arched, metal base with it nose pointed toward the gas station on the corner. In front of this memorial to the Vietnam War, a group of kindergarten children tumble about, a blur of sun dresses, jeans and cotton shirts. Encouraged by their teacher, their small hands stroke the 40 names on the granite plaque in front of the monument.

"Stephen Austin, Roy Berry, Rudy Bijl, Phillip Bridges, Rodney Carter..." the teacher recites, her soft voice entwining with the children's murmuring and the changes of high school boys exercising on a playground across the street.

The selection of a Medevac helicopter for the monument – rather than a statue of a soldier or a fighter jet – was no accident. It has been said that Porterville, a Central Valley community of 12,000 during the 1960s, lost more young men per capita in the war than any other town in the United States.

The death tally varies depending on who is doing the counting. The 58,000 U.S. war dead include 16 young men who listed Porterville as their hometown, but the Pentagon apparently never made per capita comparisons of which towns lost the most soldiers in Vietnam. The Porterville Area Vietnam Memorial bears the names of 40 war dead.

Whatever the count, too many young men from Porterville gave their lives, and for many of their families, the fact that Saigon fell, and the war ended 20 years ago this Sunday – April 30, 1975 – is just a footnote. They still live with the war every day.

Here, as in thousands of small, rural communities across the country, the war had a vivid face: The war's dead, their families, the veterans and their stories were known.

Many in Porterville knew someone who died. They went to school with the young man, knew his family, attended his church, partied with him. They also knew many of the veterans who came home.

There was the mother who kept her son's bedroom just the way it looked the day he went off to fight and die, leaving her childless. "They gave him 13 medals," the mother said, "but that didn't bring him home."

There was the veteran who lost an arm and spent two years in his bedroom before he'd agree to come out at all. There was the veteran who went to the Tulare County memorial most nights with his rosary, the veteran who one day stuck a .45 caliber pistol in his mouth and pulled the trigger.

In this town tucked up against the foothills of the Sierra, the loss was shattering.

"You will never know what Vietnam tore up in this town," said Estaline Higgins, 71 whose son, Pat, was 20 when he stepped on a land mine and died. "It wrecked people's lives."

And when Porterville came out the other side of the war, the town, like the country, was never the same.

"We lost part of our generation on this," said Richard Scearcy, a Vietnam veteran and Porterville accountant. "It's not just Porterville's loss. I think it's a loss for the country, period. It's 58,000 guys."

From her window, Eva Taylor can look across the valley to the oak-covered hills where her son, Albert, used to play soldier with other young boys. It is spring now, and the hills above Porterville are a lush, vibrant green.

"He always played like he was in the service," his 77-year-old mother said. "He got a bunch of boys and played in the hills like he was a bigshot. I look at those hills quite a bit and think, "My kid used to play there.""

After he graduated from Porterville High School, Albert Taylor enlisted in the Marines. He made a career out of it, had three children and another baby on the way when he went to Vietnam. "We all tried to get him not to sign up for Vietnam, but he said, 'Mom, I am already signed up.' He thought he would get it over with and come home."

When he first got there, the 29-year-old sergeant talked about what he fought for. "I am a Marine and an American," he wrote his parents. "If we stop (communism) here, it will someday be a help to our children."

Later, the darkness of the war crept into his accounts. He wrote of being under fire, living in foxholes, sweeping high-ways for mines, setting up ambushes, going on patrol.

On May 13, 1968, he wrote, "Mom, a couple of days ago, while I was up at hill 471, I took my platoon down to Khe Sanh village. Boy, it was really bombed out. There was bodies all over, cars, motor scooters, trucks, toys, etc. Well, I'm back up here on hill 689."

On June 18, about 2 ½ months after he got to Vietnam, Albert Taylor was killed in fighting below the country's de-militarized zone. Eva Taylor said, "I think it was hill 85 or something like that. I think he was blown up. I don't know. I don't think he knew what hit him. But sometimes I wonder if he laid there for hours hurting. That bothers me a lot." For weeks, she waited for his body to come home. "They said they didn't know exactly when Albert would arrive because they had stacks and stacks of bodies in San Francisco."

Taylor still has the yellow, tattered telegram dated July 9, 1968, from the commanding officer at Treasure Island announcing the body's arrival in San Francisco. The telegram informed her that her son's remains "are not viewable."

Today, Taylor – a big, white-haired widow whose husband died of tuberculosis complications in 1985 – doesn't see a whole lot of sense in what happened with the war. In 1989 she attended the dedication of the Porterville memorial, and she was glad they built it in honor of the young men.

These days, Taylor has a lot of time to think. Having worked as a dishwasher, nanny and house cleaner, she gets by, but she knows she wouldn't have any money worries if her son were around to help out. He was a good Marine and was always concerned about others in the family.

Taylor lives alone in a small, senior citizen apartment facing the hills in the community of Springville. Her room is crammed with stuffed animals and pictures of grandchildren. She has three other children. One of her other sons, Kenny, was in Vietnam, too. The military sent him home with his brother's body.

"I wanted Albert to be identified. A friend of ours said he would identify Albert, but they wouldn't allow it. Kenny said he was pretty sure it was Albert," Taylor said, her voice trailing off. "I don't know who made our boys go to Vietnam. I really don't."

She said she understands that the young men went to keep America free, but, "I think it is awful to take our boys over there to be killed. What did they get out of it? I guess you have to kill them or they kill you. Why they sent our boys over there? They didn't gain nothing."

When Pat Higgins was a small boy, his father used to invite his former Marine Corps buddies over, and they would sit around recalling their World War II days and the battle for Iwo Jima. A snapshot captures the men in their war days: wide grins, uniforms, Hollywood handsome. Today Albert Higgins, Pat's father, is 73 and ailing. He still has a painting of the famous flag raising by the Marines at Iwo Jima, where he drove a tank.

"My husband was a Marine," said Estaline Higgins, a tall, brown-haired woman with a quick, warm way of speaking. "The kids would hear him and his buddies. The boys emulated their father. Mike went into the Marine Corps, Pat in the Army, Chris in the Air Force."

As he grew up, Pat Higgins was full of life. The family snapshots show Pat, his two brothers and sister playing at the lake, building a snowman, swinging on a rope off a tree, frolicking in the backyard inflatable pool, licking ice cream cones on the porch.

As a teenager, Pat Higgins was tall, with blue, blue, eyes. He took his girlfriend, Elaine, when he went to have his 1955 Chevy painted, and he told the man to do it honey blond like her hair. Against his mother's wishes, Pat Higgins enlisted at 18. "I said to Pat even then, 'This isn't our war. Why don't you stay home and go to school?' But these kids wanted to do what was right. Why do you think Porterville lost so many kids? It's a small town, and there's not really that many jobs here."

Three months after he went to Vietnam in 1968, Corporal Higgins was due for a rest and recovery break, but he stayed a while longer. He died on Mother's Day when he stepped on a land mine in the remote A Shua Valley. He was 20. Estaline Higgins, sobbing steadily, said, "The Army sent their man here on Mother's Day. When the man pulled up in his truck, I knew why he had come."

Afterward, people told her she had to be strong. She had

to raise three other children, two of them younger than Pat. But she kept going over Pat's belongings in a trunk until her sister took the trunk home with her.

"It's your child," Higgins said. "It is something you carried, part of you, inside you. Do these people know what it means to be called on Mother's Day and told your son has just been blown up in a war we shouldn't have been in the first place?"

Nowadays Higgins works as a nurse. Much of the time, she tries to handle Pat's death on her own, going out to the cemetery by herself.

When the Vietnam memorial was dedicated, she attended the ceremony with her family, even though that monument fuels her pain. As she puts it, "When I see that helicopter in the park, sometimes I want to run away." But she thinks it "did open the eyes of Porterville that war was hell, and you have to give up your sons."

As for herself, she said, "You don't really ever recover. It's just a shadow on your mind about your son being blown up. Did he suffer? Did he call out for me? Those things go through my mind, especially on Mother's Day or his birthday."

One night almost two years after he was drafted, Hank Reyes and some buddies were playing with a Ouija board while Reyes was on leave. They sat still, placed their hands above the board, asked questions and watched the game's pointer to see what it indicated about their futures.

"It kept telling all his buddies they were coming back, but it told him he wasn't coming back," recalled Connie Delgadillo, Reyes' 69-year-old mother, as she described the boys gathered in her Porterville living room. "He tried to laugh it off. But I always had a feeling he wasn't coming back.

And all the others are alive today, too."

In that same period, Hank Reyes spent a night at the apartment of his girlfriend, Sally Arcure. "He was tall. Gorgeous eyes," said Arcure, who is 45 and works in job development at the state center for developmentally disabled.

Looking back, Arcure said those days seem innocent. She was a junior college freshman when she dated Reyes. Her yellow stucco apartment house was nicknamed "Sin City" because so many junior college students lived there. The crowd that Arcure hung out with would go up to Lake Success and stay late – drinking beer and making out on moonlit nights.

When Reyes returned with his stories of life as a sergeant in battle, his hurting overwhelmed her. "It bothered him to kill, it really did," she said. As they talked, Arcure said, "He begged me to take his class ring. I told him, 'No, Hank, this isn't the right time. I want you to give me the ring when you come back.' He left and never came back. And I lived with that for a long time."

In early July 1969, Reyes had been in Vietnam as an Army paratrooper for about five months. His mother flew to Mexico City, and on July 14 she visited the shrine of the Virgin of Guadalupe. She put on a black dress and crawled on her hands and knees at the shrine.

"I told her I wanted him safe. I wanted him complete," Delgadillo said. "I didn't want him missing an arm or blind, because I didn't think he could take it. He liked to have fun."

The following day Reyes stepped on a land mine in Vietnam and was killed at a place called An Khe, south of Da Nang. He was 22. Later, Delgadillo heard rumors that his death wasn't immediate. "I heard he cried in pain and said 'Mamma.' But I didn't have the courage to find out," Delgadillo said, her eyes filling with tears.

Since then, Delgadillo has continued her work as a psychiatric technician at the state center for the developmentally disabled. She has five daughters, one other son and 16 grandchildren. But she has had to struggle to move on. Little things gnaw at her. At Christmas it is the drumstick he used to demand. And then there was the rose bush that Reyes drove over once when he was trying to park the car so he wouldn't get wet during a flood. Delgadillo worried about the bush, whether it was watered. Finally, her husband, Reyes' stepfather, pulled it out.

Immediately after Reyes' death, her life revolved around the cemetery. But over time, she stopped going so much: "My mother told me it wasn't good for me. She told me, 'You don't rest, and you don't let him rest."

Six years ago, she attended the dedication of the Vietnam memorial in Porterville, and "it brought back memories that he had died," she said. "I saw some of the other boys' parents there, and I knew what they'd been through."

These days, she says she isn't as bitter as she was, but she still sees no reason for the war. "I felt he had died for nothing," she said. "If they had attacked here, but to go all the way over there…"

In September 1967, Lorene Traphagan drove to Travis Air Force Base with her family to drop off her oldest son, Marine Corporal Stephen Austin, for what she thought would be a routine tour in Hawaii. Austin was due to fly out the next day, and the family had to return home. "As we were going to the car, he was standing there alone," the 69-year-old mother said. "I ran back to him and put my arms around him and kissed him. I told him, 'This is going to have to last me a long time,' she said, her voice breaking into sobs. "I didn't know it would have to last forever."

Later, Austin was sent to Vietnam for a second tour. He

was there about five months when he was killed on June 8, 1968, south of Da Nang. It was less than a month after the Vietnamese peace talks began.

The day before he died, Austin wrote his family he was sick of all the fighting. "I've seen and helped too many boys my age and younger that was wounded or dead," he wrote. "I thank the Lord each morning I get up."

The following day, at age 21, Austin was shot in the chest, head and abdomen during the Marine Corps' Operation Allen Brook in the southern Quang Nam Province. A buddy pulled the blood-stained letter out of his pocket and mailed it home.

When the military men came to the house with the news of Austin's death, his younger brother, Allen was home. "Within two days, Robert Kennedy was assassinated, I graduate from high school and Steve was killed," recalled Allen.

Then, about two months before he died, Austin sent a letter containing his driver's license and Social Security card. "I looked at his father and said, "Now, why would he send them to us?' Yes, I think Steve knew." After he died, Traphagan said, "My husband – he had been in two wars – told me he had known Steven wouldn't come home. I guess he just had a feeling." Before Austin was sent to Vietnam, she didn't think much about the war. But later she thought a lot about it. Just lately she has been very angry about former Defense Secretary Robert McNamara's new book telling how he regrets the war. "He'll make thousands of dollars off that book, and they could have stopped that war earlier," Traphagan said bitterly. "My son would be alive. Now it's too late for the families and all their dead boys."

Years passed after Austin's death. Traphagan tried to paste her life together, raising her other two sons. Her husband, an Army veteran and former prison guard, died in 1980. She remarried in 1981 and her second husband soon died. Then, about 10 years ago on Mother's Day, Traphagan ran into the mother of her son's girlfriend at a Springville restaurant and bar.

The woman told Traphagan that Austin was the father of a daughter born to the girlfriend after Austin went off to war. Austin had never known his girlfriend was pregnant.

"I cried all day, just to know that part of Steve was still living," Traphagan said.

The next Christmas, the woman brought Austin's daughter over to meet Traphagan. The girl, Neily, was 17, and she looked a lot like Austin. Traphagan never was told exactly why Neily's family didn't reveal her existence for so many years, but Traphagan doesn't complain about that. Over the years, she has seen Neily off and on, and Neily says she wants to go to the Vietnam Memorial in Washington, so they can look at her father's name together.

Most days now, Lorene Traphagan fills her time supporting herself by caring for an elderly woman. When the Porterville memorial was dedicated, Traphagan attended the ceremony with her family.

At the ceremony she heard a speech by Army Colonel David Patton, the nephew of General George Patton and himself a three-tour veteran of Vietnam.

"Maybe the lucky ones were those brought home in an aluminum box," Patton said. "Many of us can see the faces of those who died in our arms. For some of us, the war still rages."

During the speeches, Traphagan cried a lot. "When I look at the helicopter and look at his name, I know he is gone," she said. "Years ago, I kept hoping they'd made a mistake about his death, and I guess I have tried to keep him alive. I've been sick of hearing the numbers killed over there. This boy had a name and a family. They all had a name."

You can see why I could not leave anything out of the article. As mentioned in Sward's article above, Marine Corporal Stephen

Austin was killed on June 8, 1968 during Operation Allen Brook that took place south of Da Nang. The operation lasted from May 4th through August 24th. When it concluded, 172 Marines had been killed, with Stephen being one of them, and 1,124 were wounded. Nine hundred and eleven (911) Vietcong were killed and 11 were taken captive.[2]

As you saw in a previous chapter, Operation Allen Brook was the same operation at which Ron McCarville, Porterville High School graduate from 1966, received a Bronze Star for heroism in combat. McCarville's actions that resulted in the Bronze Star were about 12 days before Corporal Austin was killed.

During those three-and-a-half weeks of the operation when the Marine Corps staff visited Stephen's mom to inform her of her son's death, 171 other mothers and fathers whose sons died in just that one operation alone were having that very same visit. Although Traphagan must have felt like she was alone in the world when she had that visit, she certainly had a lot of company.

The names of the 40 men listed above are forever etched in the long, black granite walls of the Vietnam War memorial in Washington, D. C., along with 58,000 other men and women who paid the ultimate price during the Vietnam War. If you've never visited the Wall, you should. The Wall itself may be simple in its design, but the emotions, feelings, and stories behind the Wall are profound.

Generations upon generations of people will be able to read these names and recognize who the true heroes of our country have been. These men, like those fallen men from other wars, are certainly heroes who our country will be indebted to forever.

Migalski was right.

Vietnam War and Wall Facts

It Wasn't Just the United States [4]

To make the war seem more like a multinational effort, the United States encouraged other countries to provide troops for the Vietnam War effort. The following countries provided troops in addition to the United States and South Vietnam.

South Korea

Australia

Philippines

New Zealand

Thailand

Taiwan

Spain

SECTION THREE
AFTER VIETNAM – THEIR STORIES

16

Going Back to the World

"The soldier above all others prays for peace, for it is the soldier who must bear the deepest wounds and scars of war."

Gen. Douglas MacArthur

I REALIZED SOMETHING quite interesting when I was reflecting back on my interviews with the veterans in relationship to the end of their tours of duty in Vietnam. During the interviews, the veterans never once commented that they ever felt the end of the war would be the defining moment when they were going home. None of them made any statements or shared any feeling that the end of the war would be their ticket home. Not one of them expressed any thought to the idea that they'd still be in Vietnam when the message would come that the war was over, and they would soon be going home. Not one.

To them, when they would be going home was not dictated by the end of the war but rather by the passage of time. Time left in their tour. Time left in their military service. Time left. That's it. Nothing about the end of the war. Nothing about a peace agreement being signed. Nothing about some ending ceremony in which all the GIs in the country would pack up and go home after the ceremony was over with. None of that. Just their own, personal, calendar of time marking off the days on the calendar to when their time was up.

Short-timer, two-digit midget, or just short.

These terms all meant the same thing, something the young men of Porterville High School looked forward to being called the very minute they landed in Vietnam. These terms signified that a GI's time in Vietnam was nearing its conclusion. They were getting closer to the day the Freedom Bird will lift off and carry them back home. Back to the world.

In most cases, being a two-digit midget meant that you had 99 days or less in the military. Ninety-nine, or two-digits. Your time in the service is getting short. There was light at the end of the tunnel. In Vietnam, since your tour was part of the total years of military commitment, you were generally designated a short-timer when you got to 60 days or less in the country.

Regardless, being short was a badge of honor.

Being short was a reason to celebrate. Being short meant that the GI had survived, so far at least, and each passing day was another day closer to going home. Short-timers had a certain element of stature among their peers, especially the cherries – or new recruits. They were looked upon as someone to respect, someone to hope you one day become, too. And they earned the right to be called short-timers, two-digit midgets, or just short.

Short-timers would often banter back and forth with quips such as:

"I'm so short I have to look up to see down."

"I'm so short that if I sat on the edge of a dime my feet will not touch the ground."

"I'm so short I sleep in a matchbox."

"I'm not short...I'm NEXT!"

Short-timers often visually counted down the days using various calendars or "short-timer's sticks." The calendars could be as simple as nailing or taping a calendar to the wall and crossing off each day on the calendar, beginning with the day they became short. Or, calendars were fancy, artistic displays that looked more like paint-by-the-numbers characters filling in each passing number on the calendar with various colors. A "short-timer's stick" or also called a "swagger stick" was sometimes given to and carried by the shortest man in the platoon. Carrying the stick made the GI walk with a little more swagger, cockiness, pride. Then, when that man's DEROS (Date Eligible to Return from Overseas Service) came, he would give the swagger stick to the next shortest GI.

Short-timers were often allowed special privileges, like not pulling certain kinds of duty, not walking point, or getting out of the bush entirely. Since the short-timer had survived this long, his fellow brothers wanted to see him go all the way. Make it out and fly that bird home.

Within this sense of swagger, there was also an element of concern in the hearts and minds of the short-timers. Sure, they knew when they were supposed to go home, but would they? They heard a lot of stories of guys being killed or injured on their last day of duty in Vietnam, and they didn't want that to happen to them. Yes, they were short, but they still carried with them the fear of not making it across the finish line.

Also, although they felt a certain joy in knowing they would soon be flying home, they also worried about the brothers they would be leaving behind. It is often said that there is no brother closer to you than the one in your foxhole. GIs often fought each day with the goal of keeping two people alive – himself and the brother next to him. But with you gone, who will look after your brother? A short-timer couldn't wait to leave, but in an odd sort of way, he sometimes worried about going.

Russell Vossler

Russell Vossler did something in Vietnam that he never thought would happen. He survived. He made it. He had beaten death and came out alive. His time in Vietnam was almost up and he would soon be flying on the Freedom Bird back to the world. The answer to his daily question, "Is today the day?" was "No!" and he was going home.

On the day he left Vietnam, there were about 200 GIs lined up to board the plane and Vossler was at the back of the line. He remembers, "There was some major checking the uniforms of everyone in line. One guy had literally just gotten out of the bush," Vossler said, "and he was still in his dirty fatigues and was smelly." When the major saw this, Vossler said, "The major started giving him crap about his uniform and just then, mortars started coming in. We were all in that bird in about two seconds." And, Vossler said, "The major was gone. He got the hell out of the way of the GIs running up the ramp to board the plane."

Vossler remembers how excited he was when he got short, and he said, "Leaving Vietnam was rather surreal, almost like a dream come true." And this was, indeed, a dream he was experiencing and not a nightmare. When the wheels of the plane lifted off the soil of Vietnam, Vossler said, "The whole airplane full of GIs started yelling and screaming. That was the greatest feeling in the world." And Vossler joined them in that chorus of joy and excitement. He was on his way home to Woodville.

Before arriving in the United States, the plane had a stop in Japan. He remembers something vividly that he did on that plane ride back that all of us take for granted. As he disembarked the airplane for the rest stop in Japan, he stood at the top of the stairs looking down and took a deep breath. A very deep breath. "It was my first deep breath I took in over a year," Vossler said. And unlike the breaths in Vietnam that were consumed with heat, humidity, and the smell of burning shit, Vossler said "This deep breath was cool and clean. You could take a deep breath and it would go all the way to the bottom of your feet." What a feeling that was for him. Welcome back to freedom.

When he flew into the airport in Oakland he was faced with something he didn't expect, nor did he fully understand. Protesters.

As the GIs walked through the airport, they were accosted by protest-ers yelling at them, throwing stuff at them, and holding signs with words of hatred and contempt for them. Vossler was in Vietnam be-cause his country sent him there. He did his duty as he was asked. He saw friends who died or were injured doing what was supposed to be a noble cause of halting the spread of communism. "So why the hatred of us?" Vossler thought. He then summed up his feelings about what he experienced in the airport in three words:

"It was sick!" Indeed, it was!

Roger Gibson

About 60 days before his discharge, Roger Gibson was moved to Da Nang to spend his remaining days in Vietnam. He was going home. His brother had already left Vietnam, and Gibson was awaiting their reunion back in the world. When his plane landed in California, he had the opposite effect as when he landed in Vietnam.

Like Vossler did at the airport in Japan, when Gibson stood at the top of the steps at the airport in California, he also took a deep breath. No humidity hit his face, no sweat from the extreme heat. Just plain California air. Sure, the air might have been tainted with smog, but that was nothing compared to the humidity in Vietnam. And he did something that showed his relief for being back home again.

He cried.

"I couldn't believe I was back home," Gibson explained. "I was so relieved that I didn't have to worry about war anymore." A lot of his friends had died in the war or suffered serious injuries in Vietnam. "I was so fortunate I came back okay," he said.

But while he was at the airport, he experienced what other re-turning veterans from the Vietnam War had faced as well. Protesters. For the first time, Gibson said, "I learned what a hippie was" as he walked near a bunch of guys with long, unkempt hair and unshaven faces hollering at the returning GIs as they walked through the air-port. Without the protection and direction provided by an MP who was in the airport, Gibson explained, "I might have spent my first night home in the United States in jail for doing something to that group of hippies." As Gibson further explained his initial reaction to the protesters, he said, "When seeing those protesters and hearing them hollering crap at us, I thought 'What the hell is this?'"

His brother picked him up at the airport and, "We got drunk for two days," Gibson said. He then took a plane to Bakersfield, and then a bus home to Porterville. When he got off the bus in Porterville, there was no one at the bus station waiting for him. No cheering family members. No group of friends waving at him. No signs standing tall that said, "Welcome Home." Nothing. He didn't have a car. He didn't have a ride. So, what did he do?

He walked home.

When he knocked on the front door, his mom answered it and Gibson said, "She almost passed out." There was her son, her baby boy, standing in the doorframe of the house, back home from the war in Vietnam. Alive. He made it. And then, what did Gibson do?

He got drunk.

Jim Rouch

Jim Rouch did two tours of duty in Vietnam, and it was at the end of his first tour where he had an interesting exit from Vietnam.

Rouch was in the middle of the battle of Khe Sanh when his first tour of Vietnam ended. He was scheduled to go home on leave and then return to Vietnam for his second tour. When it was time to leave Khe Sanh and then to the connecting flight back to the world, there wasn't the usual line of soldiers waiting to board the plane with someone checking their papers to make sure they were on the correct flight. And sometimes, due to their excitement about leaving Vietnam, some guys would almost run up to the plane to get in line.

Rouch ran, too, but not like they did.

Because of the shelling that was occurring on base at the time Rouch was scheduled to leave, the planes could not park on the runway waiting for people to board the plane. That was too danger-ous. Therefore, the pilots had to be creative on how to pick up the GIs who were leaving and drop off any freight the planes were carry-ing. So, if the plane can't actually stop on the runway to pick up the troops, how do the troops board the plane?

"Since the siege of Khe Sanh was going on when I was leaving to go home," Rouch said, "the plane I got on to take me off the base never really stopped to pick me up." Rouch explained, "The planes would fly into the base, land but not stop. They slowed down but kept on rolling on the runway. Then, the ramp went down and they pushed any freight they were bringing to the base out of the plane and down the ramp." Now it was the troops' turn to get on the plane.

As Rouch further explained, "After the freight was pushed off, and while the plane was rolling down the runway with the ramp down, you had to run up to the plane and jump on the ramp." There was no one there to check papers, no one there to officially welcome them aboard, and no one there to shake their hands thanking them for their service. Just a plane to jump into while it's rolling down the runway.

If you missed the jump, tough luck. The plane didn't turn around to pick you up. Needless to say, Rouch made a successful jump into the plane. And when the plane was going down the runway, faced with the possibility of a barrage of mortars and rockets being fired at it, Rouch said, "I just sat, closed my eyes, hung on tight, and hoped for the best."

Todd Pixler

About 30 days before he was scheduled to leave Vietnam, Todd Pixler was taken out of his truck and reassigned to be the driver for the first sergeant. The duty was rather boring, but relatively safe, so Pixler's last 30 days in the country were fairly uneventful. And he liked that.

"On the day I left Vietnam," Pixler said, "I was still worried." Still worried that something may happen. Still worried that his plane could be shot down. Still worried that he would join the other thousand men who lost their life on their last day in Vietnam.

As the plane began to rise from the ground and leave Vietnam, he said, "I remember looking out the window and seeing Vietnam slowly going away. What a beautiful sight that was." About a year before, he was watching the ground get closer and sitting in his seat consumed in fear of what to expect. This time, however, he was watching the ground getting smaller as he was breathing a sigh of relief knowing that he made it. He survived Vietnam and he was going home.

On his final stop home, his plane landed at Travis Air Force Base in Atwater, California. He was back in the states, and almost home. But now the big question Pixler had was, "How do I get home?" The only people there to greet him was a group of protesters. Having to endure shouts from angry protesters was one thing but having to figure out how to get home was another. It wasn't a very relaxing "Welcome Home" reception on his first day back in the states.

The military personnel at Travis gave the returning Vietnam veterans some spending money to eat and get home on. But Pixler wasn't alone. As he explained, "There were about 4 other guys from California that had just returned from Vietnam with me that also did not have a ride home. So, we did about the only thing we could do. We rented a cab."

Pixler's way home was a rather strange one. "We took a taxi from Travis to San Francisco International airport," Pixler explained, "and then I flew to LAX (Los Angeles airport). From LAX, I took a bus to Goshen." Pixler then called his dad to tell him he was in Goshen, but his dad was unable to pick him up right then. So, Pixler said, "I stayed in a motel there that night and then took a taxi from Goshen to Porterville the next day." For some reason, Pixler was dropped off at the bus depot and started to walk home.

On the way, Pixler said, "A friend of mine picked me up around Olive Street School and he took me the last couple of blocks." He was home. Pixler continued, "I was still in my uniform. I walked into the house, took off my uniform, and headed to where my friends were living. And then I stayed in hiding for about two weeks." He stayed to himself. He didn't go out and organize some family and friend gathering to celebrate his being home from Vietnam. "A lot of guys did that when they first got home from Vietnam," Pixler said. "Hiding from people gave us time to adjust to being back home."

Louis Gurrola

After 12 months in Vietnam, Louis Gurrola's tour was up. It was time to go home. Almost a year ago, he had landed in Vietnam to an airport under attack and thinking to himself, "I'm never going to make it back." But he did. He survived the war, survived the heat and humidity, survived wild boars and shit burning detail. He did what he was ordered to do, and now it was over.

Gurrola remembers the very first thing he noticed when he got on the plane. The stewardesses. "Those stewardesses were the first pretty thing I had seen in 12 months," Gurrola said. When he was on the plane flying home, he remembers that his excitement about going home was tempered by his sadness for leaving behind so many friends and fellow soldiers who were still in Vietnam. As he said, "I wished everyone could have come home with me."

Like most of the other veterans, his welcome home was met by protesters at Travis Air Force Base calling them names, holding signs, or hollering expletives in their direction. Gurrola and his fellow Vietnam veterans had been told to take their uniforms off prior to their final stop so as not to attract so much attention. But you could tell a GI a mile off, regardless if he had on his uniform or not. The GIs were told to keep walking, don't say anything to the protesters, and don't do anything that could get you in trouble later.

His parents were there to pick Gurrola up, and they were absolutely thrilled to see their son home from Vietnam. "My mom was so emotional," Gurrola said, "that she cried and cried, hugging and holding me like she didn't want to let go."

He went home for a 30-day leave after Vietnam and then was

assigned to Ft. Hood, Texas. This assignment was much like a regular job. He lived off base in the community, had fairly regular hours, and weekends off. "The interesting thing about where I lived," Gurrola explained, "was that it was a dry county. Liquor was not sold in the county, or even on the base." So, if Gurrola and his friends wanted a cold beer, they had to drive to another county to buy it.

They made the trip a few times until Gurrola was discharged.

Don Wolfram

Prior to the end of his tour in Vietnam, Don Wolfram was assigned to an area that was about two miles from the DMZ. His Seabee unit's responsibility there was to build housing for the South Vietnamese Navy. "We had to start from scratch," Wolfram explained. Preparing the foundation, pouring concrete, building block walls, etc. Then, he got his orders to go home. His tour was over.

"I was grateful that I made it through the year," Wolfram said, "I was going home." His feelings of joy about going home were, of course, tempered with the fact that so many never did or they went home with serious injuries. But Wolfram made it, and he was happy to be going home.

He flew into March Air Force Base in San Bernardino and his parents were waiting there to pick him up. When asked what the feeling was like to see his parents again, Wolfram didn't answer the question. He didn't need to. His face told it all.

His eyes teared up, his chin began to quiver, and he just smiled and nodded his head. Again, no words were needed to describe the feeling of seeing his parents again after coming back from the Vietnam War. In fact, no words could really describe the feeling any better.

Robert Johnson

After two injuries, numerous battles, hundreds of miles walked, sleepless nights in the middle of a jungle with the enemy waiting for the sun to come up, and spending months in hospitals, Johnson's time in the Army was coming to a close. However, Johnson extended his tour of duty for six months. When he did that, he got a 30-day leave where he could travel anyplace in the world. And where did he choose to go?

Back home to Porterville.

Johnson said, "Coming back home the first time was really strange." Since he knew he'd be going back to Vietnam after his leave was over, Johnson said, "Everything back home seemed so temporary." Because he had been wounded twice, Johnson did not return to the battlefields in Vietnam. Rather, he was assigned to duty on the base, far away from combat.

After that first extension, Johnson extended his duty two more times. Two more times he was given a 30-day leave. Two more times he came home to Porterville. Two more times he faced protesters at the airport. When he was leaving Vietnam for the final time, Johnson remembered, "An announcement came over the loudspeaker that we were now in international waters, and everyone started shouting and screaming." He was on his way back to the world, for a final time.

When they landed back in the states, they were met with the usual group of protesters at the airport. Again, this was not the first time Johnson had experienced the shouting protesters, but it would be his last. As they were being hollered at, Johnson said, "I wanted to say something back, but we were told not to." So, he kept his mouth shut. He felt the protesters didn't really know what they were doing. As Johnson said, "They were misinformed and just caught up in a movement. I wasn't the bad guy!"

From Travis Air Force Base, Johnson traveled back home on a Greyhound bus to Porterville. Since this was Johnson's third time coming home from Vietnam, once after his first tour was extended, and then twice more, his father said to him, "This is it!" And indeed it was. Johnson extended his tours no more, and he was finally discharged.

Greg Goble

"Imagine being in the field in Nam on Wednesday and then back home taking my first bath on Sunday." That's what Greg Goble said about the duration of time between being in a war zone to being back home in Porterville. And since the time between Vietnam and home was only about four days, Goble asked, "You're supposed to forget everything and move on to a normal life? Nope."

When Goble flew into the airport at Fresno, the first thing he did when he got off the plane was kiss the ground. He was home. And waiting for him were two people, his mother and a friend of hers. But no one else. As Goble said, "There were no parades, no parties, no nothing." As he compared the welcome home the Vietnam War veterans did not get with the welcome home the Iraq and Afghanistan War veterans often get now, he explained, "It does make me proud and happy of the recognition the young men now receive because of their service."

To make up for the lack of welcome the Vietnam War veterans experienced when they came back home, many communities, towns, and cities across the nation have tried to compensate over the years by reaching out more to Vietnam veterans and going out of their way to thank them for their service. But Goble said something quite profound about the belated welcome the Vietnam War veterans now receive. And his feeling was actually shared by some of the other veterans interviewed for this book.

"I needed it then, not now."

When Goble got home from Vietnam, he said, "A lot of my best friends were not around anymore." And like how many combat veterans felt when they returned home from the war, Goble said, "I had a hard time fitting in." He further explained very honestly, "I wasn't me."

In an effort to try and forget the war, or at least to move on from this terrible experience, Goble did something that he hoped would help him move on. "I gave my uniform and almost anything relating to the war to a friend's little brother," Goble said, "because I didn't want it anymore."

When dealing with the challenges of being back in the world after serving in combat, some veterans have nightmares and flashbacks while they are sleeping. Nightmares in which they relive the horrors of combat while in Vietnam. Goble had nightmares, too, but not ones that most others had. As he explained his nightmare, "I dreamed that my records were lost, and I was drafted again and given orders to go back in the Army, back to basic training, and back to Vietnam. No matter how much I tried, I could not prove or convince anyone that I had already done my duty." That was a nightmare indeed.

When he first got home, he said, "I did not admit that I was in Vietnam due to the unpopularity of the war and I just tried to fit in." Further explaining his efforts to assimilate back into society, he continued, "I did not do any drugs in Vietnam, but when I got home I joined the group growing long hair and doing some drugs. I was so miserable and doing stupid things that I thought would make me more accepted." But then he got the support of a friend. "Thank God with the help of an honest friend," Goble said, "who knew me before and after, told me the truth and helped me be me."

Now, that's a great friend to have.

The Army is often called "The Green Machine" because of the color of fatigues and uniforms its soldiers wear. In addition to green fatigues, GIs in the military often wear camouflage. To Goble, camouflage continues to remind him of the military and a past that he would just as soon forget. Because of that, Goble said, "I don't wear anything camouflage or the hats that advertise that I was there."

Try as he might, it has been difficult to erase some of the past from being in the war in Vietnam. But Goble also unselfishly said, "A whole lot of other vets had it a lot worse than me."

Chuck Migalski

When Migalski flew into the airport at Oakland after his tour in Vietnam, and after being injured and receiving three Purple Hearts, he was met with the usual protesters providing him an unwelcome home from the war. But the lack of a reception at the Oakland airport didn't end there. He said that when he was flying from Oakland to Visalia, "Not one person spoke to me. Not one."

No one welcomed him home. No one shook his hand. No one said, "Thanks for your service." They avoided him. They ignored him. But, due to the love of his friends and family, his lack of a welcome home changed when he got back into Porterville.

Migalski called his friend Tony Forner, himself a Vietnam War veteran, and asked that he pick Migalski up at the Visalia airport. He also asked Forner to not tell Migalski's wife that he was coming home. He wanted to surprise her. When they got into Porterville, Migalski's wife was working at a local hardware store. "When I walked in to surprise her," Migalski said, "she was overwhelmed. We both were. God it was good to see her again." Migalski also described his feelings about what it was like to be standing there in the middle of a hardware store hugging his wife, "Relief. Relief that I made it home."

As they were hugging and kissing in the middle of the store like two married couples reunited after a long and terrible experience would, the welcome home became even more special for Migalski. When he and his wife got home, Migalski got to do something he had been dreaming about the past several months.

"I met my 9-month old son for the first time."

Richard Walker

Richard Walker remembered when he was leaving Vietnam and the feeling he had as the plane left the runway at Saigon when he said, "I felt this tremendous release lifting off my shoulders." He was going home. But in just a little bit, he wasn't so sure. The joy of leaving Vietnam was soon replaced with the fear that he would be one of those he had heard about that was killed on their last day in Vietnam.

Walker flew out of Vietnam on a C-130. There were seats on both sides of the plane, and as the plane was ascending from the runway in Vietnam and heading back to the world, Walker noticed something as he was looking out the window on the other side of the plane. One of the two engines on the wing had caught on fire.

He thought to himself, "After all that I experienced in Vietnam and I have to die this way?"

Noticing that Walker was obviously distressed from what was happening, the chief sitting next to Walker said, "Don't worry, they can fly this plane on two engines." And that's what they did. The engine that was on fire was shut off and the fire was extinguished. No other engines caught on fire during the flight back, but Walker still worried about that possibility most of the way to the next stop. So, it certainly did not start out as a calm trip back to the world on his Freedom Bird.

No other engine caught on fire and Walker made it home safely.

John Alba

When it was almost time to leave Vietnam, Alba said, "I never let my guard down. I carried my pistol with me to the last day." In fact, Alba said, "When I was getting on the plane to fly home, they never even checked me for a weapon. I could have taken it with me on the plane and they wouldn't have known."

As they were lining up to get onto the plane to fly back to the world, Alba said, "New guys were coming down the ramp. I remembered what it was like when I first got there. And I felt sorry for them." But that sadness quickly turned into jubilation as he boarded the plane. Then, when the plane began to travel down the runway , Alba said, "As we were lifting off the runway, everyone started whooping and hollering. A lot of guys were crying. It was very emotional." And when they were leaving Vietnam airspace, the pilot did something unique.

Alba said, "The pilot banked the plane and then said over the intercom, 'Look out the window because you'll never see this place again.'" And what followed that announcement? More whooping. More hollering. And more crying.

When Alba's plane was about to land in Oakland, the pilot came on the intercom to warn them about the possibility of protesters in the airport. Luckily though, since it was about 1:00 in the morning, there were no protesters. Alba said, "We fought for these people (the protesters) and we are getting treated by them like this? That upset me." And there is one person that Alba still does not like very much even today. "I still can't stand Jane Fonda," Alba said.

When his connecting flight landed in Fresno, Alba's friend picked him up at the airport and he spent the night in her apartment. When he went to go to bed, Alba's friend thought he did something rather weird. But it was something that Alba did almost every night in Vietnam. "I wasn't used to sleeping on a bed," Alba said, "so I slept on the floor."

When his friend took Alba home the next day, he first walked around his old neighborhood. When he went home to see his mom and dad for the first time, Alba said, "My dad did something I had never seen him do before. He started crying."

Felix Hernandez

As his time in Vietnam was coming to an end, Hernandez was ready to come home. His found out that his unit was being deactivated and sent to Hawaii. When Hernandez boarded the plane and was about to leave Vietnam, he was a little nervous about the flight home. Not because he was afraid of flying, but because he was worrying if he would ever make it back home alive. Or, more specifically, even out of Vietnam air space. "We had heard the rumors about guys being killed on their flight out of Vietnam," Hernandez said, "and I was worried that might happen to me." One last attack from the enemy, one last death or injury, one last plane being shot down, and Hernandez worried about that.

When he boarded the plane, he strapped into his seat, listened to the instructions from the pilot, grabbed on to the seat, closed his eyes, and hoped his plane would not be shot down. Once the plane left the airport Hernandez was still not convinced they were safe. He continued to hold on for dear life. But then it happened.

The plane leveled off. It was now out of range of any rockets or mortars. They were on their way home. He made it. "When the plane leveled off and was no longer going up, that was a relief," Hernandez said.

When they got back to Hawaii, there was not much for them to do. So, as Hernandez explained the time, "We ran amok for three weeks." In other words, they partied, got drunk, and caroused around the tropical islands until it was time to go home for a well-deserved 30-day leave. Obviously, these days in Hawaii were far different than standing by an artillery piece in a rice patty in Vietnam, so Hernandez and his friends took advantage of the situation.

And when he flew home to California, his family was not waiting for him at the airport or the bus terminal like most moms and dads did when their sons returned from Vietnam. His parents were working. Climbing ladders in the orchards of Tehachapi picking pears. So Hernandez made the trip to Tehachapi to see his family. Almost his whole family was in that one orchard together picking pears. His mom and dad were there, his siblings, and many of his friends.

As the pickers were climbing up and down their ladders, loading and unloading their picking bags, working in the dust and smell of tractor diesel engines driving up and down the tree rows, Hernandez's mom noticed something in the orchard that she couldn't believe. She saw her son.

When his mom saw Hernandez walking through the trees and crews toward her, she ran to him, grabbed onto him and held her son like she was never going to let go again. And then she started crying. In fact, most of them were crying. Everyone was hugging Hernandez, shaking his hand, and patting his back. "It was great to be home," Hernandez said. For a little while at least, home was a pear orchard in Tehachapi, but that home was a whole lot better than his previous home in Vietnam.

Tony Forner

When Tony Forner's plane was lifting off the runway and flying back to the world, it had only been about two days since he was in the bush. Obviously, that's not much transition from a world of war to a world of peace.

His final plane stop in the United States was at the Marine Corps Air Station at El Toro in Southern California. From there, he took a bus to Bakersfield. In an effort to surprise his parents that their son was home from Vietnam, Forner called his aunt to have her come and pick him up at the bus station. Then, the final drive back home to Porterville.

Imagine the joy his parents felt when the doorbell rang, they opened the door, and there stood their son back from the war in Vietnam. "Mom hugged me like she wouldn't let go," Forner said, but he and his dad did something unique. Well, maybe not unique to a guy who graduated from Porterville High School in the 1960s, but maybe a little different than most.

"My dad and I drank a fifth of Wild Turkey bourbon."

After Forner was home for about two weeks, he went back to Camp Pendleton to spend his remaining few months in the service. Since he was not experiencing the combat high anymore as he experienced in Vietnam, he summed up his last few months in the service with one word: boring. As Forner said, "I was so bored, I spent more time going into Tijuana to get drunk."

"I'm going home!" No words could bring such satisfaction to a veteran of a war than those. But what did these Vietnam War veterans come home to? In most cases, the first thing they experienced when their plane landed back home, back in the world, were anti-war protesters. Hippies. Many of them draft dodgers. Hollering at the returning GIs, hurling insults, calling them baby killers, and other expletives.

How dare they!

Many of these men went into the military because they felt it was their obligation. Many went because they truly felt the cause was a noble one, to stem the tide of communism. Some went because they had no other choice except to leave the home or town they grew up in, including leaving their families. They made their decisions, just like the hippies and draft dodgers made their decision to leave the country or burn their draft cards.

The negative reception that many of these returning war veterans faced from their own fellow countrymen was a national disgrace. There should have been people clapping and cheering when they stepped off that plane. But, instead, they often got something totally different and absolutely uncalled for. And those who protested against them personally, calling them names or throwing things at them, should be absolutely and profoundly ashamed of themselves.

On a positive side, however, for most of them, the negative reception from the protesters was eventually drowned out by the hugs from friends, the crying eyes of a mother, a firm handshake and hugs from a father, clean or cool air, adoring wives, and little children. They were home, and home is where they wanted to be.

They made it.

Vietnam War and Wall Facts

Highest in the Nation [1]

West Virginia had the highest casualty rate of any state in the nation. There were 711 West Virginians killed in action, averaging about 40 deaths per 100,000 citizens. Oklahoma had the second highest casualty rate.

17

Opposition, Even at Home

"There never was a good war or a bad peace."

Benjamin Franklin

THE CITY OF Porterville is known as a city that supports its veterans and those who are currently serving. Its support is visually obvious.

Just come into town on Veteran's Day each year and attend the parade. The streets are lined with thousands of people clapping, cheering, and hollering support for the organizations, schools, political officials, or veterans who are marching, walking, or riding in the parade. Walk down Main Street and many of the adjacent streets and see the military banners showcasing those local veterans who served their country. Stop by Porterville College and visit the Veterans Resource Center (VRC) or walk through the Veterans Monument where bricks are placed in the patio with the names of local veterans, their years of service and the branch they served. Visit Veterans Park across from Monache High School. The support from the city is tremendous.

But it hasn't always been like that, at least for some of the Vietnam veterans.

Even though the Porterville community was generally supportive of its returning Vietnam veterans, some veterans still faced opposition or hostility from local agencies in town. You wouldn't think that you'd find animosity toward our Vietnam veterans in Porterville, but it was there.

Brian Rattigan

When veterans are discharged from the service, most of them find themselves immediately unemployed. Unless they have a friend or family member who owns a business or might have connections for a job opportunity, the veterans often found themselves at the local state employment agency either filing for unemployment or looking for a job. The agency's responsibility was to assist the person with resume writing, completing job applications, or recommending places that had job opportunities available. They are there to help.

But Brian Rattigan didn't receive much help at all. Why? Because he was a Vietnam veteran. "The assistance that I got from the local State Employment Development Department (EDD) office in Porterville was depressingly reflective of the negative reception that many of the Vietnam veterans received when they returned home," Rattigan explained.

After he was discharged from the Army, Rattigan made an appointment to meet with the local EDD office during which he discussed job opportunities, how to apply for a job, and other assistance that could be offered when making an application for a job opening. During the meeting, the EDD office's designated veterans' representative made a disturbing recommendation.

Regarding a job opening with the Forest Service, Rattigan said the veterans' job counselor told him with thinly veiled disgust, "If you want to get that job, you better go home, take a shower, and get cleaned up." But he had already showered. He was already clean. And he looked like any other Vietnam veteran. And thereby that was the apparent problem.

Rattigan knew, or at least could sense, that the so-called veterans' representative had stereotypes about Vietnam veterans. Rattigan later learned that other Vietnam veterans from Porterville had received the same kind of mistreatment from that same veterans' representative, so they went to the Bakersfield EDD office instead where the service was much better.

A sad commentary to helping local Vietnam War veterans.

Shortly after that encounter, Rattigan said, "I received a phone call at 4:30 in the morning requesting me to report to the U.S. Forest Service Porterville district office on Henderson Avenue for transport up to an active forest fire for several days of work as a fire crew timekeeper." With the good news of at least temporary employment, Rattigan said, "I hopped on my Triumph motorcycle with my sleeping bag and headed out. At the time of the call, I had only had approximately two hours of sleep since I spent the night down at the Mountain Lion (a local bar) drinking beer."

Rattigan mentioned that something very disconcerting happened on the way to the fire. He said, "On the way up to the fire in a Forest Service pickup, one of the career staff members from the Forest Service district office groused that WWII was a real war, whereas Vietnam paled in comparison to combat in WWII." Rattigan continued, "Apparently, the local EDD veterans' representative had advised these Forest Service staff members that I was a Vietnam veteran. Obviously, these staff members' respect for the Vietnam veterans was negligible, if not outright disrespectful."

Another sad commentary to helping local Vietnam War veterans.

Roland Hill

After leaving Vietnam, Roland Hill still had about 10 more months to serve. Luckily, he did not go back to Ft. Eustis. Instead, Hill said, "I met a guy whose brother knew me at Porterville College, and he helped me get assigned to Ft. Ord." Since Ft. Ord was close to San Francisco, the base was near some of the most radical protesters in the anti-war movement. Hill remembers on Armed Forces Day in 1969,

"They closed Ft. Ord due to the protesters outside of the gates." And, as Hill explained, "We were always told to not wear our uniforms when we went off base."

Hill was eventually discharged and returned to Porterville College where he became involved with the campus Veterans Club. His time at Porterville College, in terms of the support, or lack thereof, the college provided its veterans was "Disappointing to say the least," Hill said.

Today, most colleges and universities across the country have dedicated, stand-alone veteran centers that provide support to returning veterans. Porterville College opened its doors to a new VRC in August of 2014. The VRC is in the center of the campus and provides a place where the veterans can meet fellow veterans, a lounge area with a refrigerator, microwave, and television. There is a computer room and a dedicated counselor to assist veterans with course selections and appropriate referrals.

But the college was not always this receptive of its veterans.

When Hill returned from Vietnam and re-entered Porterville College, he became actively involved with the campus Veterans Club. "We spoke with an administrator at the college regarding the idea of dedicating a place for the veterans to gather." The Vietnam veterans were returning home in large numbers and many of them were going to college and utilizing the G.I. Bill. The club wanted a place where the veterans could gather and experience the comradery they had while in the service. A place where they could offer support when one of their fellow veterans needed a shoulder to lean on. Well, the administrator gave the veterans such a dedicated place.

A park bench on the other side of the gymnasium.

"The administrator," Hill said, "was concerned that the Vietnam veterans would be a nuisance." The administrator obviously had some certain stereotypes and prejudices about the veterans, but, admittedly, Hill said, "The Vietnam veterans at Porterville College in those days were certainly not the best ambassadors for their cause." Hill explained that the veterans drank, smoked dope, partied and raised hell, but so did many non-veteran students in those days.

Eventually, Hill said, "We commandeered a couple of tables in the cafeteria to call our own, and no one argued with us." These tables were no VRC, but they were at least a spot where you knew a veteran could be found.

Hill mentioned one time a local quarry was going to donate a boulder, and someone else was going to donate a plaque to put in that boulder, that would recognize and honor Vietnam veterans. But the administration turned this offer down. No legitimate reason was given for the denial.

Around 1971, the Veterans Club held a convocation that focused on the Vietnam War that coincided with similar convocations being held at colleges and universities across the country. Some of the campus Vietnam veterans addressed the audience about their experiences in the war. After the convocation concluded, veterans and community members marched from Porterville College, up Main Street, to City Hall to bring attention to the war, its veterans, and the ongoing support they were needing.

Some of the veterans spoke to the City Council asking for a resolution supporting the idea that no more young men from the city of Porterville would be sent to Vietnam. This request was due to the high casualty and injury rate of those from Porterville who served in Vietnam. This request was also similar to requests that were being made in other cities across the country.

Brian Rattigan remembers, "During the presentation of the veterans, one of the City Council members sarcastically dismissed the request by quipping that 50,000 Americans had died in car accidents that year and suggested that the vets do something about that instead." Incredible. Their request for a resolution was turned down.

This was not a very supportive welcome home. "The denial of our request for putting a memorial on campus and the denial of a resolution by the City Council, soured many of the Vietnam veterans on campus, leaving us feeling disrespected by certain members of the college and community," Hill explained. And fifty years later, Hill is still bothered by that, as well as others are who took part in these requests.

But Hill took that anger and disappointment and helped to ensure that the returning GIs of today do not experience the same indifference by the college administration like he experienced back in the late 60s. Hill became involved in the development of the current campus VRC and served on the college's Veterans Advisory committee. He made a difference and continues to make a difference for those veterans attending Porterville College today.

The campus learned its lesson, and now is one of the most veteran supportive community colleges around thanks to Vietnam veterans like Roland Hill.

Don Dowling

Two of the nationwide organizations that serve and support fellow veterans are the Veterans of Foreign Wars (VFW) and the American Legion. Both organizations have had chapters in Porterville for many years. There are some differences in eligibility requirements for each organization, however. Depending on his or her military service history, a veteran could be eligible for membership in the American Legion, but not the VFW. The main difference in membership requirements is that the American Legion allows members to be veterans of either peacetime or wartime, and stationed anywhere in the world, including stateside. On the other hand, the VFW requires its members to have served in a combat area.

Understanding those requirements, Vietnam War veterans would be eligible for both organizations. However, they may have been eligible, but back in the late 60s and early 70s they weren't necessarily welcomed, at least not in the VFW.

When he was fresh out of the Vietnam War, Dowling went to a local VFW meeting to find out more about the organization and to possibly join its membership. But what he heard made Dowling "fighting mad" as he defined his feelings. Dowling said, "I was told, 'You're not welcome here.'" But why?

Dowling continued, "They told me that I was not welcome in the

VFW because Vietnam was not really a war. It was more of a conflict." Not really a war? "I had bullets firing at me just like they did," Dowling said, "and I was shot in the ass, legs, and belly. I have a box full of medals. I saw friends get killed. That's not a war?" Without a doubt, Dowling's anger at such an attitude was understandable.

Certainly, not everyone in that VFW meeting felt the same way, but, Dowling said, "No one came to my defense."

You would probably never think that an attitude such as this from one group of veterans to another would exist, but it did. Thankfully, for the most part, that attitude has changed, but what a sad commentary to the continued struggles for acceptance the Vietnam War veterans experienced upon their return home from the war. Yes, the war.

It was there. It might have been subtle to some, and maybe most didn't notice. Or maybe they didn't want to notice. Sure, not all of the returning veterans faced hostility, but some did. And we cannot ignore the fact that it was here in our community. Certainly, the hostility they faced in Porterville was not as severe as they would have faced in other cities across our country, but it was there, nonetheless.

Making disparaging remarks in a meeting of the City Council. Getting no support from the college administration for placement of a Vietnam veterans memorial on campus. Staff at the employment agency making comments about taking a shower and getting cleaned up. Employees from the Forest Service and veterans from WWII indicating that Vietnam was not really a war.

These might not have seemed like big deals to most, but they were big deals to the veterans who experienced them. Especially those who felt the country had turned their backs on them at the time when these veterans needed their support the most.

But, thankfully, things have changed and Porterville is now one of the most supportive communities around when it comes to its veterans.

Vietnam War and Wall Facts

Family Connections [1]

There were 3 sets of father-son combinations
that were killed in Vietnam:

Air Force T-Sgt Richard Fitzgibbon, Jr. was killed on
June 8, 1956 while his son, Richard, was killed on
September 7, 1965. The father is also the first known
casualty of the Vietnam War.

Leo Hester Sr. was killed in an aircraft crash on March
10, 1967 while his son Leo Hester Jr. was also killed in
an aircraft crash on November 02, 1969.

Fred C. Jenkins died April 2, 1968, while his son Bert
M. Jenkins was killed in action on April 28, 1969.

There were 31 sets of brothers killed in Vietnam
(another list has 40 sets of brothers).

18

The War's Impact on the Families and Friends of the Veterans

"When the peace treaty is signed, the war isn't over for the veterans, or the family. It's just starting."

Karl Marlantes

WHEN WE CELEBRATE the homecomings of our loved ones returning back home from a war like Vietnam, when we deal with the aftermath of their receiving medical assistance from the physical or psychological damages they may have incurred, or when we mourn the loss of those who may have died, we often forget about the impact these events have on the family members and friends of those veterans.

It's like dropping a rock in the middle of a still pond. One rock makes little waves, and then those waves grow and spread. That one little rock eventually impacts a large part of that pond; much is the same with a returning veteran. One veteran's homecoming, injury, or death, impacts many, many people. Family and friends alike. We should remember those who were impacted, too, by the Vietnam war.

They may not have fought in the war, but they certainly felt, and in many cases, continue to feel its impact in their lives.

Here are some of their stories, too.

Reba Wolfram, mother of a PHS Vietnam veteran

Since many of the Vietnam War veterans are now in their early 70s, most of their parents have long since passed away. Some of the parents who may still be living are oftentimes struggling with the effects of dementia or Alzheimer's or battling through challenging physical ailments that have hindered their ability to move about freely, if at all.

I had the opportunity to have a conversation in the home of a mother of a Vietnam War veteran. She may be losing her physical strength, but her mind is as sharp as a tack.

Reba Wolfram is 91 years old. She is unable to move around her house without a walker, and she requires daily supervision and assistance that is provided by her children. But she is mentally alert and still able to carry on conversations about most any topic. Her son, Don, a Vietnam War veteran from Porterville High School, lives in Arizona and comes to Terra Bella periodically with his wife to stay with his mother and assist with her daily care.

Prior to the war in Vietnam, Reba was used to the ravages of war and its effect on the lives of the family and friends of those who may be serving. Her husband, Bob, served during WWII and the Korean War. Even though she had the experience of living through two wars already, that experience did not make the challenge of having a son go to the Vietnam War any easier.

As I interviewed Reba, I had a different feeling when speaking with her than I did when I interviewed the veterans. You see, each veteran had a somewhat different story to tell. Some experienced combat in the jungles, some in the air, some on the rivers, some on the roads, or some not at all. But with Reba, I believe her story is one that is shared by countless mothers across our country. A story of heartache as the son she bore is off in a foreign country fighting in a war most in the country did not support. A story of fear or concern as she watches the news on television every night with reports from the war zone where her son is now living. A story of sadness or hopelessness that her child is so far away and she cannot do much to protect him as she did when he was younger.

So, in essence, the story of Reba Wolfram is a story that most mothers of GIs in our country would tell about that time. With that, Reba is almost like a representative or spokesperson for all mothers who had a son that served during the Vietnam War. She speaks for them almost as much as she speaks for herself.

After her son, Don, graduated from Porterville High School in 1965, the war had not really been a major topic of discussion around the Wolfram house. But after Don graduated from high school, started going to college and working, the war began to escalate. When we talked about the feelings she had about her son possibly going to Vietnam, Reba said, "I knew it was going to happen. I expected it, but what can a mother do?" However, Reba did something any mother can do, and something that brought her some relief to the anxiety of worrying about her son going to a war.

"I prayed a lot," Reba said. "I prayed that he wouldn't have to go to Vietnam." But Don was eventually sent to Vietnam. His going to Vietnam, however, did not affect her faith in God when she said, "God gave me an answer that was different than what I wanted." And then she said, "But if it was God's answer, then it was the right one. I just had to accept it."

When it was time for Don to fly to Vietnam, Reba said, "It was so hard when he left. I held him and hugged him and didn't want to let go." And what else did she do? "I prayed," Reba said, "and I cried." And she did something that helped her handle the pain of watching her son leave to a war, "I relied on my faith."

Even at 91 years old, Reba said, "I can still remember the day Don left like it was yesterday. It was so hard, and I was sad. And scared, too."

While Don was in Vietnam, he did something that helped his mother with the pains of missing her son. He sent her tape recordings almost every week. "Those tapes helped a lot," Reba said. But one tape scared her. Reba said, "On one tape as Don was talking there was a loud sound in the background and Don said, 'Well, there goes another bomb.' And, boy, that scared me." So what did she do then? She prayed.

Reba also did something to help Don. "I sent him an Angel Food cake almost every week," Reba said. And Don interjected, "And cookies, too." Reba sent a lot of cakes and a lot of cookies while her son was in Vietnam, but she wanted her son to do something with those culinary delights. Reba said, "I wanted him to share it with the other guys he was serving with."

Since the war was on television every night, every night was another reminder that her son was in a war zone. "It was hard watching the news," Reba said, "because you knew something about Vietnam would come up. And what came up was never any good." But, finally, something about Vietnam did come up that was good. Very good. And that was the news that her son was going to be coming home. "When we found out Don was coming home I couldn't wait for that day to get here," she said.

When Don flew home from Vietnam, his parents met him coming off the plane at March Air Force Base in Southern California. "It was so exciting when he came home," Reba said, "It was such a joyful time. And when I saw him for the first time I started crying and I couldn't wait to hug him." As she further explained the feeling of having her son home again, "I was so thankful that he came home alive. And I absolutely prayed to God and thanked Him for bringing my son home." This time, the Lord gave her the answer she wanted, too. Don was home.

But Don's coming back home didn't stop the fear and concern that Reba had about the Vietnam War. She had two younger sons and the war was still going on. Her next oldest son, Ken, was now of the draft age. And Reba said, "I really thought that Ken would have to go, too. And that worried me. It worried me a lot." But something happened that was another answer to a prayer to God from a worried mother. "They stopped the draft and started the lottery system," Reba said, "and Ken got a high number." Her worries were over.

Reba Wolfram was like most mothers of young sons who were of the draft age during the Vietnam War. She worried about her son. She cried for her son. She held her son and didn't want to let him go. But she did something else. She prayed. And for the most part, her prayers were answered in the way that she hoped. However, she also relied on her faith to comfort her in case her prayers were not answered in the way that she wanted. But she knew the answers to her prayers were God's and she would accept the answer He made.

As Reba said, "God's in charge of everything. I just had to accept His decisions." And accept them she did.

When I retired a few years ago, I began to spend more time at our church property, mowing lawns, spraying weeds, and doing anything that related to the maintenance and upkeep of the grounds. In what may seem like an odd feeling to have, one of the pleasures I have when working on the property is spending time at the cemetery. It is there that I feel the presence of the dear departed that gave so much of their time, talents, and treasures to our congregation over the years. Almost every time I go to the cemetery, there is something that I find that brings a certain satisfaction and profound respect.

American flags.

Among the nearly 300 headstones in the cemetery, there are almost always at least two that are adorned in American flags. It does not matter the season or the weather, the flags are there. It does not matter if it's a holiday or not in the church or secular world, the flags are there. It does not matter if it is a period of celebration or a time of mourning, the flags are there. And the two headstones that are almost always adorned in American flags both have the last name of Wolfram.

Edward Wolfram, born in 1893 and died in 1982, served during WWI, the war that was supposed to end all wars. And his son, Robert, Reba's husband, who was born in 1924 and died in 2014. Robert served during WWII and Korea. And as mentioned above, Edward's grandson and Robert's son, Don, served in the Vietnam War. The service of the Wolfram family is a testament to their love of country and pride in the service of their great-grandfather, grandfather, father, husband and son during times of war and times of peace.

Our heartfelt thanks to the Wolfram family, and the countless other families like them, who have served our country spanning several generations. And, especially, our thanks to Reba and the other mothers who waited, hoped, and prayed for their sons to return home from their generation's war.

Carol Vossler, wife of a PHS Vietnam veteran

Post-Traumatic Stress Disorder (PTSD) affects many of the veterans who served in Vietnam. The majority of the veterans interviewed for this book have been diagnosed with PTSD and most are still receiving services through the VA for this condition. What we often forget, however, is that the families of these veterans often suffer with them.

The families also live with the flashbacks, mood swings, anger, or other behaviors. The spouses often ride with the veterans to the hospital or doctor appointments, make sure the veterans are taking their medications, and explain to others who may not understand why their husband acts the way he does in certain circumstances. In addition to the spouses, we often forget that children are affected by PTSD, too. Watching their father react as he does is often a confusing and stressful time for their children. They often struggle trying to understand the behaviors, feelings, and experiences of their father.

Carol Boydstun was almost 18 when she first met Russell Vossler while they were in a bank in Porterville. When they first met, Russell was a police officer. On Christmas Eve, Carol's 18th birthday, Russell sent her a dozen red roses. That evening, Carol sang a solo during her church's candlelight service, and when she stood up to sing the solo she said, "There was Russell, in a suit and tie, sitting at the back of the church." Thinking back on when she saw Russell in the back of the church, Carol said, "That was the moment." And it surely was. "We have been together for almost every day since," Carol said. In fact, Russell and Carol have been married now for over 40 years. Congratulations.

But their marriage has been filled with serious challenges. Challenges because of the Vietnam War.

When Carol first met Russell she knew he had been in the military but had no idea that he suffered from PTSD. In fact, at that point in her life, she really had never even heard of PTSD. But she would soon learn about the condition and how it would impact their family for the next four decades.

When they were first together, Carol began to recognize various behaviors in Russell that she eventually learned were the result of his service in Vietnam. She said, "Russell wasn't comfortable in crowds, even small ones, and he needed to have his back to a wall so he could scan the room." She also said that Russell warned people not to approach him from behind or pat him on the back for fear he would physically hurt them. Carol said, "His startle reflex was extremely high. I also began noticing his restless sleep, often kicking and yelling out." And she further said, "I didn't put the pieces together at that point. Russ had some serious health issues and injuries, another piece I didn't connect with his military service."

A few years later when Russell had a major back injury and surgery, he was unable to work or do much of anything. Carol said, "The nightmares became much more frequent and serious. One night he broke windows out in our bedroom. Another time I found him cowering in the closet. He said the Viet Cong were all around and the helicopter was on fire."

Obviously, Russell needed help. He finally began seeing a therapist connected to the VA. Carol said, "The therapist was the first person to say anything about PTSD." But it wasn't really enough, however. Since Russell was unable to work, he was given a 100% service-connected permanently disabled status. When Carol found out her husband was now considered permanently disabled she thought, "This was scary!"

At this point in their marriage, Russell and Carol had three children. Their oldest son was in college, their daughter was in high school and their youngest son was in junior high school. "The children were very sensitive to and affected by all of this," Carol said, "and their dad's moods were devastating." Due to his condition, Russell didn't attend church with his family anymore and was not able to be part of many of their children's activities at school. He couldn't attend sporting events, school banquets, help with fund raisers, and do the kinds of things most parents at schools participate in. "Even family gatherings became almost impossible for him," Carol said.

As Russell's behaviors became more pronounced, difficult, and challenging, Carol said, "I struggled with staying or leaving." She had to determine what was best for the children, herself, and Russell, too. But her decision on whether to stay or leave was determined by her faith in God and her strong religious foundation. As Carol said, "I was raised with Christian morals and felt that divorce wasn't an option. I had said 'till death do us part' and that's what I meant, and I loved Russ."

Certainly, Carol felt responsible for Russell's safety and well-being. He needed help and she felt it was up to her to make sure he got what he needed. So she stayed. "There were many times that I felt hopeless and felt like giving up. But our children are what kept me going." At the same time, however, Carol said, "None of us understood what was happening."

In an effort to help financially, Carol had taken a second job at night. On Christmas Eve 2009, while Carol was at work, she received a call from Russell. He said that he needed her to come home right now. Carol said, "Russel said he couldn't do this anymore." Carol further explained, "He was very emotional and said that he was holding a hand full of pills and ready to end the misery and torment." Russell told her that he couldn't continue to hurt them and thought that suicide was the only option.

When she heard what he said, Carol immediately went home. "After I got home and was able to assess the situation, I told Russell to get in the car. He was either going for help or we were done. I couldn't, we couldn't, do this anymore." Carol said, "We were going to the National Center for PTSD!"

They had learned of the PTSD center after many years of struggle with a psychiatrist at the VA. Carol and Russell had previously received an application for the national center, completed it, but the new psychiatrist that Russell had been assigned to at the VA said that he had "just been too busy" to fill out his part. Feeling more determined than ever to get the services Russell needed, Carol said, "We weren't waiting anymore!"

So they drove four hours late at night to the emergency room in Palo Alto near the location of the national center. After they evaluated Russell, he was admitted to the psychiatric ward until things were stable for him. In order for Russell to be accepted into the program at Menlo Park, they had to get him off of some of the medication the doctors at the VA had put him on. "I remember leaving him and going to a hotel to try and sleep a couple of hours before driving back home," Carol explained, "Christmas - here we were. I could barely move. The whole world had fallen apart, and I hadn't been able to fix anything! I cried myself to sleep."

After a couple hours, Carol managed to pull herself together and drive back to Porterville. As she explained, "I had to move forward, whatever that was, or who that would include."

Russell began receiving the psychological assistance that he needed through the national center. But the road to recovery, or at least to some degree of improvement, would be long and difficult. And for the Vossler family, each day is different. Carol said, "There are times that I do everything for Russ and then there will be a period where he interacts and helps with life's day-to-day." As she further explained,

"There is no pattern or consistency. It's challenging because rarely are there two days alike."

Although Russell usually manages his own medical appointment schedule and prescriptions, she drives him to his appointments most of the time. Carol said, "He pretty much has appointments every week. Russ doesn't drive much anymore, especially on highways or out of town." She also explained that Russell's PTSD and anxiety has disrupted his ability to process so she goes to the appointments to help him remember what the doctor said. So, Russell's appointments have become her appointments, too.

In terms of how services to the family could be improved, Carol said "I really feel that the psychologist and psychiatrist should consult with the spouses and families occasionally to get another view of how things are going, to be sure all of the information is given regarding the veteran's situation." As she said with Russell, "I'm fairly confident Russ feels he is much more present and doesn't isolate, but I see it very differently. TV and Bronco (his service dog) are his focus the majority of his day."

In addition, Carol said, "There is basically no help for spouses and families through the VA system. Our children and I were included for about an hour on two days during Russ's time at Menlo Park. At Russ's request, I have been present with him and his psychologist maybe five sessions over all these years."

As life and time have progressed since the war in Vietnam, Russell's physical and mental health have been seriously compromised and affected not only by the war, but by the medications he's been prescribed by the doctors, and, of course, from time itself. Describing his ongoing health challenges, Carol said, "Russ's memory is not so sharp, he has tremors in his hands which are becoming more severe, and severe neuropathy that began in his feet, but now has moved into his legs, buttocks, and hands."

Carol continued, "Life is definitely much different than any of us had envisioned. I am pretty much always with him. He isn't able to travel away from our home much anymore." And his inability to travel affects his extended family, too. "In the past," Carol explained, "I might leave to go see our other grandchildren, being gone maybe a week, but that seems to be less of an option as time goes on. I feel very responsible for Russ's care, safety, and wellbeing." She doesn't want to leave him alone anymore and has to manage her household accordingly. As she explained, "All of this has very much affected the day-to-day. It's very hard to make plans even if they don't include Russ. If he's not doing well then I can't leave him. He doesn't participate in life very much, so I feel very lonely trying to continue on 'normally.'"

And her concern is not a selfish one either. "My concern," Carol said, "hasn't been me. First and foremost, my concern is for our children and Russ. My faith in God and occasionally a good friend's ear have been my lifeline." Her concern is also for those families in the country who are struggling with the effects of the war, and, specifically, dealing with PTSD.

Carol then provided some recommendations and pieces of advice.

She encourages families to take advantage of group or family counseling that may be provided in local vet centers, if there is a center nearby. She also recommended various resources of information that the veterans and their families should avail themselves to. Some are included in the epilogue in the back of the book. And then she reiterated, "It's not the veteran nor the family's fault! It's not just the veteran that needs healing. Talk to others about what you are dealing with. Stuffing this won't help anyone. No Shame! Do not become part of the isolation. Have a life!"

Great words of advice.

Her final words about Russell and his condition are rather poignant. "Watching the strong, calm man that I fell in love with slipping away is heartbreaking. The damage to relationships and Russ's feelings of worthlessness are most challenging. His focus tends to be on all of his health issues. Often it's very difficult to determine if it's PTSD or other health issues. He continually is working on his mindfulness."

Russell is obviously very lucky to have such a determined and caring wife. I wish all veterans struggling with PTSD or other psychological or physical injuries would have such a strong person to support them like Carol Vossler.

Cheryl McCarville, wife of a PHS Vietnam veteran

"Always there for 50 years."

That was a statement Cheryl McCarville made during our interview that was actually a very profound statement when you think about it. "Always there for 50 years." But what has always been there for 50 years that Cheryl was referring to? Could it be the love for her husband, Ron? True, they've been married for 50 years and she has certainly loved him during that time but that's not what she was referring to. Could it be bills, house payments, or car loans? Sure, their life, like the life of any couple that's been married for 50 years, is often burdened with bills, financial commitments, or monetary concerns. But, again, that's not what she was referring to. So, what has always been there for 50 years?

PTSD.

Cheryl Springmeyer was born in Cortez, Colorado and raised in Porterville. She attended Hope Elementary School before enrolling at Porterville High School where she graduated in 1968. While she was in high school, her future husband, Ron McCarville, was in the graduating class of 1966, two years before Cheryl. "We didn't actually meet in high school," Cheryl said, "but we met after Ron returned from Vietnam."

The first time they met, McCarville was working with the Forest Service at the Needles lookout point tower scouting for fires. One day, some friends of McCarville's made a trip to visit him in the lookout tower to bring him some supplies, and Cheryl joined the group. Shortly after that visit, McCarville called Cheryl to ask her out. Then, only three months later, they were married. When I asked her if it was love at first sight, Cheryl laughed and said, "It must have been. We only dated for three months." Regardless if it may have been a short dating period, their love for each other has certainly been proven by the length of their 50-year marriage.

In the early stages of their marriage, Cheryl began to notice some behaviors in her husband that would later be attributed to his experiences during the Vietnam War. Cheryl said, "Sometimes we'd just be sitting around, and everything would be okay. But then he would just go off on someone or something. He would get really angry." At first, her husband's behaviors surprised her, and his outbursts got worse as time went by. Not knowing the reason why he would act in such a way, Cheryl said, "It was confusing while it was happening, and I began to think that maybe I did something wrong that caused him to get angry."

Blaming yourself is a common reaction when trying to come up with a reason for a spouse's behaviors such as what McCarville was displaying. Back in the late 1960s, the term PTSD was a diagnosis that not many had heard of, but that's exactly what her husband had. Cheryl said, "I had no idea what PTSD was. Never heard of it. So I thought he got angry because of something I did."

The realization that the behaviors her husband was displaying had an actual label came to her as she was reading an article in a magazine one day.

"About two years after he was back from Vietnam, I was reading an article written by a wife whose husband had PTSD," Cheryl said, "and I thought to myself, 'Wow, that's me.'" But rather than reach out to someone who might understand what she and her husband were going through, Cheryl kept things to herself. "I didn't want others to know the difficulties we were dealing with," Cheryl said. When I mentioned to her how hard that must have been dealing with it by herself, her eyes teared up and she said, "You can see I'm crying." But Cheryl dealt with it the only way she knew how. "I began to withdraw a lot," Cheryl said, "and I didn't talk about it very much. Still don't actually."

During the early years of their marriage, they reached out to the VA for assistance, but what they received was rather negligible. "We went to the VA and got Ron evaluated, but we never heard back from them," Cheryl said. Several years later when Ron had an appointment with a person at the VA, Cheryl said, "They asked Ron, 'Did you know that you were diagnosed with PTSD?'" So, the diagnosis was made that Ron had PTSD but they were never contacted. Explaining their frustration with this, Cheryl said, "We never got a letter or anything from the VA that said he had PTSD. We should have been informed when he was first diagnosed with it."

They began to hear and read more about PTSD and the services available to help deal with the condition. And they began to finally receive appropriate services from the VA. In addition, Cheryl said, "The groups at Porterville College that Cliff had (referring to Cliff Davids, a Vietnam War veteran and former counselor for disabled students at Porterville College) also helped in getting Ron started on the right road."

Like other households that have a husband struggling with PTSD, Cheryl has had to make some adjustments in their lifestyle. "We didn't take a lot of long trips out of town," Cheryl said, "because I was not sure how he would react." She further explained, "We never went to a lot of parties or social gatherings our friends had, because Ron didn't like crowds or being around a lot of people." When they ate in a restaurant, she said, "Ron would need to sit with his back to the wall so he could see everything."

Even some things in their house were affected, too. Cheryl said, "When the sun went down, the blinds went down." And Ron would often do something at home he probably did a hundred times in Vietnam, "He would walk the perimeter of our lot at night to make sure everything was okay."

Cheryl and I spent some time not only talking about what has been in their lives, but also talking about what others can do in the future. Cheryl provided some words of advice for wives and families of a husband or father who struggles with PTSD. Her first words of advice, and words she expressed rather forcefully, she said, "Go to the VA." Too many veterans and their families try to struggle through the effects of PTSD or other related health issues on their own. Sometimes veterans don't seek out assistance because while they were in the service, asking for help was a sign of weakness. But asking for help can be a sign of strength, too.

Cheryl did offer, however, a word of criticism about the services of the VA and a suggestion for improvement. She said, "The VA takes care of veterans, but does nothing for the wives or families." That was a similar concern expressed by Carol Vossler. So, in a way to counteract that deficiency in service, Cheryl offered a great recommendation. "It's helpful to have someone to talk to because I've often felt so alone. But there are others like me out there, too." She recommended starting or finding a group of wives or family members of the veterans who are struggling with PTSD where they could have the chance to share feelings and experiences, lean on each other for support, or learn about related services available. Cheryl also made an observation that was somewhat funny but probably is very true.

"Find a veteran on PTSD and you'll find a wife on anti-depressants."

Cheryl mentioned that Ron has gotten better over the years. And she has also learned from her experiences and from the literature she has read about PTSD. About Ron, she said, "That warm, loving person I married 50 years ago is still there. He's just been affected by the war." In addition, she feels that she is now better able to manage her reaction to his behaviors. She said, "When Ron acts out, he is remorseful, and I know now that he can't control himself sometimes. So I've learned to manage my reactions." And, contrary to how she felt in the early years of their marriage, she's also learned that any expressions of anger or strong emotions by her husband are not her fault either.

When thinking about the whole Vietnam War experience, Cheryl said, "While they were in Vietnam, many of these guys were in charge of platoons and making life and death decisions on the battlefield. They had an awesome responsibility. Then when they came home, they were given menial jobs like washing cars and having to prove themselves. These guys weren't treated very well after the war."

At one point, she beamed with pride and said, "I am very proud of Ron for serving in Vietnam."

Cheryl, so are we.

Diane Johnson, fictitious name, friend of the PHS Vietnam veterans

Diane Johnson is actually a fictitious name of a friend of the Porterville High School veterans who requested anonymity when telling the following stories. In addition, the name of the veteran she references in one of her stories is fictitious, too, out of respect for the privacy of the family. Both of them are graduates from Porterville High School and friends to many of the veterans who served in Vietnam.

Diane told a story about Jack Mills, who graduated the year before her. Diane said that she didn't really know Jack that well in high school since he was a year older than she was, but she ran into him after the war when she was working back East. Diane said, "My cousins came to visit me so Jack must have heard from them that I was in the area. Jack called me one time and we became friends." She doesn't remember where Jack must have been stationed, but she felt it was somewhere near where she lived since it was close enough that he could visit her periodically.

Like many who live far away from the place where they were raised, Diane said, "It was always nice to find someone from home in a strange city, and I loved seeing people from Porterville while I was living back East." But it was during one visit from her new friend that Diane witnessed how the Vietnam War could continue to affect those who served in it years after the war was over.

As she explained what happened, Diane said, "One night I had just gotten back from a date and Jack was waiting for me at my apartment. My date and I just sat around and talked to Jack for a while." She said that her roommate had already gone to bed and when her date left, Jack stayed, and they continued to talk. But then something happened that scared her.

"As Jack and I were talking, he suddenly looked at me with a strange look on his face," Diane explained, "and he stood up from the couch and crouched over like he was walking with a rifle in his hand. He opened a few doors and looked inside. And even though I was asking him if he was okay, he ignored me, like he didn't hear me." Thinking back on the situation she summed up her feelings by saying, "It was scary." And indeed it was.

Then she said, "Finally, he opened the front door and walked out." Not knowing what to do, Diane called Jack's brother who lived in the area. "He told me that Jack was suffering from PTSD and was having a flashback," Diane said, "and said that if he came back I should call the hospital."

Not only was it scary, Diane said it was something else, "It was so very, very sad. That's what Vietnam did."

Thinking back on her friend, Jack, and remembering how he struggled with the effects of the war, Diane said, "I tried to look him up a few years ago to see how he was doing. But I couldn't find him." Later, Diane found out that shortly after her failed search for her old friend, he died.

Diane also described a conversation she had one time with Jack when she said, "Jack described to me how he was riding in a truck with a buddy of his and they hit a mine and the truck blew up. I believe Jack was partially deaf as a result." Diane described something that Jack said that really impacted her, "What struck me most was how open he was about seeing his buddy decapitated, and how he could describe it. No wonder he had PTSD." As Diane further said about the war in general, "We are taught killing is wrong and then go to war and see killing, and you kill!"

Diane described herself as being rather naïve about the war at that time, but after losing so many of her friends in the war, or losing them to psychological disorders such as PTSD, she wasn't really naïve anymore. She didn't just lose friends from Porterville High School either. Diane had a friend from Visalia who was going to be a helicopter pilot in Vietnam. She said, "I can still remember him telling me before he got shipped over that he would probably not be coming back because the life expectancy of helicopter pilots wasn't long." And what happened to her friend?

Diane said, "Not long after I moved back East I was notified that he had been killed in Vietnam. I wish I would have saved his letters."

Almost 50 years later, Diane still remembers. She remembers her friends. She still mourns their loss. She still feels sad that the war could affect someone like Jack and others in the way that it did. Yes, Diane is correct. That's what Vietnam did, and it is so very, very sad.

Steve Durtsche, classmate and friend of the PHS Vietnam veterans

"Why did that bastard have to do that on Mother's Day?" exclaimed Steve Durtsche. He asked that question with 50 years of pent-up frustration built up inside him.

Durtsche was not asking about a spouse who forgot to get flowers for his wife on Mother's Day. He was not asking about a child who didn't remember to buy his mom a present on Mother's Day. He was not asking about a chef messing up an order for the family dinner on Mother's Day. He was asking about something much more serious.

On Mother's Day in 1968, Albert and Estaline Higgins received a visit from an Army representative to inform them that their son, Pat, had been killed in Vietnam. "Couldn't they have waited another day?" Durtsche wondered. "Why tell them on Mother's Day?"

Pat Higgins and Durtsche were best of friends. They had known each other from kindergarten, went to school together, played on the same streets, and attended high school together. Durtsche got to know Higgins' parents and siblings so closely that they were almost like his surrogate family.

Durtsche remembered Higgins' love for bluegrass music, often playing the banjo and harmonica at social events, high school parties, or just around the house. Durtsche said, "Pat liked to kid around and loved the mountains." Durtsche said that when he and Higgins would go backpacking, "Pat often carried his banjo along, slung across the 45-pound pack he was carrying on his back."

Geary Baxter, one of the veterans interviewed for this book, said this about Pat, "Pat was the first friend I made when I moved to Porterville. He was such a great guy."

Durtsche did not enter the military right after high school but Higgins did. Higgins went into the Army and was initially stationed in Germany. When Higgins came home for a 30-day leave, Durtsche picked him up at the bus depot in Fresno. During the next 30 days, they partied, talked, listened to Higgins on the banjo or harmonica, and just did what friends do. But during his leave, Higgins made an announcement that brought great concern and fear to Durtsche and to Higgins' mom and dad.

Durtsche said, "Pat told us that after his 30-day leave was over, he was going to Vietnam." And when he said that, "It scared the crap out of me." The war was in the papers and on television every night, "And the news was awful," Durtsche said.

This announcement upset Higgins' mom so much that she encouraged her son to go to Canada. On the other hand, being a Marine Corps veteran, his father disagreed with his wife. Their son was called to Vietnam and that's where he should go, his father felt. Against his mother's wishes, and following the feelings of his father, Higgins went to Vietnam.

While Higgins was serving in Vietnam, Durtsche was working for the Forest Service. "We exchanged letters frequently," Durtsche said. "I'd let Pat know about life back in Porterville and he'd let me know about life in Vietnam." One day at work, Durtsche was told to go the office. When he got there, one of his supervisors told him that he needed to go home, right now, and his supervisor would drive him. The supervisor did not tell him why, and Durtsche could only imagine. His mind was racing with all kinds of possibilities. Then, just before they got back into Porterville, the supervisor broke the news to Durtsche.

His best friend, Pat Higgins, had been killed in Vietnam.

"When he told me that Pat had been killed, I was stunned,"

Durtsche said. Shocked. He couldn't believe it. He said, "I remember tearing up and feeling such a profound loss. My best friend was gone." Durtsche was confused with a headful of questions. And Durtsche said, "When Pat died, that changed my life."

When further thinking about Higgins' death and trying to adjust to the loss, Durtsche said, "His death was enough for me. I will always respect the flag. I will always respect my country. But I had no respect for the war."

As a pallbearer at the funeral, Durtsche carried his best friend to his grave. It was a trip that he would never forget. Durtsche hated the war, and when given the opportunity to participate in it, he refused.

The year following Higgins' death, Durtsche got drafted. He was one of the last guys drafted prior to the beginning of the draft lottery in 1969. When the first lottery was held, Durtsche's lottery number was a high one. A number high enough that he would have avoided being drafted if he was under the rules of the lottery. But he didn't have the luxury of using the lottery number since he had already been drafted under the previous conscription process. So, to the draft board he went.

"Since I was the father of twins, with a third child on the way," Durtsche said, "I went to the draft board to appeal my draft notice." He could have gone to Vietnam, but he had no use for the war. His best friend had been killed there and he hated the war. So, Vietnam was the last place he wanted to be. Sure, his children were the main reason for deciding to appeal his draft notice, but the memory of his friend Pat impacted his decision almost as much.

His appeal was approved.

Fifty years later, Durtsche still remembers. He still remembers his other friends from Porterville High School who served in Vietnam, some dying, some being injured, and some still feeling the effects of the war today. He still remembers the feelings, emotions, and fears that many of the mothers and fathers of his friends were struggling with while their sons were fighting in the war. He still remembers how the city of Porterville and the surrounding communities were affected by the war in so many ways.

And, most importantly, he still remembers Pat.

Susie and Lance Goble, wife and son of a PHS Vietnam veteran

The memories of and reactions to the Vietnam experience can surface almost at any time and in ways that no one could imagine they would. And family members are often there to deal with these unexpected reactions. Susie Goble remembers an incident that happened about 30 years after she first met her husband, Greg, who was a veteran of the Vietnam War. Thirty years.

"One day," Susie said, "while doing daily household chores, Greg offered his help by sweeping the kitchen floor. Several minutes into this while I was in the next room doing laundry, I suddenly heard a loud bang and a burst of yelling in a language I didn't understand." Susie may have not understood what Greg was saying, but she recognized that the language he was speaking in was Vietnamese.

When this happened she was obviously concerned and a bit confused on what was going on. She continued, "I immediately went to the kitchen, only to see the broom on the floor and Greg in what looked like a trance walking into the back yard. He just stood staring in a trance." She asked him if he was okay. He was confused, of course, but said he was fine.

Susie was obviously concerned about what was happening so she went to get their teenage son, Lance, who was a high school student at the time. Susie told him about her concern about the incident and asked Lance to check on his dad.

Describing the incident, Lance said, "I remember sitting at my computer, and my mom came in and asked if I could check on my dad." Lance remembers being confused by this request because it was not a normal thing he ever had to do before. Lance continued, "I walked into the kitchen, there was a broom on the floor and the back door was open. I go outside and I see my dad on the far side of the patio, and he was mumbling." Lance was obviously concerned about his dad's behavior and had never seen him act this way. So he asked his dad, "Hey, dad, are you okay?"

Lance said that his dad didn't respond to his question. Rather, his dad put his hand up to Lance as if to tell his son not to come any closer. Although he was not in any danger, Lance felt his father just needed some space. Lance continued to describe the incident, "Dad then puts his hand to his mouth, started mumbling again, then loudly spoke in what I could only guess was Vietnamese." But then his dad stopped and screamed in English, "F_ _ _ you, you mother f _ _ _ er!" His dad then made a motion like he was shooting.

Lance remembered, "I didn't know what to do, so I walked back inside and told my mom that I didn't know what to do and that I thought he was having a flashback." And his dad certainly was. When later asked about the incident, Goble did not remember any of it.

Flashbacks like that are sometimes common in those who have experienced traumatic experiences in their lives, such as combat. And sometimes flashbacks are triggered by memories, or stress. And, at that time in his life, Goble was under a tremendous amount of stress.

When thinking back to that instance, Susie has a theory on why she believed her husband reacted in that way. And that reason has to do with stress.

Susie said, "Greg was going through an enormous amount of stress at the time, and I think that was a major factor for his flash-back." She continued, "Greg had earned his way up to a high position with his company at the time, with several men under him." And she proudly said, "He was a great boss and his guys loved him."

But then Greg got an assignment from his superiors that Susie feels was the catalyst for his flashback. "One day," Susie said, "with very little notice, Greg was informed that the company was down-sizing and he was to let 10 guys go. The pressure of this task was so overwhelming as you can imagine."

From a personal perspective, I can certainly imagine the stress that Goble was going through with that assignment. I, too, was given the same directive when I was in my first few years of management at Porterville College. Due to the budget, we had to reduce our expenditures, and some classified staff positions were being eliminated. The president gave me the responsibility to meet with each person whose position was being discontinued to let them know of the decision. I couldn't sleep at night, irritability permeated my interactions with people, and my mood was not a pleasant one.

Goble, with a mind and memory full of horrendous experiences in Vietnam, and the combination of these experiences along with the stress placed upon him to do an extremely difficult task, reacted in such a way. And understandably so. Thankfully, he has not had a flashback since.

I must say, his wife Susie has an interesting past herself. Back in the 60s, she was a self-described hippy. And, yes, she was an anti-war protester, too. I guess Greg and Susie are proven examples that opposites attract. Who would have thought of a Vietnam War veteran marrying an anti-war protesting hippy? One day, Susie put her anti-war mentality to work when her brother received his draft notice in the mail.

Susie opened the envelope, read the letter indicating that her brother was being drafted, and then took a pen and wrote the following word across the top of the letter: "Deceased." She then sent the letter back. A few weeks later, Susie's mom walked in with a letter in her hand and wanted to know why the government was asking for a death certificate for Susie's brother who was still alive.

Okay, her plan didn't work, but it was a creative attempt.

The family of PHS Vietnam veteran Barry Jackson

Barry Jackson died on July 6, 2014 in Fresno, California from cancer. But his sister, Beverly said, "We lost Barry in Vietnam."

When we think and speak of the casualties of war, we sometimes focus exclusively on those who died in combat, or those who had been physically injured. But not all the causalities of the Vietnam War were from physical wounds. Some suffered and died from the result of psychological wounds, too.

In the case of those veterans with psychological wounds, there was usually a friend or family members who suffered with him as he dealt with the psychological challenges he was faced with. One such family who cared for, worried about, and struggled with someone with psychological injuries from the Vietnam War was the family of Barry Jackson.

Some of the adjectives that described Jackson are loving, kind, gentle, sensitive, thoughtful, caring, and strong. Everyone he knew loved him. His little brother, Jerry, said "Barry was a great big brother" and his sisters agreed. Barry's sisters, Joan and Beverly, and his brother, Jerry, met with me to speak about their brother and the impact the war had on him and his family as well. Jackson's other sister, Linda, passed away in January of 2018.

Yes, Barry died from cancer, but he lived many years in care facilities due to the mental and psychological challenges that dramatically surfaced while he was in the service. At some point during his time in Vietnam, Barry suffered a psychological crisis and was eventually medically and honorably discharged from the Army. He then lived the remainder of his life in care facilities and VA hospitals.

No one really knew what caused his mental breakdown in Vietnam. Very little was shared with his family about what happened. Maybe no one really knew. Jackson seldom spoke about his time in Vietnam, but something happened that changed his life.

Jackson was drafted in 1967. When he got his draft notice, his sister, Joan, said, "I can still remember how upset and worried dad was." And she also remembers, "I was scared, too." Jackson was drafted the year prior to the deadliest year in Vietnam, 1968, so he would be entering the Army at almost the worst time.

After receiving his draft notice, Jackson filed for Conscientious Objector status. According to the Merriam Webster dictionary, the definition of a conscientious objector is a "person who refuses to serve in the armed forces or bear arms on moral or religious grounds." Jackson did not support the war, nor did he want to participate in a war he felt might have been unjust. In addition, he did not want to kill anyone in combat, or risk being killed. When he completed his conscientious objector application, one question asked was, "Would you kill to protect your family?" Jackson answered "Yes." And because of that answer, as his sister, Joan, explained, "His application was turned down."

He was now faced with a dilemma. Go to Vietnam and fight in a war he did not want to participate in or leave his family in Terra Bella and move to Canada. He considered both options, and later decided to stay home and take his chances with the draft. He was eventually drafted and began his training to be a soldier in a war he wanted no part of.

Jackson went to basic training in Ft. Ord, California, and then to his AIT at Ft. Eustis, Virginia. His family did not remember his exact MOS, but whatever it was, he eventually found himself in Vietnam. Since he was stationed at Ft. Eustis for his AIT, Jackson would have been trained in water, air, or land transportation-related responsibilities, including motor vehicle operations and helicopter maintenance. When reviewing the history of Ft. Eustis, it shows that the 7th Transportation Brigade was activated at the base on July 1, 1966. This was about a year prior to Jackson being drafted.

When Jackson was being processed at Ft. Eustis, he mentioned in a letter home:

"Myself and some others are being held over for further testing instead of being directly sent to our assignment. It seems that there may be a chance that we can get a better assignment such as teaching, etc. since we have high scores or are college grads."

Jackson was still hoping for an assignment that did not put him in harm's way. It was his conscientious objector belief that was still guiding his thoughts about the military and the war. When he received his orders at the end of AIT, his worst fears were confirmed. He was going to Vietnam.

When he went to Vietnam, the family remembered that he was assigned to work on some sort of supply vehicle that traveled through the regions of Vietnam, including the Mekong Delta, delivering supplies, ammunition, and related equipment to the troops in the jungle. When writing back home to his mom, Joan said, "He mentioned about times when his vessel came under enemy attack. And we were so worried."

This kind, gentle and caring young man, who in his core was a conscientious objector, not wanting to kill or be killed, not wanting to fight but still willing to serve, was, as Beverly explained, "thrust in the middle of the very thing he wanted to avoid." And then something happened. As stated previously, no one really knows what happened. What did he do? What did he see? What did he experience? These are questions with few answers, but whatever he did, whatever he saw, or whatever he experienced resulted in psychological trauma.

When he was discharged and came home from Vietnam, "We could all tell a difference in him," Joan said. Their son and brother who left just a few months before, came back not as the same person they had known. He had episodes of aggression and anger. He couldn't hold down a job. This was not the Barry Jackson they knew. And when his aggressiveness was one time directed at his mother, Joan said, "It became obvious that he needed serious help." Help his family could not provide.

Jackson underwent numerous psychiatric evaluations, was admitted to a care home, and eventually became of conservator of the county. In the treatment to manage his behavior, Jackson was heavily medicated, maybe sometimes too medicated. As with many individuals with psychological or mental conditions, there were years of trial and error in the application and administration of the necessary medications to control his behaviors.

Jackson lived in several care facilities in the Central Valley of California, so he was close to his family and home. As Jerry said, "We were by his side every step of the way." His family visited with him often, and he, when he was able to, visited them at their homes on occasion. Eventually, Jackson died of cancer while living at the VA convalescent home in Fresno.

In 1977, about nine years after he returned from Vietnam and while he was in a facility in Angwin, California, Jackson sent the following letter to his father.

"Dearest Father, Thank you for your letter. Your words of help and understanding are well appreciated. This place is really building me up to be a stronger person but in doing so one day is as much a trial as another. Forgive me for not having written to you sooner. I just don't know if or when I'll ever get well enough again to make it on my own. These people are giving me security and understanding, but what's best is the freedom they give me to relax and try to recover. Well, that's about all I can think of to write now. Please write whenever you can. Love, Barry."

Jackson's letter was one of hope, but also one of realization about the challenges that he faced on his road to recovery.

Even during his most difficult times, his sister, Beverly, still remembered him to be a smart, intelligent brother. For example, Beverly explained, "One time, as we were walking together along the beach, Barry knew every plant and weed we came across during our walk." Information that was still stored in his brain from his days as a Marine Biology undergraduate student.

Beverly also said that even with his psychological challenges, Barry still possessed something that was more important than a sound mind and body. She said, "He kept his soul and his great faith in the Lord, always keeping his Bible near him." His body now rests in peace, and his one-time troubled and anguished mind is now living in the solitude and comfort of heaven with his Lord. Peace at last.

Jackson's name will not be found etched into the Vietnam Veterans Memorial Wall in Washington, D.C., or on any other monument dedicated to those who died in Vietnam. But maybe his name should be.

Jackson is a casualty of the war in many ways like those who suffered physical injuries or death. His mental challenges are a reminder that not all injuries suffered in a war can be seen. These unseen injuries can be just as devastating to the persons who suffered them as well as to the families who had to live in their aftermath. I'm glad that Barry is now resting in peace. He certainly deserves it.

And Jackson's family deserves peace, too. "We struggled along with him," Jerry said, as they witnessed and experienced the digression in their brother and son's psychological condition. They supported him as best they could as he was transferred from one care facility to the next. Jackson certainly suffered, and so did his family.

Bobbie Barber, classmate and friend of the PHS Vietnam veterans

After graduation from Porterville High School in 1966, Bobbie Barber said, "Vietnam was getting more and more in the news, and with family and friends in the service, I thought I could do some good. So, I enlisted in the Army." Barber further said, "I was a medic, and when I got my orders for Nam, I was ready to go. Better me than some poor guy with a family." With the war almost at its height at that time, soldiers with an MOS as a medic, as Barber had, were desperately needed on the battlefields in Vietnam. But before Barber would ship out, the Army realized it had made a mistake and rescinded Barber's orders to Vietnam.

Why were Barber's orders to Vietnam rescinded?

You see, in the Vietnam War, medics were males only. Barber is a female. When they were looking for medics and saw her name on the list, Barber explained, "They didn't see the 'Sue' part of my name, I guess." Bobbie Barber's full name is Bobbie Sue Barber.

When Barber was in high school, Vietnam was not much of a discussion around her house. Her older brother was in the Air Force and was eventually sent to Thailand. As a family, they were certainly aware of the conflict in Vietnam, but it was a subject they generally avoided discussing around the house. Barber's father was a sergeant in the Army during WWII. She remembers a discussion they had regarding draft dodgers when she said, "My dad understood the fear of being sent into combat, so he was pretty compassionate about the draft dodgers."

As she was entering her senior year in high school, the war was becoming more intense, but she and her friends tried not to worry so much about Vietnam. Barber said, "Most of the people I knew planned on staying in school and staying out of Nam." Some of Barber's friends were successful in using college deferments to avoid Vietnam, while others weren't.

After she graduated from high school, Barber went to work at the local state hospital. She eventually quit that job and then worked at a variety of jobs around Porterville. She then decided to enlist into the military.

Initially, Barber wanted to join the Marine Corps, which, ironically, is the branch of service many of her male counterparts in high school tried to avoid. As she said, "If I would have been male, I would have joined the Marines." However, the Marine Corps used Navy medics and she didn't want to enlist in the Navy. The Air Force was out since her brother was currently in that branch of the service. So, almost by process of elimination, Barber enlisted into the Army and became a medic.

Back in the late 1960s, the Women's Army Corp (WAC) was still in operation and all females in the Army were sent to Ft. McClellan, Alabama, for boot camp. Regarding her experiences in boot camp, Barber said, "It was nothing like today's Army. We didn't train with weapons but got most of the other stuff. Gas chamber, standard first aid, military etiquette." Obviously, Barber excelled in boot camp as she was awarded for her abilities. "I got my first stripe out of basic," Barber explained, "as the Outstanding Graduate." Well done!

After boot camp, Barber was sent to Ft. Sam Houston in Texas for her AIT. Since she already had a Psychiatric Nurse Technician license from her work at the state hospital in Porterville, she only stayed at Ft. Sam Houston for a few weeks, and then was sent to Ft. Ord in California that served as her duty station during her military service. She described her living conditions at Ft. Ord as "a little creepy at night." The hospital was an old WWII wooden barracks style, and all of the females were housed in the same area, with female officers in charge. She said, "It was a fairly protected environment then. If you had a problem, there was another woman to talk to."

She remembered a couple of incidents while at Ft. Ord. "I was on the drug ward," Barber said, "and at that time, the government decided that the guys coming back from Nam that had drug problems weren't going to be released to a VA near their homes even though they were near the end of their service or had already reached it." This policy made no sense, so those guys on her ward tried to talk to the administrators of the hospital, and even the VA representatives, but to no avail. In an effort to display their disagreement with the policy, those on her ward did something rather creative.

"They took over the ward and held us 'hostage,'" Barber explained. "Before they did," she said, "they asked if any of us wanted to leave and told us what and why they were doing this." And what did Barber and the other workers on her ward decide to do? "We stayed," Barber said. Barber's showing of solidarity and support for the psychologically injured soldiers was certainly a commendable one. She should have received a medal or another stripe for that, too.

Another time she described was an incident involving a new recruit. As Barber explained, "Ft. Ord was a training base and most of it was infantry. So, most of them were headed for Nam." She said one day, "A guy on our ward got a hold of a gun and threatened to shoot himself, or any of us that tried to stop him." The new recruit was scared thinking about what he was going to face in Vietnam. He felt that since he was probably going to get killed in Vietnam, he might as well die in the ward at Ft. Ord. Die here or die there. Those were the only two choices this scared recruit felt he had in front of him.

"One of us managed to sneak off the ward while the rest of us kept him busy and called the MPs. He surrendered peacefully when they showed up," Barber said. She further explained that the recruit who threatened to kill himself was eventually medically discharged.

Barber was not only an outstanding graduate at boot camp, but she was also an outstanding GI in her service in support to the soldiers. Barber was discharged from the service in 1975, and after a short time back in Porterville, she transferred to the University of Arkansas to be near her parents who had retired there.

When looking back on the years since the Vietnam War, Barber remembers two things that stand out in her memory - drugs, and how the veterans were treated when they came home from Vietnam. "Drugs were everywhere," she said, "and I think one of the reasons there were so many drugs was because of the treatment received by the guys when they came home." She further explained, "People saw what they went through over there and still treated them like shit instead of giving them the resources and respect they needed to get through it. And by their own government."

Commenting more on the impact of the war, Barber said, "My mother's best friend lost her son to friendly fire. Medics that I met at Ft. Ord never came home from the war. It affected a whole generation in so many ways. And I hope to whoever you want, you never have to go through it."

I hope not either.

Steve Cha, admirer of all American Vietnam veterans

The final story in this chapter does not come from a personal friend of a Vietnam veteran. It does not come from a family member of one of the veterans either. Actually, this final story is more than just a story. It is a statement of appreciation from someone whose family experienced the Vietnam War up-close and personal. And this person not only considers the Vietnam veterans to be his friends, he considers them his heroes.

Steve Cha's grandfather fled Laos with his family during the Vietnam War. When he did so, he certainly would not have envisioned that a grandson of his would someday enlist in the United States Marine Corps. But he did.

The Cha family came to the United States as refugees, fleeing the communist influence in Laos and Southeast Asia so they could enjoy the freedoms of America. The family first stopped in Hawaii and then to Southern California where they began working in the farming industry. Although they remained in the Central Valley of California, the family moved around a lot working in the fields, orchards, and packing houses. Eventually, the Cha family started their own farm in Lindsay, growing oranges and olives.

Cha was born and raised in Lindsay, in addition to his two brothers and two sisters. After graduation from Lindsay High School, Cha enlisted in the Marine Corps. He completed his boot camp in San Diego, advanced training at Camp Pendleton, and then went to the Marine Corps Air Station in New River, North Carolina where he was trained as an electrician on the V22 Osprey helicopter. The Osprey is the helicopter that transitions from a helicopter to the airplane mode while in flight. A technological marvel.

After he completed his training, Cha was assigned to remain at the Air Station working on the Osprey helicopters. As Cha said, "I would have preferred to be deployed to another country so I could experience all that the military had to offer." But the Marine Corps wanted him there in North Carolina, and that's where he stayed.

Upon his discharge, Cha came back to Lindsay and eventually enrolled at Porterville College to work on his Associate degree. In the fall semester of 2014, the VRC at Porterville College officially opened its doors to its veterans on campus. One day during that semester, Roland Hill, a Vietnam veteran and, at that time, a member of the campus Veterans Advisory Council, came into the VRC to speak with me. During our conversation, Cha came into the center, too. Knowing that both Hill and Cha worked on helicopters, I introduced them to each other. When I told Cha that Hill was a Vietnam veteran, Cha put down his books, stuck his arm out to shake Hill's hand and said, "I honor you!"

Hill looked stunned. No one before had ever said such a thing to him about his service in Vietnam. Cha mentioned, "Because of the American veterans, I am where I am today." And he said that he owed so much to the American veterans. Hill left the center still pondering the unexpected words of thanks.

When I was in the process of writing this book, I remembered that brief conversation between Hill and Cha, so I contacted Cha to see if he would agree to meet with me and tell me further about his personal story. Since Cha's story is one of appreciation from someone whose family was embroiled in the conflict in Vietnam and Southeast Asia years ago, I wanted to conclude this chapter with Cha's words of appreciation.

There is no narrative or summary below about our conversation. These are simply direct quotes from Cha during my conversation with him as he remembered the American Vietnam veterans:

"The Americans came across the world to fight for freedom and democracy, and that inspired me to join the Marine Corps."

"All Vietnam veterans are my heroes."

"I have so much respect for them."

"They did something they may not have wanted to do, but they did it because their country told them to. They were certainly dedicated."

"They stood up to defend other countries from communist rule, and we should be thankful to them for that."

"They inspired me."

"I enlisted in the Marine Corps as a way to honor the American Vietnam War veterans."

"I would not be where I am today without the American veterans."

And, finally, I asked Cha if I could get all the American Vietnam veterans in the room right now, what final words would he say to them? Without any hesitation whatsoever, Cha emphatically said:

"THANK YOU!"

When we remember on Memorial Day those who have fallen during their military service, or when we remember on Veterans Day all those who previously served in the military, or when we think of those on Armed Forces day who are currently serving around the world, we must not forget the families and friends who, in essence, served right along with them.

The fathers, mothers, brothers, sisters, sons, daughters and other relatives of the Vietnam War veterans were often impacted by their service, too. The family members struggle through the loss, through the medical appointments, through their rehabilitation, and through the various challenges these veterans face because of what they experienced during the war.

In addition to the family members, their friends are impacted, too. Friends lost friends in the war. Some of the buddies they played with in elementary school or partied with in high school, lost their lives in Vietnam. Or, the friend that they remembered during high school is not really the same friend anymore. Combat has changed him. Combat has hardened him. Combat has affected him. So, friends need to be part of the recovery as well. They, too, oftentimes need support and understanding.

The ripple affect from a death or a psychological injury due to a horrendous experience touches the lives of many, not just the veterans, and not just for a moment, but often for a lifetime.

Vietnam War and Wall Facts

Civilians on the Wall [1]

Although there were American civilians working for the government who were killed in Vietnam during the war, there are no civilians listed on the Vietnam Veterans Memorial Wall in Washington, D.C.

The wall is dedicated solely to military personnel who lost their lives in Vietnam.

19

Lessons of Vietnam from Those Who Were There

"Above all, Vietnam was a war that asked everything of a few and nothing of most in America."

Myra MacPherson

AT THE END of their interviews, the veterans were asked what they would have done differently if they were the president, defense secretary, or the general in charge of the war. They were asked to express their feelings about the war, the country, or the aftermath. Their comments are summarized below into various "lessons" we could learn from their experiences in the Vietnam War.

As a point of comparison, it was interesting to read the book, *"In Retrospect: The Tragedy and Lessons of Vietnam,"* by former Defense Secretary, Robert S. McNamara. Secretary McNamara was known as the "architect of the Vietnam War" and in his book he did sort of a mea culpa, but never really said he was sorry for his and the administration's failures in Vietnam. He admitted, "We of the Kennedy and Johnson administrations who participated in the decisions on Vietnam acted according to what we thought were the principles and

330

traditions of this nation. We made our decisions in light of those values. Yet we were wrong, terribly wrong."[1]

Yes, Secretary McNamara, you were wrong, but were you sorry too?

In addition to a historical review of the circumstances surrounding the decisions they made during the war, he also provides a listing of the major causes for what went wrong in Vietnam. If you read his book and compare what these veterans said to what McNamara said, you will see that the veterans from Porterville High School knew almost as much about the causes of what went wrong in Vietnam as McNamara did.

He should have listened to them.

PHS Lesson #1:

We should have never gotten involved in Vietnam.

"I wouldn't have done it. It was their place. There was no way we could really defeat them." Robert Johnson

"We shouldn't have been there in the first place." Louis Gurrola

"We shouldn't have gotten involved in a land war in Asia." Todd Pixler

"I never really understood why we were there." Melvin Braziel

"We shouldn't have been there." Vince Arcure

"We couldn't change things there." Ron McCarville

"...a very questionable war." Brian Rattigan

"We never should have gone." Geary Baxter

"It was a senseless war and all for nothing." Greg Goble

It was a universal feeling among the veterans that we should never have been in Vietnam in the first place. Some still ask the question, "Why were we there?" Sure, the purpose for our involvement centered around the domino theory, but the domino theory became muddled later as the war dragged on with no outcome in sight. The North Vietnamese eventually took over the country shortly after we left. Regardless of the reason we were there, the veterans generally felt the purpose of our being there was not worth the end result.

PHS Lesson #2

Our politicians should have gotten out of the way of the generals.

"Keep politicians out of it and let the generals do their thing." Russell Vossler

"Let the generals run the war. Keep politicians away." Joe Souza

"There was too much politics in the war." Chuck Migalski

"McNamara lied his ass off." Joe Souza

"Those responsible for the Vietnam debacle have in no way been held accountable." Brian Rattigan

"They tried to run the war from Washington D.C." Richard Walker

"The politicians put too many boundaries on us. We could only do so much." John Alba

"The military didn't lose, the politicians did." Don Dowling

"There was too much politics in the war." Alfred Alba

"Our government set us up to fail. Too many rules that should not have applied during a war." Greg Goble

Too often, the decisions about the prosecution of the war were made by politicians or policy makers far away from the battlefields. With that, war decisions were often affected too much by politics or world events happening on the other side of the world.

Without a doubt, the overwhelming feeling among the veterans was that the further away the politicians are from the battlefield, the better. The more you can keep politics out of the decisions on the field the better for those who are fighting in it. Therefore, the responsibility for making the decisions regarding the war should rest on the shoulders of the generals, not on some elected official in Washington D.C.

In addition, the veterans felt that if there is no clear objective, or no clear feeling the war can be won, then stay out of it. Some of the veterans expressed their opinions about how the Americans were often not told the truth by our government and were often not informed about the progress of the war and what it was going to take to win it.

PHS Lesson #3:

Since we were in a war, we should have been there to win, not lose or tie.

"We should go in and kick ass." Chuck Migalski

"There were too many rules that restricted us. Sometimes you had to ask for permission to shoot back." Greg Goble

"Whatever we took, we should have kept it." Todd Pixler

"If we take a hill, keep it. Don't give it back to the North Vietnamese by leaving it." Roger Gibson

"Fight to win and get out as soon as possible. We didn't lose any major battles. We pulled out." Richard Walker

"We could have won the war much earlier if they didn't put so many restrictions on us." John Alba

"We should have used more air power and less on the ground." Ron Crabtree

"We fought a war of attrition that never worked. We could have ended the war early by invading North Vietnam and dropping into Hanoi." Don Dowling

"We should have finished them off." Alfred Alba

"We should have bombed the hell out of them even more." Felix Hernandez

The veterans were clear in their feelings that our country should never go into a war unless we go in to win. Not to tie, not to lose, or not to withdraw until the war has been won or our objectives have been met. And, if we are in it to win it, we should give our military personnel all the tools necessary to do just that.

If territory is won, then keep it. Too often during the Vietnam War, hills that were won by the Americans were eventually taken back by the North Vietnamese when the Americans pulled out of the area. What was the point of fighting, being injured, and dying for territory if we eventually gave it back anyway?

PHS Lesson #4:

We shouldn't fight for someone who doesn't want us there.

"The people wanted to be left alone." Vince Arcure

"The Vietnamese people I met didn't want us there." Russell Vossler

"The people we were fighting for didn't even like us. The South Vietnamese seemed to dislike us almost as much as they disliked the North Vietnamese." Melvin Braziel

"The Vietnamese didn't even want us there. Why fight for them?" Louis Gurrola

"Those poor Vietnamese were victims. They were just trying to survive." Geary Baxter

If the purpose of the war was to save the South Vietnamese from communism, you would have thought the South Vietnamese people would welcome the American soldiers with open arms. But they didn't, at least not universally.

They saw their people killed in the war, too, and their land was ravished by bulldozers, bombs, defoliants and Agent Orange. This destruction helped to exasperate their dislike for Americans or soldiers from any other country that might have been fighting in the war. They wanted to live their lives, grow their rice, and basically be left alone. But being left alone was an impossibility.

PHS Lesson #5:

Our country should know and learn from the history of the country it is considering fighting for or against.

> "We should have learned from history before we committed ourselves. France got their asses kicked in Vietnam. Couldn't we see that coming?" Todd Pixler

When considering our involvement in future wars, our country should always consider the history of the country that we will fight against, and how the chance for victory can be affected by that history. Prior to our combat involvement in Vietnam, many politicians in America, France, and other countries, were warning about the possibility of a quagmire that the United States may find itself in if it commits to a war in Vietnam.

The French had spent years fighting in Vietnam and were eventually driven out of the country. What happened to France was a lesson we should have learned from.

PHS Lesson #6:

Our country should welcome its returning GIs home regardless of its feelings about the war.

> "It (the protesting) was sick." Russell Vossler

> "If I could have, I would have done something to those hippies." Roger Gibson

> "They didn't know what they were doing. They were just caught up in the moment." Robert Johnson

> "We fought for these people (the protesters) and we are getting treated by them like this?" John Alba

335

"Bastards" (describing the protesters). Chuck Migalski

"I was never spit on. I would be in jail if I was." Greg Goble

If there was anything that pissed off the returning Vietnam veterans, it was the reception they received when their plane landed back home. Most landed in Oakland or Travis Air Force Base. Regardless of where they landed, the reception was often the same. Assembled to welcome them back was a group of angry protesters, hollering expletives at them, calling them baby killers, or holding signs disparaging them specifically or the war in general.

Most of the protesters were young hippies who hadn't shaved in a year, gotten a haircut in two years, or taken a bath in a few months, if any. Luckily for the protesters, they were often sectioned off in an area of the airport away from physical contact with the returning Vietnam veterans, and the veterans were ordered not to say or do anything. If they would have had the opportunity, or the permission, I'm sure the veterans would certainly have taught those hippies a lesson or two. A couple of the veterans said they'd do something rather graphic if given the chance, but not for print here. And I wouldn't have blamed them.

Certainly, our constitution allows for freedom of speech. However, in the case of the Vietnam War, much of the protesting in the latter part of the war was misguided. Protest the government or the war all you want, but don't protest against or blame those who fought in it. Never again should we welcome home our returning war veterans with such disdain as they felt from the protesters in the airports.

PHS Lesson #7:

Our country should provide adequate support for veterans and better inform them of the services available.

"A lot of guys lost their minds, but not their lives. And they needed help." Roger Gibson

"He did not receive adequate VA services." The Barry Jackson family said of their brother.

"I didn't know what VA services were available to me when I got out. No one told me." Jim Rouch

"At first, the VA kept losing things and cancelling appointments." Ron McCarville

"Dealing with the Veterans Benefits Administration during the disability process fostered justifiable frustration and anger." Brian Rattigan

Our country sent these men to fight in the war. Most didn't choose to be there. One of the travesties of the Vietnam War was the lack of quality support our country provided our veterans when they returned home from Vietnam. It is our country's responsibility to support our veterans by providing them with the necessary physical, psychological or vocational services they may need.

What I also found interesting during the interviews, was the lack of knowledge many of these veterans had regarding the services that were available to them when they first returned from Vietnam. But this lack of understanding was generally no fault of their own. The VA rarely reached out to them to inform them of the services available. So, some did not begin receiving services until 20, 25, or 30 years after the war. Services they should have received soon after they returned from Vietnam.

Like what was shown through the protesters and the indifference of many of its citizens at that time, our country should never again turn its back on our veterans regardless of the popularity of the war they may have fought in. It appears, however, that this attitude has changed in our country. Finally.

PHS Lesson #8

Consider changes to the previous draft or current volunteer military.

"The politicians who vote to send us to war should be required to go themselves." Russell Vossler

"Perhaps, when a greater portion of society is obligated to serve our country, we will be less prone to casually commit military force..." Brian Rattigan

"Our country should have kept the draft going." Dan Boydstun

Vossler and Rattigan both offer interesting ideas to consider regarding the draft, compulsory service, and committing our country to war, while Boydstun feels the draft should have continued so that everyone could be subject to a draft. One of the intended consequences within their ideas is the feeling that politicians will not be so quick to send our young men and women to war if there is the potential they, or their children, will be sent there as well.

Rattigan also expressed the feeling that the draft during the Vietnam War was inherently unfair due to the variety of deferments that were available to those who wanted to avoid military service. In his opinion, Rattigan said, "The plethora of deferments resulted in only a small segment of draft age young men unfairly bearing the burden of military service." In order for a draft to be equitable and fair, his feeling is that our country should adopt a compulsory service in which all young men and women would be required to serve two years of military or civilian service. "If this were the situation," Rattigan said, "the general public would have a more realistic understanding of the responsibilities and costs of pursuing our nation's proffered interests at home and abroad."

In addition to making the draft more equitable, Rattigan also feels that if our country had across-the-board compulsory service without deferments during the Vietnam War, things would have been much different. He explained, "An across-the-board draft may well have limited the Vietnam War in both its intensity and duration. Simply put, the more influential elements of society most likely would not have tolerated their sons being drafted and sent off to Vietnam."

As he further explained how compulsory service would have changed the Vietnam War, Rattigan said, "Once the bodies of the sons of the more privileged began being returned to their families, the outcry against the war would have been much more intense and effective."

Our country's current and future policy makers should listen to these veterans from Porterville High School. And, like him or not, they should also listen to Defense Secretary McNamara.

McNamara's book may have come too many years too late for some, but at least it came. In his book, he did not say he was sorry or ask for forgiveness for some of the decisions that were made or lies that were told, which he should have. However, even though he may at times be passing the buck to others, he does provide a detailed account in his book of what went wrong in Vietnam, regardless of who should take the blame or not.

We too often repeat our problems when we do not learn from our past. So, we should learn from McNamara and the mistakes he made, as well as from the Porterville High School veterans who were there and were affected in one way or another because of those mistakes. If we do not listen to them, if we do not heed their advice, if we choose to ignore their input, we will be doing a disservice to the future GIs of our country who may someday find themselves in the middle of their generation's war.

I wonder what the impact of Vossler and Rattigan's ideas would have had on the Vietnam War and our country in general. Maybe there wouldn't be over 58,000 names on the wall in Washington D.C. Maybe there wouldn't be 28 names on the Hillcrest memorial or 40 names on the memorial at Veterans Park in Porterville.

And maybe there wouldn't be a need for me to write this book.

Vietnam War and Wall Facts

Still Unaccounted For [2]

As of July 29, 2019, there are still 1,587 American GIs that remain unaccounted for in Vietnam.

20

The War Never Ends

TO MANY, THE official end of the Vietnam War was April 30, 1975 when Saigon, the capital city of South Vietnam, fell to the North Vietnamese. But for many of the veterans from Porterville High School who fought in Vietnam, the war has never really ended for them. Or, at least, if it did end, it ended many years after 1975.

Roger Gibson said something most appropriate when remembering the aftermath of the war and those who fought in it. He said, "Everyone that comes home from combat needs help." He recommended that every combat veteran immediately go to the VA after their return from war to be evaluated and provided with necessary services. "They need those services," Gibson said, "and they certainly deserve them."

We must always remember and understand that most of those from Porterville High School who served in Vietnam were teenagers when they entered the military. They were young men, or older boys. They were anxious, scared, fearful, or apprehensive. Before being drafted or enlisting in the military, their lives were relatively stress free, concerned only with partying, chasing girls, and cruising Main Street. But then, within only a few months after graduation from high school, some were being shot at on the battlefields of Vietnam.

Before they could legally buy beer or vote in the upcoming election, they were making life and death decisions on a battlefield in a country eight thousand miles from home, shooting at an invisible enemy while lying in elephant grass, wading through insect-infested marshes and rivers, or dodging bullets fired from snipers in the trees. They experienced horrendous things. They saw their friends die right next to them. They loaded body bags that covered their friends onto helicopters or trucks. They saw what a booby trap could do to an unsuspecting soldier who happened to trip the wire. It was awful.

Like McCarville said, "How can you not be affected by that?"

But Gibson was also right. Everyone who experienced what these Porterville High School graduates experienced in Vietnam should at least investigate the services that are available to them. Luckily, most of these veterans who were interviewed for this book have utilized VA services, while some have been receiving services for decades.

Russell Vossler

Did the war really end for Russell Vossler when his plane from Vietnam landed back home?

Vossler's brother-in-law picked him up at the airport when he flew back from Vietnam and took him to their home to spend his first night in the United States on their couch. This couch was a thousand times more comfortable than a cot in Vietnam. Vossler said, "When I got to my sister's house, I couldn't believe it." He said, being back in the states "was better than Christmas or anything I could imagine."

He looked forward to his first night back home in the United States knowing that he could now sleep with no fear of mortars, no battles, and no worries about the threat of death. But then sometime happened during the middle of the night.

Vossler's sister woke him up. "She told me that I was screaming in my sleep," Vossler said.

This nightmare, on his very first night back in the world, was an indication of what was yet to come. Yes, he was not physically in Vietnam anymore, but he was still there in his mind. The actual war in Vietnam was over for Vossler but the war in his mind was not over, not by a long shot. The doctors didn't have a common name for it yet back then, but this nightmare was the first indication that Vossler had PTSD. He was fine for now, but the effects of PTSD would later become almost unbearable.

Vossler said, "When I got home from Vietnam, I felt like a mess." But in those days, Vossler said, "No one talked much about Vietnam, so I kept what I experienced mostly to myself." Everyone tried to move on. But talking is exactly what veterans need who have been through such a horrendous experience; however, after the war was over, the subject was generally avoided.

After serving his remaining time in the Army at Ft. Sill, Oklahoma, Vossler was discharged in 1971. He came back home and started working in a variety of jobs around the Porterville area. At one point, he served as a police officer with the Porterville Police Department. "I enjoyed being a police officer," Vossler said, "but the realities of the job became too much for me. I couldn't leave work at the station and often brought work home with me." He became obsessed with the job to the point that it, and his PTSD, affected his first marriage, which ended in divorce.

He resigned from the police force and then went back to work at the ranch. "I was short-tempered with my dad," Vossler said, "and we often got into arguments." Although the signals of his involvement with PTSD were noticeable, they were not as pronounced as they would later become. Soon, PTSD began to roar its ugly head in ways no one could have anticipated. "Sometimes in my nightmares," he said, "I thought I was fighting the Vietnamese in downtown Porterville."

In 1990, the first Gulf War began. The buildup of troops, equipment, and endless commentary consumed the news channels on television. President Bush, General Schwarzkopf, Saddam Hussein, video images on guided missiles, the liberation of Kuwait. It made for fascinating television. Vossler said, "I watched the war on television every night. I followed the war closely. And it was then that my PTSD began to flare up."

His agitation grew. His sleepless nights increased. Flashbacks brought the Vietnam War back into his living room. "Arguing became rather common in conversations I had with my family and friends," Vossler said, "and my behaviors were affecting my second marriage." He needed help, and he knew it.

After evaluation at the Veterans Administration (VA) hospital in Fresno and receiving some PTSD-related services, "I was not improving as I had hoped," Vossler said. The symptoms were still there and, in some ways, getting worse. "At one point," he said, "I even thought about suicide, but I never attempted it." However, he admitted, "It scared me to know that I even thought about it."

He needed something else. He asked for, and eventually, was referred to the National Center for PTSD. Vossler said that the center "saved his ass and his marriage." He was not cured by any means, but he was doing better.

He improved enough to realize that others could benefit from his experiences. "I went to the veteran's center in Tulare to see how I might be able to help fellow veterans dealing with PTSD," Vossler said. He got involved in the vet-to-vet peer support program, receiving his certification as a specialist. "I then began to conduct PTSD groups for combat veterans," he said.

As he explained, "The national PTSD center saved my ass, but my work at the Tulare center changed my life." Through his work as a PTSD specialist, he could see that he was making an impact in the lives of many who were suffering as he had. He felt fulfilled. He felt useful. And he was.

Although Vossler's involvement in the Vietnam War ended 50

years ago, the war may never be over for him. He still struggles. He still needs assistance. But he will succeed, too. I have no doubts. Vossler is one of the thousands upon thousands of Vietnam War veterans who are struggling with PTSD, in addition to other physical challenges because of their experiences in that terrible war. For Vossler, and the thousands who are struggling like him, their war has never really ended. But I pray for a time that it does.

Robert Johnson

Robert Johnson was very upfront and direct about his condition when he returned from Vietnam when he said, "I was pretty messed up when I came back." A very honest assessment of his condition, but one that is not too surprising. After all, he had spent months in the jungles of Vietnam humping the bushes while fighting in horrendous combat situations and crawling into tunnels as a tunnel rat not knowing if death was staring him in the face as he entered the hole. He saw death and destruction up-close and was injured not once, but twice in the process.

Who wouldn't be messed up after experiences like that?

As Johnson said, "When I returned home, I had the classic symptoms of PTSD." He couldn't sleep, nightmares and flashbacks interrupted his sleep, and he was aggressive at times with others. "Relationships were hard for me," Johnson said, and he was unable to resurrect a relationship with a girlfriend who had written him every day for two-and-a-half years. He just couldn't see her when he got back home.

Due to the symptoms of his PTSD, Johnson was unable to maintain steady employment. "I went through a lot of jobs," Johnson said, "and I couldn't hold one down for very long." He explained, "As soon as a supervisor told me what to do, and I didn't feel like the order made any sense, I'd tell him to f_ _k off." Not exactly the kind of reaction a supervisor would want to receive from one of his or her subordinates.

To compensate for the symptoms he was experiencing, Johnson resorted to the same self-medications that others who suffer from PTSD sometimes do. "I was doing drugs and drinking alcohol a lot," Johnson admitted. He was struggling both physically and psychologically. After years of struggling with PTSD, Johnson finally realized he needed help, and began to see a therapist which helped him tremendously. He was making progress. The symptoms of his PTSD were becoming more controllable and he was able to better manage his feelings and emotions. But then he found out he had another battle to face.

Johnson said, "I was diagnosed with cancer."

After many tests and evaluations, he explained, "It was determined that my cancer was a result of my exposure to Agent Orange while in Vietnam." Agent Orange was a defoliant that was sprayed on Vietnamese jungles to strip the trees bare and expose the enemy who used the jungle foliage as cover or places to hide. It got its name from the orange stripe that was on the drums in which it was stored.

During the use of Agent Orange, American authorities and chemical company executives insisted there was nothing to worry about in terms of the effects of these chemicals on the health of those who came in contact with it. These assurances, however, were later proven to be false as researchers found evidence of health issues and birth defects in laboratory animals. Eventually, more and more scientists began to speak out and oppose the use of Agent Orange. The use of it was stopped in 1970, but the spraying of other chemicals continued until the entire herbicide program was terminated a year later.[1]

The VA now officially links various health-related issues, diseases, and cancers due to exposure to Agent Orange. Johnson is one of many veterans who have been affected by this exposure and, sometimes, the veteran may not suffer from any illness, but his offspring could. A couple of the veterans interviewed for this book indicated their suspicions about illnesses that have been found in their children and grandchildren. They believe there is probably a link between their family health issues and the veteran's exposure to Agent Orange.

To battle this cancer, Johnson said, "I had a stem cell transplant two years ago and now I'm being monitored and treated at the Cancer Center in Porterville." Johnson's recovery from the war and his illnesses and injuries continues.

Ron McCarville

As he thought back to when he left Vietnam, Ron McCarville said, "I remembered the flight home was not fast enough." He always wanted to be a Marine, and he followed his goal in life all the way to the jungles of Vietnam. But now, he was ready to go home.

McCarville didn't really have much time to debrief from the horrors of war to the peace of being back home in Porterville. He said, "It was only a little over a week after my last time in combat to when I was flying out of Vietnam going home." And when he got home, he found out that he might have left the war, but the war had not really left him.

He was different when he got home as compared to when he first left for Vietnam. The war had certainly affected him. McCarville said when dealing with people, "Sometimes, I'd just blow up and go off on people." He described his sleepless nights, and how he had nightmares, profound and extreme nightmares. "I'd try to sleep, and I couldn't breathe," he said. "A lot of times I'd sweat so much during my nightmares that I could wring the sweat out of my shirt."

He needed help, but he didn't receive any assistance from the VA for about 25-30 years after he came home from the war in Vietnam. "One day," he said, "I saw an ad in the paper about a PTSD group in Visalia and I made an appointment." Finally, he began receiving services from the VA that he so desperately needed. But the medical effects of the war did not end with his PTSD.

McCarville had a heart attack. And the doctors eventually established a link between the heart attack and his exposure to Agent Orange while in Vietnam. McCarville's war goes on.

Ron Crabtree

Ron Crabtree's war has never really ended for him either. Because of the war, he now lives with PTSD, heart disease, hearing loss, and diabetes. Even with these challenges that are a result of his service in Vietnam, Crabtree still maintains an infectious sense of humor and a positive disposition about life in general.

When Crabtree's time was up in Vietnam, he was given an offer to stay an additional 28 days. By doing so, he could then be discharged from the service while in Vietnam at the end of those 28 days. Otherwise, he would have to go back to the states to serve out his remaining six months in the military. Crabtree told them, "I'll take the six months."

He was ready to come home. Crabtree said, "When I got on the plane to leave Vietnam, it was like I had a huge sigh of relief. I was so happy to leave." He left alive, but he wasn't so sure about his friends. The war has been over for over 50 years and Crabtree still thinks of them.

Looking back on his years in Vietnam, Crabtree said, "I wouldn't do it again, but I wouldn't trade it, either." He then got emotional when talking about the guys he served with. He said this about his fellow soldiers, "We went through hell together. And I was so lucky when so many others weren't." In addition to those who were killed, Crabtree had friends who were injured, or who were still in Vietnam when he left. Of those, Crabtree said, "I never saw them again. I never heard from them again. And I'm not sure if they ever made it out. I'll never forget them."

He started crying. And I almost did, too.

Think about it. Has the Vietnam War really ended for the veterans from Porterville High School?

Did the war really end for Robert Johnson while he has spent years undergoing therapy and counseling sessions trying to deal with his PTSD? Or did the war really end for him when he found out that he has cancer due to his exposure to Agent Orange while in Vietnam?

Did the war really end for Russell Vossler as he continues to deal with the profound effects of PTSD that has affected not only his life, but the life of his wife and children?

Did the war really end for Todd Pixler when he still avoids bumps or objects in the road for fear they may be landmines planted in the ground? Or did the war really end for him when, at the sound of a helicopter flying overhead, he goes to his window to look outside to make sure everything is okay?

Did the war really end for Roland Hill as he struggled with PTSD issues years after the war? Did the war really end for him when he still recalls the disrespect he found from city and college officials in their lack of support for the returning Vietnam veterans? Did the war really end for him when he can't shake the memory of seeing two helicopters collide resulting in the death of their crews?

Did the war really end for Roger Gibson as he struggled with nightmares, readjustment issues and PTSD to the point where some friends, he said, didn't like him anymore? And did the war really end for Gibson as he continues to deal with health issues resulting from his exposure to Agent Orange?

Did the war really end for Vince Arcure when he suffered wounds from battle which were serious enough that resulted in an early discharge, and later found himself receiving VA assistance to help in dealing with PTSD and the physical recovery from his injury?

Did the war really end for Joe Souza when he had to spend months in the hospital dealing with a shattered jaw from a bullet, serious enough to be medically discharged, while remembering friends who he watched being killed in a helicopter accident? Or spending the next several years after the war dealing with PTSD-related issues? Or did the war really end for him when, even today, 50 years later, he still expresses vivid animosity toward Defense Secretary Robert McNamara and Jane Fonda?

Did the war really end for Melvin Braziel when he still feels a sense of guilt for getting a hardship discharge only 70 days into his tour in Vietnam while his friends were still fighting, dying, or being injured in the war that he left behind?

Did the war really end for Louis Gurrola when he still remembers his friends who came back from the war "pretty messed up" and, especially, his one friend who came back from Vietnam with psychological challenges and was killed while driving erratically on a motorcycle?

Did the war really end for Steve Durtsche, not a veteran but the best friend of Pat Higgins who was killed in Vietnam, while he still remembers his friend and continues to feel deep and profound sadness for his loss?

Did the war really end for Diane Johnson (fictitious name), not a veteran but a friend of a veteran who was experiencing flashbacks in her apartment to the point she was scared and afraid? Did the war end for her as she still thinks back with sadness about her classmates and their families who were devastated by the war?

Did the war really end for the family of Barry Jackson whose life was spent in care homes due to his mental challenges he developed while in Vietnam? His life is over now, but his family continues to live with the painful memory of how Barry's war experiences affected his life, and theirs. Has the war ended for them?

Did the war really end for Brian Rattigan when he was diagnosed with PTSD and has, as he explained, some residual low-grade survivor's guilt? Or has the war ended for him as he still has lingering anger that those responsible for the debacle in Vietnam have not been properly held accountable, and anger at the fact that after his discharge more and more GIs were needlessly killed and wounded?

Did the war really end for Chuck Migalski as he continues to receive medical attention for the physical injuries he received that resulted in three Purple Hearts and the continuing emotional effects of PTSD? Has the war ended for him when he thinks daily of his two best friends that were killed in Vietnam?

Did the war really end for Greg Goble when his wife and son found him one day talking in Vietnamese while walking out of the house? Or did the war end for him when he still does not wear anything camouflage as soldiers wear or clothing that advertises he was in Vietnam?

Did the war really end for Greg Goble's wife, Susie, or their son, Lance, who, decades after the war was over, watched their husband and father having a flashback and not knowing what to do?

Did the war really end for Ron McCarville who has suffered from PTSD since his tour in Vietnam and when he suffered a heart attack because of his exposure to Agent Orange? Has the war ended for him as he still remembers with profound emotions his fellow GIs who lost their lives in the battles he survived?

Did the war really end for Cheryl McCarville as she has spent every day for the last 50 years dealing in some way with the effects of PTSD that her husband has struggled with?

Did the war really end for Jim Rouch as he continues to receive services for his PTSD and still has a hard time getting close to anyone? Did the war really end for him as he still remembers the death and destruction at Khe Sanh and watching two planes that crashed killing all the crews on board and he could do nothing to help?

Did the war really end for Don Wolfram when he thinks back to when he saw his mom and dad again for the first time after returning from Vietnam, and he couldn't describe the feeling in words, but rather through a quivering chin and teared up eyes?

Did the war really end for Reba Wolfram as she can, after 91 years of life, still vividly remember the day her son left for Vietnam and how scared she was for her son, and how she relied on her faith in God to pull her through the fear and sadness?

Did the war really end for John Schultz as he remembers missing the last days of his father's life because he was on a ship in the middle of an ocean when his dad died? And the fear of almost losing his life as they struggled to pull him from the ship during a violent storm so he could fly home for his father's funeral, a funeral that he almost missed.

Did the war really end for Richard Walker as he still vividly re-members with profound emotions the first time he saw the human equation of the war while seeing a friend die on a table due to serious burns from an attack, and how that attack changed his perspective on feeling sorry for the Vietnamese people?

Did the war really end for Geary Baxter as he remembers having to often maneuver his helicopter when he was landing onto a hot LZ around dead American GIs that were being extracted from a battle? Or did the war end for him as he still remembers the almost helpless feeling he had when he dropped off troops into an area where they might be killed or injured?

Did the war really end for Tony Forner as he still remembers in detail the death and destruction that he witnessed during some of the most horrendous battles he was involved in during the Vietnam War? Or when he can still smell the smell of death over 50 years later? Or did it end for him when he has struggled with the inadequacies of the VA in trying to get assistance for his PTSD and hearing loss?

Did the war really end for John Alba as he still remembers the sight of when his medic died from a white phosphorous RPG and they couldn't extinguish the fire? Or when he still feels the guilt for not being able to tell a dead soldier's mother that her son died while subbing for him when he was recuperating from an injury back on base?

Did the war really end for Ron Crabtree as he still wonders with emotion what happened to the soldiers he served with, whether they lived or died? Or has the war ended for him when he not only suffers from PTSD, but also hearing loss from exposure to deafening sounds, and diabetes and heart disease from his exposure to Agent Orange?

Did the war really end for Don Dowling when he spent not one tour in Vietnam but three-and-a-half tours during his 23-year career in the Army, being involved in a multitude of horrendous experiences while in Special Forces and now living with PTSD and physical ailments resulting from his exposure to Agent Orange? Or did the war end for him as he can still remember with emotion the disrespect he received from his fellow veterans at the VFW?

Did the war really end for Felix Hernandez when he still thinks about Vietnam every day? Sometimes his thoughts are good, sometimes they are bad. Did it end for him when he brought home serious anger issues and struggled with the effects of PTSD?

Did the war really end for Dan Boydstun as he still remembers the endless number of caskets he processed knowing there was a body inside? Or did the war end for him as he later learned that his diabetes is a result of his exposure to Agent Orange?

Did the war really end for Alfred Alba as he lives today with diabetes because of his exposure to Agent Orange while in Vietnam and the lingering memory of so many injured or dead soldiers he transported from the battlefield back to the base, often under enemy fire?

Did the war really end for Bobbie Sue Barber as she still recalls with emotion the disrespect so many of the Vietnam veterans were met with when they returned home from the war?

Did the war really end for the families and friends of the two Vietnam veterans from Porterville High School who committed suicide?

Did the war really end for the veterans who declined to be interviewed for this book because they still can't talk about their experiences in Vietnam that happened over 50 years ago?

Did the war really end for the families of those 40 men whose names are engraved on the Vietnam Veterans Memorial at Veterans Park? Those families continue to live today with the sadness of their loss, and also with confusion, disillusionment, and anger about the war in which their children died.

Did the war really end for the city of Porterville who lost so many of her sons in that terrible war in Vietnam?

So, has the war really ended?

For some of the Vietnam War veterans from Porterville High School and their families and friends the war has ended, but for others, their war continues. For those who are still marching through their personal hells 50 years after their service during the war, I hope and pray that their war ends sometime soon.

They certainly deserve peace.

Vietnam War and Wall Facts

Medals of Honor to Non-combat Personnel [2]

Two U.S. Army chaplains, Charlie Watters and Angelo Liteky were awarded the Congressional Medal of Honor.

Corporal William T. Perkins was a Marine Corps combat photographer. He is the only military photographer to be awarded the Medal of Honor. He was killed in action on October 12, 1967.

Corporal Thomas W. Bennett was an Army medic and was the only conscientious objector to be awarded the Medal of Honor during the Vietnam war. He was killed in action on February 11, 1969.

21

Where Are They Now?

"It's the soldier, not the poet, who has given us freedom of speech."

Zell Miller

Alfred Alba

Alfred Alba today - 2019

Alfred Alba did not have much transition time from flying his medevac helicopter picking up dead and wounded soldiers to flying home to the states. He had about one day. Prior to his last mission, Alba was told, "Today's your last day." He said he didn't get too excited about the news because, "We still had a mission to fly." When Alba came back from the mission, he packed up the next day and was then on a flight back to the world. When he flew into Ft. Lewis, Washington, they were told that if they all followed orders, they'd be processed out by the afternoon. "I certainly followed orders that time," Alba said. When Alba got to Fresno, he and another guy from Dinuba had no way home. So, they rented a taxi. The taxi driver, in a nod to our deserving Vietnam veterans, said, "Give me $10 apiece and I'll drive you home." For only $10 he got a ride all the way to Woodville in a taxi. When he got home, Alba said his dad put him to work the next day, pruning trees. For the next several months, Alba worked in a variety of jobs around the Porterville area. He eventually got a job as a mechanic in a muffler shop in Porterville where he worked for the next 30 years until his retirement. Due to his exposure to Agent Orange while in Vietnam, Alba was diagnosed with diabetes about 20 years ago. Of the services he's received from the VA for his diabetes, Alba said, "They've been very good to me."

John Alba

John Alba today – 2019

After John Alba was discharged from the military, he struggled somewhat with his adjustment from his war experiences to being back home. Alba said he often walked around the house at night, looking outside through the windows, checking to make sure everything was alright. It was more difficult for him when it rained, because the sound of the rain reminded him of Vietnam. When he first returned home, he attended Porterville College. Alba then worked at a variety of jobs around the Porterville and Lindsay area, working as a bus driver and janitor at his alma mater, Porterville High School. He then worked as a mechanic for six years and later was employed at a tractor dealership for 32 years. He retired from the dealership approximately five years ago and currently lives in Porterville. Due to his experiences in

Vietnam, Alba is receiving VA services for his loss of hearing. In addition, he also has diabetes that the VA attributed to his exposure to Agent Orange.

Vince Arcure

Vince Arcure today – 2019

When Vince Arcure returned from Vietnam he said, "I had a hard time adjusting to civilian life." He said that he had problems dealing with anger issues while often getting into fist fights. Although not diagnosed yet, Arcure was suffering from PTSD. He often had nightmares when he slept and said that during his nightmares "someone was always trying to kill me." He attended Porterville College with the goal of transferring to California State University, Fresno. After working in a variety of jobs around Porterville, including as a substitute teacher at the elementary school level, Arcure eventually was hired to work with the Tulare County parks and road departments. He then was hired with the Porterville Courthouse to serve as the marshal, a position he held for 29 years until his retirement. He currently lives in his cabin at Camp Nelson. Due to the injury he received in Vietnam and the PTSD he was eventually diagnosed with, Arcure has been receiving services from the VA.

Geary Baxter

Geary Baxter today – 2019

After he was discharged from the military, Geary Baxter enrolled at Fresno City College (FCC) in their aeronautics program. Baxter wanted to continue flying as a pilot; however, at that time, the market was flooded with people looking for pilot positions. He eventually received his commercial pilot license to fly multi-engine, fixed wing, and rotor wing aircraft. Baxter also received his certification as an aircraft mechanic. He was hired with an independent contractor as an inspector for gas lines, working across the country. He continued his flying by working part-time with a local helicopter company that contracted with PGE flying powerline patrols, setting telephone poles, and flying with the National Parks Service and Forest Service dropping water onto forest fires, and similar responsibilities. He worked with this company for approximately 16 years on his days off from the fire department. Baxter was hired by the City of Clovis Fire Department while also serving as an adjunct instructor at FCC. He retired from the fire department after 30 years in 2007. After retirement, he continued to serve as the adjunct coordinator for the FCC Fire Academy until 2018.

Dan Boydstun

Dan Boydstun today – 2019

When Dan Boydstun was discharged from the Air Force, he became part of the transition program the Air Force implemented for its veterans who had recently been discharged. The program would connect the veteran with a job and the Air Force would pay the employer for hiring the veteran. Boydstun got a job near Travis Air Force Base working as a light mechanic. He worked in that job for about six months and then returned to Porterville. He became employed with the Jostens plant, but then the business moved to Tennessee. Boydstun was then hired at Office Max where he worked as a store manager for 10 years. He then was hired at Target, where he worked for five years until he was able to pay off his house. Once the house was paid off, Boydstun retired. In just a few short years, Boydstun and his wife will be married 50 years. When he was in Vietnam, he said he periodically saw a C-130 flying over or near the barracks spraying some sort of chemical. Well, that chemical was Agent Orange, and because of his exposure to Agent Orange, Boydstun was later diagnosed with diabetes. In addition to his diabetes, Boydstun also receives services from the VA for his hearing loss.

Melvin Braziel

Melvin Braziel today – 2019

Approximately 70 days after Melvin Braziel landed in Vietnam, he was flying home on an emergency leave. His father had gotten sick and Braziel needed to return home. In order to help care for his father, his mom had to quit work and doing so would leave the family in severe financial hardship. With the assistance of the Red Cross and his local congressman, Rep. Bob Mathias, Braziel was able to get a hardship discharge from the military. Due to his early discharge, Braziel suffered from "survivors guilt" since he came home before his tour of duty was up and while his friends were still in Vietnam. Continuing to work in the same MOS as he had in the Army, Braziel drove truck for many years, delivering and transporting agricultural produce throughout the western states including Arizona, Colorado, California, Oregon, Washington, and into Canada. He drove for a trucking business, and then purchased his own truck and worked independently. After he retired, he continued to drive part-time with the Forest Service delivering water to the crews fighting forest fires. He and his wife live in Porterville.

Ron Crabtree

Ron Crabtree today – 2019

"When I got on the plane to leave Vietnam," Ron Crabtree said, "it was like I had a huge sigh of relief. I was so happy to leave." Crabtree spent the remaining six months of his military service at Ft. Lewis, Washington. When he was discharged from the military and returned home, he found a job at a local auto parts distributing company. He worked in that same dealership in its parts and accounting departments for the next 22 years prior to his retirement. But Crabtree's retirement has not been spent traveling the country in a motor home, hunting, fishing, or spending time at the beach. He became a foster parent. And not just a foster parent to a handful of children. "We've had about 200 kids go through our house," Crabtree said. One of his foster kids was born in prison to an incarcerated mother. Crabtree and his wife brought the child home from prison when he was only two days old. For some reason, this child was special. They fell in love with him and eventually adopted him as their own. Their adopted child is now in high school. Those 200 foster kids who passed through the Crabtree house were certainly loved and cared for. Yes, Crabtree was lucky in Vietnam like he said he was, but these kids are lucky in Porterville to have such loving and caring foster parents as the Crabtree family. Around 1999 Crabtree began receiving VA services for PTSD and a hearing disability. In addition, Crabtree also has diabetes and underwent heart bypass surgery. The diabetes and heart ailment have been attributed to his exposure to Agent Orange while in Vietnam.

Don Dowling

Don Dowling today – 2019

Don Dowling served three-and-a-half tours in Vietnam. He was with the 1st Brigade of the 101st Airborne Division for one year, and Special Forces for two-and-a-half years. When he returned from Vietnam, he re-enlisted at Ft. Bragg, North Carolina and became an instructor at the Special Forces training school. His birthday continued to be a day of anguish rather than a day of celebration. As mentioned in the first part of this book, Dowling landed in Vietnam on his 18th birthday. And then, on his birthday in 1974 when he was stationed in Germany, at 10:05 a.m. to be exact, Dowling broke both of his legs during a demonstration jump at the Special Forces training school. Regarding his career in the military, Dowling said, "Special Forces was a way of life," but that way of life was coming to an end. After a 23-year career in the Army, he retired. Dowling came back to Porterville and began working in construction, insulating houses. When he finished his career in the Army, local educator Bob Perez talked with him about completing his high school education. Dowling successfully passed the required tests and was awarded his high school diploma in 1988. He was eventually hired by the State Hospital as a California State police officer. He worked in that position for 27 years until his retirement. Dowling continues to serve his fellow veterans by his active involvement with the local branch of the American Legion, currently serving as its commander. He has been receiving assistance from the VA for PTSD and physical injuries from his experiences in the military, including diabetes and other health issues due to his exposure to Agent Orange while in Vietnam.

Tony Forner

Tony Forner today – 2019

When he was discharged from the military, Tony Forner began to work in various jobs around the Porterville area. He drove a bulldozer for a while, breaking his leg during a working mishap. He was then hired to work with the Tulare County Parks Department at Lake Success east of Porterville. He later worked with the road department in Terra Bella, eventually becoming Road Superintendent for Tulare County. After 38 years with the county road department, Forner retired, and currently lives in Porterville. He is a hunting enthusiast, doing a lot of hunting in the mountains of Idaho, Colorado, and Montana. And he proudly displays the efforts of his hunting on the walls of his house that are decorated with numerous heads and horns of animals he's shot. It has only been about 10 years since he began receiving services from the VA for his PTSD and other medical issues. His dealings with the VA have been challenging and sometimes frustrating. He also has a hearing loss from his exposure to deafening sounds while in combat.

Roger Gibson

Roger Gibson today – 2019

Speaking about the personal impact his Porterville High School friends had on him when he came back from Vietnam, Roger Gibson said, "A small group of people kept me sane." After he returned from Vietnam, Gibson worked at the Porter Theater, and then moved to San Jose where attended San Jose City College, eventually being hired to work with the State of California's employment office in San Jose. He later returned to Porterville where he attended Porterville College and received his certificate in Psychiatric Technology. Following the completion of his certificate Gibson worked at the development center in Porterville for 37 years. He has since retired and is living with his wife in Porterville. During the years following his return from the war, Gibson experienced flashbacks, nightmares and had a quick startle reflex. All of which are classic symptoms of PTSD. Fortunately, however, these subsided several years ago. Due to his exposure to Agent Orange while in Vietnam, Gibson has developed cancer, diabetes, and problems with his lungs. He continues to receive services from the VA.

Greg Goble

Greg Goble today – 2019

Upon his discharge from the military, Greg Goble attended college in Fresno and majored in Criminology. He went to college under the G.I. Bill that helped with school expenses but was not enough to also pay the bills. So some friends helped him get a part-time job at a mini-mart in Fresno that was robbed once. Due to several plane hijackings at that time, the U.S. Deputy Marshals created a position called Sky Marshal. The responsibility of this position was to sit on planes and be the security in case of hijackers. Goble took the tests for entrance into the Sky Marshal program and was successful in making the cut. He was instructed to report back in 11 months and the training would begin. He felt he no longer needed to be enrolled in school since he was accepted into the program, so he quit school and moved to Lake Tahoe. He worked there part-time and said that while in Lake Tahoe, "The best thing that ever happened to me was meeting my future wife, Susie." When he later returned to Fresno to find out when the Sky Marshal program was to start, he was informed that he was no longer a candidate for the program due to affirmative action policies. He then began to work in the auto parts manufacturing industry, working in the San Francisco Bay Area. He eventually moved back to the Central Valley and became the western regional manager of 14 states for an auto parts manufacturing company before it was sold. He then worked for a filter company for 10 years, and retired in 2016. He is currently living in Southern California with his wife, Susie.

Louis Gurrola

Louis Gurrola today – 2019

When Louis Gurrola returned from Vietnam he went right to work in the Terra Bella area and has stayed there until today. Gurrola continued to work in the farming business when he returned from Vietnam, being employed with an irrigation business in Terra Bella. When the business eventually closed, Gurrola continued to work independently and then started his own irrigation and farm supply business. He still owns and operates the business in Terra Bella. Almost every farmer in Terra Bella knows Gurrola, because he continued in his hometown doing the kind of supply work he did in Vietnam by providing farmers with supplies, equipment, and the support they need in order to effectively do their jobs.

Felix Hernandez

Felix Hernandez today – 2019

When Felix Hernandez was about to be discharged, he decided that he wanted to reenlist, but his wife didn't want him to. However, when he could not get assurance that he would not be sent back to Vietnam if he reenlisted, Hernandez decided to take the discharge and not reenlist. When he was still in the military, he met his wife in Hawaii for an R and R. Eventually, they found out they were going to have a baby. Hernandez said they called his son,

"The Wanderer." He was conceived in Hawaii, born in Washington, and raised in California. When he was discharged from the service, Hernandez worked in packing houses and picking oranges, and then worked in building mobile homes and conveyer systems. He eventually bought his own diesel truck and drove for agricultural businesses. He's now retired and living in Porterville. He was diagnosed with PTSD and has been receiving VA services. Regarding the services he has received from the VA, Hernandez said, "The VA has been there for me."

Roland Hill

Roland Hill today – 2019

Roland Hill finished his degree at Porterville College and then transferred to Cal Poly, San Luis Obispo and received his bachelor's degree. He then went to law school in the San Francisco Bay Area. When his first wife died, he returned to Porterville with his eight-year-old daughter so she could be cared for by both sets of her grandparents. He later remarried and became employed as an appraiser in the Tulare County office where he has worked for almost 40 years. He is currently serving as the Tulare County Assessor/Clerk-Recorder, which is a county-wide elected official. He lives in Visalia and is involved in many civic organizations in the community.

Barry Jackson

After spending the bulk of his adult life in group homes and care facilities resulting from his psychological trauma in Vietnam, Barry Jackson died of cancer on July 6, 2014. Although it was suspected, it was never determined if his cancer was related to his exposure to Agent Orange while in Vietnam.

Barry Jackson in mid to late 1980s

Robert Johnson

Robert Johnson today – 2019

After he returned from Vietnam, Robert Johnson spent a year living in Canada. While he was in Canada, he sometimes ran into draft dodgers. You would think that a Vietnam veteran with two Purple Hearts and a memory ravaged with the horrendous experiences of combat in the jungles would be antagonistic toward the draft dodgers. But not Johnson. Rather than being upset with the draft dodgers, Johnson could empathize with them. In fact, about the draft dodgers Johnson said, "They made a better choice than I did." Johnson eventually went to work on his family's ranch. He later went to Porterville College and then transferred to California State University, Fullerton where he received his bachelor's and master's degrees in Psychology. He then attended the California School of Professional Psychology where he has an ABD (all but dissertation). Johnson worked with the Tulare County Veterans Services Center providing therapy and counseling to veterans with PTSD. He also taught part-time at Porterville College where he was eventually hired full-time to teach mental health-related courses. He retired from the college in 2016 after teaching there for 14 years. He is now battling cancer due to his exposure to Agent Orange.

Ron McCarville

Ron McCarville today – 2019

When Ron McCarville returned from Vietnam, he said, "I got drunk for about a month." He then went to the local Employment Development Department looking for work. They found a part-time job for him working with the Forest Service doing road work and other general assignments. He stayed in the mountains during the week and came home on the weekends. It was during his work in the mountains that he experienced his first PTSD-related nightmare. The guys in the bunkroom with McCarville found him screaming in his bed one night, and McCarville said, "I woke up soaking wet." That began his long, difficult battle with PTSD and other health issues related to his time in Vietnam. He later got a job with a packing house in Lindsay, and then with the local Volkswagen dealership in the parts department, where he eventually worked up to being the parts manager. He then was employed with the Tulare County road department, working in the office and doing such things as payroll. McCarville worked there for 21 years until his retirement. In addition to his PTSD, McCarville had a heart attack, and it was attributed to his exposure to Agent Orange.

Chuck Migalski

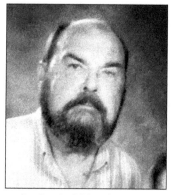

Chuck Migalski today – 2019

When Chuck Migalski returned from Vietnam, the name Vietnam was not mentioned in his house. He didn't want to relive the horrors of the war and tried to move on from the experience. The Navy tried to get him medically discharged due to the injuries he received in Vietnam. However, Migalski wondered how he would ever get a job if he was medically discharged from the military. So, he didn't accept the discharge. He spent his remaining time in the Navy at Long Beach and was honorably discharged on September 1, 1970, the opening day of dove season. Migalski then spent many years as a truck driver for various businesses around the Porterville community. After successful completion of various vocational and aptitude tests, Migalski was hired by the State Department of Fish and Game as a fish culturalist. He is retired and living in Arizona. He continues to receive VA services for the physical injuries he suffered during Vietnam, in addition to his PTSD.

Todd Pixler

Todd Pixler today – 2019

Todd Pixler's first job after Vietnam was working at the local Josten's company making trophies, plaques and announcements. He briefly tried to resurrect his track career at Porterville College, but then transferred to De Anza College to complete his Associates in Arts degree. He eventually completed his bachelor's degree in Psychology at California State University, Fresno, and worked in a variety of jobs locally, as well as in the San Francisco Bay Area. He then taught in the prison system at Corcoran and with the California Youth Authority in Norwalk. He is currently retired, living with his wife, Tina, in Porterville. Pixler is also involved with the Porterville High School Alumni Association.

Brian Rattigan

Brian Rattigan today – 2019

After his discharge from the Army, Brian Rattigan enrolled at Porterville College and earned his Associate Degree in Liberal Studies in 1972. While at the college, Rattigan was involved with the campus Veterans Club and wrote for the campus newspaper. He then transferred to the University of San Francisco where he earned a Bachelor of Arts degree in Government in 1974. He also volunteered during the 1970s at Swords to Plowshares, a San Francisco-based veterans advocacy organization. Today, Swords is one of the premier veteran advocacy groups in the country. In 1984 Rattigan earned his Juris Doctor degree from the University of Santa Clara School of Law. During law school, he worked as a law clerk for the California Rural Legal Assistance organization in Gilroy. In the mid-1980s he was diagnosed with PTSD. However, he vehemently denied the diagnosis for 22 years. He finally filed a claim for PTSD disability out of anger and frustration due to the failure of the VA to provide proper health care. After graduating from law school, he worked for two criminal defense law firms eventually becoming a sole practitioner as a criminal defense attorney. Rattigan and his wife met as law school classmates. He is currently retired and living with his wife in Fairfield, California.

Jim Rouch

Jim Rouch today – 2019

When Jim Rouch returned from Vietnam he went back East for a couple of years. He then returned to Porterville where he worked in his family's truss company. Rouch later opened up a lumber yard in Bakersfield. His family then hired him back into the family business to help start a plant in Paso Robles. Later, he started his own crane business where he worked for 18 years until his retirement. He suffers from PTSD and heart problems, and only began receiving VA assistance about five years ago. He currently lives in Visalia.

John Schultz

John Schultz today – 2019

After he was discharged from the Navy, John Schultz continued his education at Porterville College and was a member of the Veterans Club while on campus. He then transferred to Chico State University to continue working on his bachelor's degree. Schultz then came back home to Terra Bella where he worked in a variety of jobs around the Porterville area. For many years he was employed as a truck driver with a local fuel distribution business. Schultz was later hired at Porterville College where he worked in the maintenance department for several years prior to his retirement. He and his wife, Becky, live in Porterville and travel around the country in their RV.

Joe Souza

Joe Souza today – 2019

When Joe Souza was discharged from the Army and decided to not make the military his career, he returned to the family farm near Poplar where he worked until his retirement. He received services from the VA for his PTSD and assistance for his physical injury when he was shot in the mouth. Souza credited his wife for being so understanding and caring as he dealt with the issues he brought back with him from Vietnam. He has since used those strong, Portuguese hands to develop a very detailed and skilled craft of making tables, cabinets, and various ornate forms of furniture.

Russell Vossler

Russell Vossler today – 2019

When Russell Vossler returned from Vietnam he went back to work on the family farm. He also worked at the local Rockwell plant, loading trucks and a variety of other responsibilities. He was hired with the city of Porterville's Police Department. After several years working as a police officer, Vossler quit his position and began to deal more directly with his PTSD adjustment issues. He went back to work on the family farm and then eventually received his certification to work as a PTSD specialist, specifically providing group counseling sessions for combat veterans. He has since retired and moved with his wife, Carol, to Idaho, where he is living today. He continues to receive services from the VA for his PTSD. In addition to his wife, his other close companion at home has been his service dog, Bronco.

Richard Walker

Richard Walker today – 2019

When Richard Walker returned home from Vietnam, he was stationed on a ship in San Diego. Soon thereafter, he was discharged. He started dating a girl who he eventually married, and they are still married today. Since he loved Terra Bella so much, Walker did not go to college or leave the area to establish his career or home. He wanted his family to grow up in the area, too, just like him. With that, upon his discharge from the military he began to work in various places of business around the Terra Bella and Porterville area. He worked with an agricultural chemical company, a lumber company, an air conditioning business, and then in construction. In 1983, he was hired with the Porterville Unified School District to work in their maintenance department, where he eventually retired. Walker has a shop on his property where he tinkers, doing such things as building a small-scale replica of the PBR he was assigned to in Vietnam.

Don Wolfram

Don Wolfram today – 2019

After he returned from Vietnam, Don Wolfram was stationed in Los Alamitos, California and had about a year and three months left in the service. At that time, the military was offering Vietnam War veterans early outs, which Wolfram took advantage of, and he was discharged nine months early. While he was still in the Navy and stationed at Los Alamitos, Wolfram applied to be a police officer in Santa Ana. When he went into the police academy he did not find it to be that difficult since it was much like basic training in the Navy. After passing several tests and background checks, Wolfram was hired by the Santa Ana Police Department where he worked for 31 years. He retired in 2004 and now lives in Arizona. He enjoys traveling the country with his wife and assists in the ongoing care of his mother.

★ ★ ★

When these men came back from the Vietnam War, they each continued on with their lives, taking different directions in their personal or vocational pursuits. As they enter their seventh decade of life, some of their classmates have already passed on. Therefore, it is important for us to continue to listen to their stories, because these men are an important part of our country's history.

They lived, while some died, through a horrendous war, and it is incumbent upon each of us to value their stories and treasure their experiences during that time. And we need to pass their stories on to the next generation. God bless each and every one of them.

Vietnam War and Wall Facts

The Last One Killed [1]

The Vietnam Veterans Memorial Wall website lists Kelton Rena Turner, an 18-year old Marine, as the last American soldier killed in the Vietnam War. He was killed in action during the Mayaguez incident on May 15, 1975, two weeks after the evacuation of Saigon. The Mayaguez incident is considered the last battle of the Vietnam War.

Other sources list Charles McMahon, Darwin Judge, Gary L. Hall, Joseph N. Hargrove and Danny G. Marshall as the last to die in Vietnam.

SECTION FOUR
REFLECTING ON THEIR STORIES

22

The Author's Opinion and Reflections

"Spending time with America's soldiers is always inspiring."

John Boehner

My Opinion

I could not agree more with Boehner's quote above. The time I spent in conversations with these veterans was truly an inspiration to me. I hope others have that same opportunity. Make the effort. You won't regret it.

But permit me to shift focus slightly from the men of Porterville High School who served in the war, to a statement about the outcome of the war, whether we won or lost. I need to say it. Since this book centers around the Vietnam War, I feel it necessary to provide some personal opinions regarding the war, specifically about its outcome.

Some people say that Vietnam was the only war America ever lost. Many books and articles have been written with references to how we lost the war, the media has sometimes portrayed the results of the war as an utter failure on the part of the American military, and colleges and universities across the country have taught in their history classes that our forces were run out of the country by the North Vietnamese army.

For many years, I believed we lost, too. But not anymore.

The evolution of my feelings about the outcome of the war was profoundly affected by the writing of this book. The research I conducted, the articles and books that I read, and, especially, the conversations I had with the veterans who were there, all brought me to a realization that what I believed for so many years may not be true after all. Sure, we all have different opinions, and I had mine. But my opinions have changed.

Many people look at the fall of Saigon on April 30, 1975 as the epic moment when America lost the war in Vietnam. Others, however, consider different dates as the end of the war, such as January 27, 1973 when the Paris Peace Accords were signed; March 29, 1973 when our combat troops left Vietnam; May 7, 1975 which is the ending date of the Vietnam Era as determined by Congress for VA purposes; or May 15, 1975 which was the last day of the Mayaguez incident that is considered the last battle of the Vietnam War.

When searching the various dates that may be considered as the official end of the war, it seems that the most common date agreed upon is when Saigon fell and South Vietnam surrendered on April 30, 1975. Scenes of helicopters rushing to the embassy to save U.S. personnel and local Vietnamese from the onslaught of the North Vietnamese forces who were closing in on the embassy were played on television night after night. Hope for a different outcome to the war had finally run out. Reporters told stories of Saigon being overrun, soldiers and civilians running for their lives as the North Vietnamese pushed them out of the country once and for all.

And that's when we lost the war in the minds of many within our country and the world. But not so fast.

To illustrate my feelings about the outcome of the war, I'd like to use a sports analogy.

A game between the Los Angeles Dodgers and the San Francisco Giants is being played in Dodger stadium in Los Angeles. The starting pitcher for the Giants pitches eight strong innings but his arm was getting tired after throwing so many pitches during the game. He is taken out of the game after the eighth inning, with the scored tied 0-0. A relief pitcher comes in to take his place at the bottom of the ninth. Since the starting pitcher is done for the day, he takes a shower, puts on his street clothes, boards a plane, and flies back to San Francisco.

With the Dodgers up to bat in the bottom of the ninth inning, the relief pitcher for the Giants gives up a couple of hits, a walk, and the bases are now loaded. The next two pitches are balls. There is now a 2-0 count, the bottom of the ninth inning, bases loaded, with the game tied at zero. Here comes the pitch, a hanging curve ball over the middle of the plate. The batter smashes the ball over the left field fence that lands in the adjacent parking lot. The Dodgers win 4-0.

Who gets the loss in the game? The starting pitcher for the Giants or the relief pitcher?

Well, if you follow baseball, you know that the relief pitcher gets tagged with the loss. Why should the starting pitcher be blamed for the loss if he left the game when it was tied? He shouldn't, and he doesn't. The loss is on the relief pitcher. The starting pitcher does not get the loss because he was pulled from the game when the score was tied. So, since he didn't win or lose the game, his achievements are recorded as an appearance.

The same goes with the Vietnam War, in my opinion.

As mentioned above, according to many the end of the war happened on April 30, 1975. But the last of the American ground troops departed from Vietnam on March 29, 1973. Take a look at those dates again, a hard look, and you will realize something that may be subtle at first glance, but something that is very important in the debate about whether we won, lost, or tied the war.

Our ground troops left Vietnam two years before the fall of

Saigon. I'll say that again. Our ground troops left Vietnam two years before the fall of Saigon. So, how can America be blamed for losing a war that it stopped fighting in two years before the fall of Saigon, the event that is designated by many as the official end of the war?

The treaty that was signed in Paris, France on January 27, 1973 included various conditions regarding our departure from Vietnam. Some of these conditions included our withdrawal from Vietnam, the prisoners of war would be released, certain limitations or restrictions were placed on what the opposing sides could do within South Vietnam, and a commitment regarding a peaceful reunification of Vietnam was agreed upon.[1] The United States generally did what the treaty required us to do, and we left. The North Vietnamese cheated.

Again, we have been told for many years that the United States lost the war in Vietnam. But I don't believe that anymore. So then, if the United States did not lose the war, who did?

South Vietnam.

They took over when the score was tied. By the time our combat troops left, the Americans had won the most battles and secured the most individual victories on the ground and in the air. And most importantly, South Vietnam was still its own country. But then the Americans went home, and the war became the South Vietnamese's to handle. And they got blown away.

If the South Vietnamese lost the war, then who won?

North Vietnam.

Let's be honest. When the Americans left, and their formidable foe was no longer in the game, it was only a matter of time before the North Vietnamese would dominate the South, push them out of Saigon, and establish a communist government. The South was just not strong enough or adequately equipped enough to hold off the North by themselves for very much longer.

If South Vietnam lost the war, and North Vietnam won the war, then that means the United States tied the war. Correct? Wrong again. How can you tie a game that has already been won by someone else?

The slogan on the shirt that I mentioned at the beginning of this book, "We did not lose the Vietnam War. We withdrew from it" is actually a very fair conclusion to the outcome of our participation in the war. Take another look at Richard Walker's comment in Chapter 19, PHS Lesson #3, and you will see that he agrees with this assessment, too. We did not win, we did not lose, we did not tie, we withdrew.

No one wants to be on a losing team. To be called losers has a demoralizing effect. So, to say that we lost the war, or that the men who fought in Vietnam were losers is, to me, a disservice to those who fought in it, were injured, still suffer from the effects of the war and, especially, those who died. It is a disservice to the parents of those young men, most of their children being teenagers back then, who worried night after night about their sons who were fighting in a dirty war thousands of miles from home.

Those young men from Porterville High School, most of them now in their early 70's, should not bear the burden of being known as participants in the first war that the United States ever lost. Because, in my opinion, the Americans didn't lose the war. We were winning the majority of the battles while we were in it, but then we withdrew.

You may not agree with me, and that's okay. But that's my opinion.

My Reflections

Although it has been a privilege to write this book and, especially, for having the opportunity to get to know these veterans, I'm glad it's over. I never expected this, and I am thoroughly exhausted. I am not exhausted from the actual writing of the book, but I am emotionally exhausted from reliving with these veterans the challenges of their experiences, both while in Vietnam and here at home. And if I'm feeling this way after only hearing about their experiences, I wonder how difficult it is for these veterans to have lived them.

The interviews included the gamut of emotions. I experienced anger, sadness, pride, and bitterness. I saw 70-year-old men cry, and I often cried when I was back home telling my wife about the interview. Most spoke openly, but some could not go on any further. And some couldn't stop talking either. For them, it was almost like the floodgates were open and they took the opportunity to share their experiences. No ego-driven braggadocios. Just guys telling about their experiences to someone that wanted to listen. One veteran said after our interview, "Steve, you know more about my experiences in Vietnam than my wife does."

During my interviews with the veterans, it was quite obvious to me that these men were, in fact, not a bunch of egomaniacs bragging to me about their exploits during the war. Quite the contrary. Most of them were humble and some were almost embarrassed talking about themselves or their heroics while in combat. In fact, when I inquired about any medals they may have received, most hesitated on even talking about that. So, for the most part, I did not ask them about medals, but let them share only if they felt comfortable in doing so.

One reason why I decided early on to not ask them about medals they were awarded was because of something rather poignant that one of them said. He was speaking about being injured in a battle and how he then declined the Purple Heart he should have received. I asked him why he would decline an award he was entitled to.

He said, "How can I take a medal for living, when so many died?" He started crying after saying that.

I think it's important, however, to understand the bravery and sacrifice that these young men from Porterville High School exhibited during the war that resulted in being awarded a medal. Since I'm not exactly sure how many medals were totally awarded, I used the term "at least" regarding the number of medals in this group of war veterans. Some told me about their medals, some didn't. So, I added the number of those who did. Remember, my totals are the minimum. I'm sure there were more, many more.

Here goes.

There were at least 14 Purple Hearts awarded to these war veterans from Porterville High School because of an injury they suffered during combat. At least four of them received more than one Purple Heart. There were at least eight medals of valor awarded for bravery or heroism on the battlefields.

I believe it's also important to understand something else they brought back home. In addition to medals on their chests, they also brought home with them injuries and illnesses as a result of their experiences in Vietnam. Injuries or illnesses that require on-going rehabilitation.

At least 18 of them brought back from the war a mind affected with PTSD; because of their exposure to Agent Orange, at least six developed diabetes, three cancer, two heart ailments, and two with lung conditions; at least three developed substance abuse problems and other illnesses or conditions that required medical and psychological assistance after returning from the war.

Purple Hearts, medals of valor, substance abuse, illnesses and injuries. They experienced it all. And like I said in a previous chapter in this book, and I mean this sincerely: "These guys were studs."

I am proud to join these men in the distinction of being called a veteran. I served in the United States Army, enlisting in late 1974 and then going into boot camp in January 1975. Technically, I am considered a Vietnam-era veteran since I served in the military before the official end of the conflict. But my duty station was in Germany. Sure, when I went into the service the official end of the Vietnam War was a few months away, there was the Cold War happening, with upheaval in the Middle East and other parts of the world, but nothing of any significance that caused me to worry like these men worried back when they were in Porterville High School during the Vietnam War. As I look back on my service, I've often searched for an answer to a question that I've asked myself a thousand times.

Could I have done it?

Could I have done what these guys from Porterville High School did on the battlefields of Vietnam? Could I have stared death in the face and physically or psychologically survived the ordeal? Could I have remained cool enough under the pressures of combat to call in air strikes, make sound decisions, or provide support to a fallen troop? Sure, I went through the same boot camp as these Vietnam veterans did, I attended the same AIT school in Georgia as a couple of those who were interviewed, I was deployed like they were, put on KP, walked guard duty on Christmas night, ran hundreds of miles, wore the same outfits, got the same haircuts, and marched the same roads. From a training perspective, I was ready.

But was I ready for a war?

From talking with each of the veterans who had experienced combat, it was clear that you are never totally prepared for a war until you are faced with it. Nothing can really prepare you for the chaos of the battlefield. The fear. The stress. The injury. The death. Robert Johnson, an infantryman, a tunnel rat, an airborne paratrooper, and a veteran with two Purple Hearts, honestly described his feelings when he was first faced with combat by saying, "It scared the shit out of me." And take another look at Roland Hill's graphic yet precise description of what it was like to be scared. You can't really be prepared enough for that.

But going back to my question, "Could I have done it?"

The answer to that question finally came to me as I was reflecting on the interviews I had with these veterans. And they inadvertently helped me come up with the answer. I now believe, without a doubt, that, yes, I could have done it. But under one condition.

I could have done it with more confidence if any one of these veterans from Porterville High School was by my side. I could have done it if I knew that any one of these veterans would have been there with me on the battlefield. After hearing their stories, after feeling their emotions, I know for a fact that these guys would have pulled me through. They would have had my back. They would have provided me with the confidence and ability to handle such a horrendous experience like that is found in combat.

As John 15:13 (ESV) in the Bible says, "Greater love has no one than this, that someone lay down his life for his friends." In the spirit of this Bible verse, I came to the conclusion after interviewing these veterans that each of them would have laid down his life for me. I believe that in my heart. So, yes, I could have done it. But I could have done it with more confidence if they were there with me.

Knowing them as I do now, I'd trust every single one of these veterans with my life.

Like their fathers before them, I wish the Vietnam veterans could have experienced their war's equivalent to the raising of the flag at Iwo Jima. Or participated in historical fights like the Battle of the Bulge that they could brag about to their children and grandchildren for years. Or to have flowers tossed at them and be smothered in kisses by the citizens of another city that they liberated from the communists.

But these young men of Porterville High School got none of that, and I'm sorry they didn't. Instead, they fought in a war as their country ordered them to do and then were chastised, ridiculed and shamed for doing so.

As noted earlier in this book, when Chuck Migalski's granddaughter asked him if he was a hero in Vietnam he said, "No, all the heroes' names are on the Wall." Migalski certainly earned the right to be called a hero. After all, he received three Purple Hearts, was under enemy fire six days out of seven, and has since spent many years of his life dealing with the physical and psychological injuries he suffered during the war. But his response was a selfless answer to a little girl's question. He placed the honor of being called a hero not on himself, but on his fellow brothers who paid the ultimate price. And he was right, to a point.

You see, I am going to slightly disagree with Migalski, and I hope he understands me for doing so.

The Vietnam War veterans served with honor. They did their duty with courage and distinction. They were brave, courageous, and selfless. They fought like hell. Just like their fathers did in Germany,

France, Japan and Iwo Jima. The WWII veterans were the heroes of our fathers' generation. And to me, the Vietnam War veterans are the heroes of my generation. Therefore, I consider all Vietnam War veterans to be heroes. Especially, the ones from Porterville High School that I got to know through the writing of this book.

So, in addition to the names on the Wall, Chuck Migalski is a hero to me, and so is Vince Arcure, Todd Pixler, Joe Souza, Russell Vossler, Brian Rattigan, Greg Goble, Don Wolfram, Roland Hill, Robert Johnson, Melvin Braziel, Barry Jackson, Roger Gibson, John Schultz, Louis Gurrola, Ron McCarville, Jim Rouch, Richard Walker, Tony Forner, John Alba, Geary Baxter, Don Dowling, Felix Hernandez, Ron Crabtree, Alfred Alba, and Dan Boydstun.

Some Vietnam War veterans declined to be interviewed for this book, a couple pulled out after the interview process began, while others may not have known this book was even being written. And some have already passed away. These veterans are certainly heroes, too.

At the end of a longer statement about war in general on June 19, 1879, William Tecumseh Sherman, acting United States Secretary of War and former Commanding General of the United States Army, said these three concluding words: "War is hell."[2] And it certainly is. Yet these young men from Porterville High School marched through hell and served with honor, bravery, and heroism. We should be thankful for their service and proud of them for the job they did. I know I am.

Now, I'd like to conclude this book with two simple words.

Two simple words that if said 50 years ago, may have drowned out the disgusting chatter thrust upon these veterans by the protesters at the airports they flew into. Two simple words that could have made a difference in their psychological transition from a world of war to a world of peace. Two simple words that Greg Goble said, "Would have brought tears to my eyes" if he would have heard these words when he first came back from Vietnam.

Two simple words.

To those of you reading this book who are Vietnam War veterans, you may not have heard these words 50 years ago when you returned home from the war but hear them now. These words come not just from me, but from a country that has struggled with a profound sense of guilt over the years for not saying these words to you when you first came back after marching through the battlefields of hell in Vietnam.

"Welcome home!"

Epilogue

*"The worst part about being strong is that
no one ever asks if you're OK."*

Unknown

WHEN I WAS done with the interviews and almost finished with editing and reviewing the chapters, I was ready to send the manuscript to the publisher to complete the final stages of getting the book published. But my satisfaction that I had finished the book was hampered with a feeling that I left something out. I had this gnawing feeling there was something incomplete about the book. Something was missing. And after going back through the book, looking at my notes, and reviewing its content, I finally realized what that missing piece was.

I read again what Roger Gibson said about his feeling that everyone who has been in combat needs help or should at least be evaluated. And that's when it hit me. As I considered more about what Gibson said, and thought back on the interviews I had with those who had been in combat, I then realized he was right. Almost every combat veteran I interviewed for this book had PTSD, or at least had previously received services for the condition.

I realized then that I needed to take a step away from the personal stories about the Vietnam War, and address some of the resulting symptoms of their experiences in combat. And, hopefully, through the experiences of these veterans other veterans and their families can face the effects of the war with greater strength and a better understanding about the services that are available.

The statement above at the heading of this epilogue is so true. We assume that soldiers are strong, especially combat veterans, so they can handle whatever they experienced. There's no need to ask how they are doing, right? No, that's wrong because there are many injuries that you cannot see. So, it doesn't hurt to ask. In fact, asking may save someone's life.

As I mentioned above, almost every one of the veterans interviewed for this book who experienced combat has been diagnosed with PTSD. Most had never heard of PTSD when they returned from the Vietnam War and felt their reactions to life when they got back from Vietnam would fade away like their memories of their experiences. So they rationalized their behaviors, feelings, and attitudes as adjustment problems that would eventually dissipate. But, finally, most of them went to the VA and began receiving services.

They may have finally gone to the VA for help because they couldn't handle it anymore. They may have finally gone because of the encouragement of a fellow veteran. They may have finally gone because their wives gave them an ultimatum. Or they may have finally gone because they could see how their behaviors were affecting their families and, especially, their children. Regardless of why they went to get help, they went, and that's all that mattered.

Most of the veterans were diagnosed with PTSD many years after the war, not right after they returned. Because of that, they struggled for years with a condition that was affecting themselves, their marriages, and their children. But at least they now had a reason, a label for their moods, a better understanding of their flashbacks, nightmares, and irritability, and knowledge of the services that are available to them. The Vietnam War affected them, and, thankfully, most are now getting the help they need.

So, in order to feel that this book is complete, I wanted to include some information about PTSD and suicide – the latter sometimes being a result of the former. The following is only a brief explanation of each issue, and I encourage veterans, family members, and friends who may be struggling with PTSD or considering suicide, to reach out.

Disclaimer - The information below is not intended to be a substitute for medical advice from a licensed therapist, psychologist, or physician. The reader should consult with the VA and his or her therapist, psychologist or physician in any matter relating to his or her medical and physical health.

Post-Traumatic Stress Disorder (PTSD)

The following bits of information are excerpts from the National Center for PTSD website (www.ptsd.va.gov). There is a ton of information on the website, so please spend some time browsing through it.

What is PTSD?

PTSD is a mental health problem that some people develop after experiencing or witnessing a life-threatening event, like combat, a natural disaster, a car accident, or sexual assault. It's normal to have upsetting memories, feel on edge, or have trouble sleeping after a traumatic event. At first, it may be hard to do normal daily activities, like go to work, go to school, or spend time with people you care about. But most people start to feel better after a few weeks or months. If it's been longer than a few months and you're still having symptoms, you may have PTSD. For some people, PTSD symptoms may start later on, or they may come and go over time.

How common is PTSD in veterans?

It is estimated that about 30 out of every 100 (or 30%) of Vietnam Veterans have had PTSD in their lifetime. (It is interesting to note, however, that the percentage of Vietnam veterans from Porterville High School that were interviewed for this book who have been diagnosed with PTSD is 70% - almost two-and-a-half times higher than the national average.)

What are some of the related problems of PTSD?

Anger, depression, chronic pain, sleep problems, substance abuse, suicide.

Why get treatment?

The decision to get care for PTSD symptoms can be difficult. You are not alone if you feel nervous. It is not uncommon for people with mental health conditions like PTSD to want to avoid talking about it. But getting help for your symptoms is the best thing you can do. PTSD treatments can work.

There is no need to suffer with PTSD. There are good treatments that can help. You don't need to let PTSD get in the way of your enjoyment of life, hurt your relationships, or cause problems at work or school.

"Getting better" means different things for different people, but people who get treatment improve their quality of life. In many cases, PTSD treatment can get rid of your symptoms. For some, symptoms may continue after treatment, but you will have learned skills to cope with them better.

Treatment can also help you make sense of the trauma, learn skills to better handle negative thoughts and feelings, reconnect with people you care about, and set goals for activities, like work or school, that you can handle.

The above is only a small fraction of the information about PTDS that is found on the website. There is so much more. Spend some time on the website. The time you spend could be the difference in your life or the life of a veteran and his or her family.

For referrals to appropriate services and agencies, a good place to start is with your County Veterans Service Officer (VSO). Google search for the VSO in your county, if there is one. They can provide you with information about the services that are available to veterans.

Suicide

On June 18, 2018 the Veterans Administration released its "National Suicide Data Report."[1] Their data included information from every state in the nation, including the District of Columbia. Some of the insights gained from this report include:

- The average number of veterans who died by suicide each day is 20 (a few years ago, the number was 22.). Twenty veterans a day commit suicide!
- Although this number was a slight decrease from previous reports, this latest report indicated that the rate among young veterans, those who are between the ages of 18 to 34, increased by more than 10 percent from 2006 to 2016.
- Since most veterans are older, nearly 60% of veterans suicide in 2016 were from individuals 55 years or older.
- Veterans who have regular contact with VA health services are less likely to commit suicide than those with little or no interactions.

The last insight is important to restate: "Veterans who have regular contact with VA health services are less likely to commit suicide."

Remember that.

To respect his privacy, his name will remain anonymous, but one of the Gulf War veterans I worked with at Porterville College spoke openly about his consideration of committing suicide. Very seriously considering suicide. And this happened years after he was in Afghanistan. He was having tremendous difficulty dealing with the effects of PTSD – anger, sleepless nights, flashbacks, and anxiety. It was just too much to deal with. He began to feel that suicide was the only way out.

Every now and then he would look into his desk drawer to find a loaded pistol staring him in the face and he'd wonder. Sometimes he would take it out and hold it, other times his palms would be sweaty thinking about the decision to end his life or not. He was better when he was drunk, and worse when he was sober. Drugs and alcohol reduced his feelings of hopelessness. But he couldn't stay drunk or loaded for the rest of his life. He needed help.

Luckily, however, he recognized he needed help before he made the final decision to carry through with his thoughts of suicide. He eventually went to the VA and got help. But there are many others who choose to deal with this condition alone, trying to battle through it with self-medication using drugs or alcohol. And too many of them are losing the battle.

On a personal note, one of my friends is a Vietnam War veteran. He suffered greatly from PTSD, with sleepless nights, flashbacks, anger, and depression consuming his thoughts about life. Like many who suffer from and experience the ups and downs of depression, he had a setback one night. And to deal with this setback he got drunk. He drank so much that he passed out on his mattress. This time, getting drunk and passing out saved his life. He woke up the next morning, hung over from the night before, and found something that horrified him.

He found his gun lying on his chest with bullets scattered around him. He apparently passed out before he could load his gun and commit suicide. He came as close to death in a lonely garage as he did in the jungles of Vietnam. And it scared him. He eventually reached out to others for help and I am eternally grateful that he did. He is not cured of his PTSD, but he has made tremendous strides in his recovery. After learning more of his experiences in Vietnam and his struggles afterwards, I grew to respect and admire him profoundly, and I am thankful for his friendship.

According to some of the veterans who were interviewed for this book, two of their classmates from Porterville High School committed suicide after they returned from Vietnam. And their suicides were not soon after Vietnam, but several years later. There may have been more who committed suicide, but these are two that the veterans who were interviewed knew about. And their names will be left anonymous in this book.

For these two veterans who committed suicide, their war continued to rage in their minds for many years after Vietnam to the point they felt they could no longer continue. Dealing with the mental and psychological anguish and turmoil that can result from an experience like the Vietnam War is difficult enough to handle even with the assistance of a therapist. But dealing with it alone is almost impossible for some.

Previous to the latest VA report on suicide, the data suggested that 22 veterans committed suicide every day. Twenty-two a day. To try and stem this terrible tide, Phil Luciano, a Marine Corps Gulf War veteran, started a nationwide effort a few years ago called "Buddy Check 22."[2] The effort is simple. On the 22nd of each month (the day being the same number as those who committed suicide daily) you call up a veteran and ask how he or she is doing. Simple as that.

When I was the coordinator of the Veterans Resource Center at Porterville College I started our own Buddy Check 22 effort. I had shirts made that said in large print on the front "Buddy Check 22" and then on the back, the following words: "22 Veterans commit suicide every day. That's 22 too many! What can YOU do? On the 22nd of each month, check up on a veteran and ask, 'How are you doing?' Remember – not all wounds are visible."

A simple effort that could have profound results. I have never known if the effort has been successful or not, if anyone decided against suicide because someone checked up on him or her, but I hope it has helped someone somewhere.

One day, I stood in line at the bank for a while waiting for my turn at the window, wearing my Buddy Check 22 shirt. As I concluded by transactions and left the bank, a couple came up to me in the parking lot and said, "Great shirt. We are going home right now to call a veteran friend." I hope that their call, and the shirt I was wearing, may have saved the life of a struggling veteran.

For any person, veteran or not, who might be considering suicide, please reach out to someone who cares. Reach out to someone who will listen. Reach out to someone who can refer you to the appropriate services.

If you are in a crisis

Veterans who are in crisis or having thoughts of suicide, or those who know a veteran in crises, should call the Veterans Crisis Line for confidential support 24 hours a day, seven days a week, 365 days a year at 800-273-8255. You can also visit the website at www. suicidepreventionlifeline.org.

When I was recently at the Tulare Veterans Clinic awaiting my audiology appointment, I noticed a poster on the wall about suicide. It stated: "It takes the courage and strength of a warrior to ask for help." So, warriors, show your courage. Show your strength. Call someone.

You are not alone!

Glossary of Terms

This was the vocabulary of the veterans during the Vietnam War

A

A-gunner	An assistant gunner.
AIT	Advanced Infantry (or Individual) Training – the more specialized training received after Basic Training.
Agent Orange	An herbicide dropped on the forests and bush in Vietnam to defoliate (strip the leaves from plants and trees) an area. This was done to expose hiding enemy troops. Many Vietnam veterans who had been exposed to Agent Orange during the war have shown an increased risk of cancer and other health issues.
AK-47	Soviet assault rifle supplied by the Russians to the North Vietnamese and Viet Cong.
ALPHA	Military phonetic for the letter 'A.'
AO	Acronym for "area of operation."

APC	Acronym for "Armored Personnel Carrier" used to transport troops on the battlefield.
ARVN	Acronym for "Army of the Republic of Vietnam" (South Vietnam's army).
ATC	Acronym for Armored Troop Carrier.

B

Beaucoup	Many.
Boom boom	Sex with a prostitute.
Boom boom girl	A prostitute.
Boondock (boonies)	Term for the jungle or swampy areas in Vietnam.
Boot	A new soldier in or just out of boot camp.
BRAVO	Military phonetic for the letter 'B.'
Bug juice	Insect repellant.
Busting caps	A term for firing a weapon.
Butter bar	A term for a second lieutenant. Also known as brown bar.

C

CHARLIE	Military phonetic for the letter 'C.'
Charlie	Slang for Viet Cong (VC). The term is short for the phonetic spelling (used by the military and police to spell things over the radio) of "VC," which is "Victor Charlie."
Cherry (boy)	A slang term for new, inexperienced soldiers.
Chinook	A CH-47 cargo helicopter.
Cobra	An Army helicopter.

D

DELTA	Military phonetic for the letter 'D.'
DI	Acronym for "drill instructor."
Diddy-bopping	A term for someone who was walking carelessly.
DMZ	Demilitarized Zone. The line that divided North Vietnam and South Vietnam, located at the 17th parallel. This line was agreed upon as a temporary border agreed upon in the 1954 Geneva Accords.
Domino theory	A U.S. foreign policy theory that stated, like the chain effect begun when even just one domino is pushed over, one country in a region that falls to communism will lead to surrounding countries also soon falling to communism.
Dove	A person who is opposed to the Vietnam War. (Compare to "hawk.")
DRV	Acronym for "Democratic Republic of Vietnam" (Communist North Vietnam).
Dust off	A medical evacuation helicopter. Usually a Huey.

E

ECHO	Military phonetic for the letter 'E.'
Elephant grass	Tall, sharped-edged grass found in the jungles.
EM club	Acronym for the "Enlisted Men's Club."
ETS	Acronym for "Estimated Termination of Service." Or the day you got out of the military.

F

FNG — Acronym for "f_ _ _ ing new guy." Similar to cherry or boot.

FOXTROT — Military phonetic for the letter 'F.'

Frag — A fragmentation grenade.

Freedom Bird — Any airplane that took American soldiers back to the U.S. at the end of their tour of duty.

Friendly fire — An accidental attack, whether by shooting or by dropping bombs, upon one's own troops, such as U.S soldiers shooting at other U.S. soldiers.

FUBAR — An acronym for "f_ _ _ ed up beyond all recognition." When some event gets really messed up.

G

GOLF — Military phonetic for the letter 'G.'

Gook — Negative slang term for Viet Cong.

Grunt — Slang term used for an infantryman.

GR — Graves Registration. The place on a military base where dead GIs are identified, embalmed, and processed.

H

Hanoi Hilton — Slang term for North Vietnam's Hoa Loa Prison which was notorious for being the place where American POWs were brought for interrogation and torture.

Hawk	A person who supports the Vietnam War. (Compare to "dove.")
Ho Chi Minh Trail	Supply paths from North Vietnam to South Vietnam that traveled through Cambodia and Laos to supply the communist forces fighting in South Vietnam.
Hootch	Slang term for a place to live, either a soldier's living quarters or a Vietnamese hut.
Hootch girl	A slang for a young Vietnamese woman who is employed by the military to serve as maids or laundresses.
Hot LZ	A landing zone that was under enemy fire.
HOTEL	Military phonetic for the letter 'H.'
Huey	The helicopter that became the face of Vietnam.
Hump	Carry.

I

In country	Vietnam.
INDIA	Military phonetic for the letter 'I.'

J

Johnson's war	Slang term for the Vietnam War since Johnson escalated our involvement in the war.
JULIET	Military phonetic for the letter 'J.'
Jungle rot	Fungal infections due to moisture.

K

K-bar	A military knife.
KIA	Acronym for "killed in action."
KILO	Military phonetic for the letter 'K.'
Klick	Slang term for a kilometer.

L

LIMA	Military phonetic for the letter 'L.'
Lyster (or lister) bags	36-gallon, canvas water bags.
LZ	Acronym for "landing zone."

M

M16	The standard rifle used by the infantry.
M60	A machine gun.
M79	A grenade launcher.
Mamma-san	Slang term for an older Vietnamese woman.
MIA	Acronym for "missing in action." A term that means a GI is missing and his death cannot be confirmed.
MIKE	Military phonetic for the letter 'M.'
Mike-mike	Term used for millimeter.
MOS	Acronym for "Military Occupational Specialty." Someone's job while in the military.

N

Napalm	A jellied gasoline that when dispersed by flamethrower or by bombs would stick to a surface as it burned. This was used directly against enemy soldiers and to destroy foliage in order to expose enemy troops.
NCO	Acronym for "Noncommissioned officer."
NLF	Acronym for "National Liberation Front" (the communist guerrilla forces in South Vietnam). Also known as "Viet Cong."
No bic	I don't understand.
NOVEMBER	Military phonetic for the letter 'N.'
NVA	Acronym for "North Vietnamese Regular Army."

O

OIC	Acronym for "officer in charge."
OSCAR	Military phonetic for the letter 'O.'

P

PAPA	Military phonetic for the letter 'P.'
Papa-san	Slang term for an older Vietnamese man.
Peaceniks	Early protesters against the Vietnam War.
Point	The first man in line when a squad or platoon is walking along a trail or through the jungle.
Pop smoke	To light a smoke grenade for identification and location.

POW	Acronym for "prisoner of war." A GI that has been taken captive by the enemy.
PTSD	Acronym for "Post-Traumatic Stress Disorder." A psychological disorder caused by experiencing a trauma.
Punji stakes	A booby trap made out of a bunch of sharpened, short, wooden sticks placed upright in the ground and covered so that an unsuspecting GI would fall or stumble upon them.

Q

QUEBECK	Military phonetic for the letter 'Q.'
Quick reaction force	Infantry on helicopter gunships able to react to enemy attacks.

R

R and R	Acronym for "rest and recuperation," a break or vacation while in the military.
Rack	A cot or bed.
ROMEO	Military phonetic for the letter 'R.'
Round eye	Slang for Caucasian girl.
RPG	Acronym for "rocket propelled grenade."
RTO	Acronym for "radio telephone operator."
RVN	Acronym for "Republic of Viet-Nam" (South Vietnam).

S

Sampan | A small boat the Viet Cong often used to transport weapons and ammunition to the enemy.

Sapper | An enemy soldier who would try to infiltrate a base camp to destroy lives or property. Term also used for combat engineers who assist team members when tackling rough terrain in combat situations.

Short timer | Someone who has 60 days left in his tour of Vietnam, or 99 days left in his military service commitment.

SIERRA | Military phonetic for the letter 'S.'

Six-by | A large flat-bed truck with a canvas covering used to transport troops or equipment.

Slick | Slang word for helicopter.

T

TANGO | Military phonetic for the letter 'T.'

Tet Offensive | The massive attack on South Vietnam by North Vietnam's army and the Viet Cong, begun on January 30, 1968, the Vietnamese new year. Also just called Tet.

Top | The top sergeant.

Tunnel rats | Soldiers who explored the dangerous network of tunnels that had been dug and used by the Viet Cong.

Two-digit midget | Same as short timer.

U

Unbloused	Pants that are not tucked into the top of the boots.
UNIFORM	Military phonetic for the letter 'U.'

V

VICTOR	Military phonetic for the letter 'V.'
Viet Cong (VC)	The communist guerrilla forces in South Vietnam, NLF.
Vietnamization	The process of withdrawing U.S. troops from Vietnam and turning over all fighting to the South Vietnamese. This was part of President Richard Nixon's plan to end U.S. involvement in the Vietnam War.
Vietniks	Early protesters against the Vietnam War.
Ville	Short term for village, small town, or group of thatched huts.

W

WHISKEY	Military phonetic for the letter 'W.'
WIA	Acronym for "wounded in action."
Willie Pete	White phosphorous round or grenade.
the World	The United States - or real life back home.

X

XO	Acronym for "eXecutive officer." (X capitalized). The second in command.
X-RAY	Military phonetic for the letter 'X.'

Y

YANKEE   Military phonetic for the letter 'Y.'

Yankee Station   Tonkin Gulf area of the South China Sea pa-
                          trolled by the Navy.

Z

ZULU   Military phonetic for the letter "Z."

Zulu   Casualty report.

Endnotes

INTRODUCTION

1. Wikipedia contributors. (2019, November 20). Porterville California. *In Wikipedia, The Free Encyclopedia.* Retrieved 10:36, December 14, 2019, from https://en.wikipedia.org/wiki/Porterville,_California.
2. *Porterville Recorder*, "Vets Day Brings Back Memories," by Rick Elkins, November 14, 2013.
3. Wikipedia contributors. (2019, August 16). Tet Offensive. *In Wikipedia, The Free Encyclopedia.* Retrieved 18:45, August 20, 2019, from https://en.wikipedia.org/wiki/Tet_Offensive.
4. Wikipedia contributors. (2019, August 11). Walter Cronkite. *In Wikipedia, The Free Encyclopedia.* Retrieved 20:00, August 14, 2019, from https://en.wikipedia.org/wiki/Walter_Cronkite.
5. National Archives, "Vietnam War U.S. Military Fatal Casualty Statistics," April 30, 2019, www.archives.gov/research/military/vietnam-war/casualty-statistics.

CHAPTER 1
Profiles of the Porterville High School Patriots

1. National Archives, "Vietnam War U.S. Military Fatal Casualty Statistics," April 30, 2010, www.archives.gov/research/military/vietnam-war/casualty-statistics.

CHAPTER 2
Coming of Age in the 1960s

1. The Vietnam Veterans Memorial, The Wall-USA, "Names on the Wall," www.thewall-usa.com/names.asp.

CHAPTER 3
Making the Choice: Enlist, Draft, College, Canada

1. Wikipedia contributors. (2019, June 14). 1968 in the Vietnam War. *In Wikipedia, The Free Encyclopedia.* Retrieved 19:50, July 30, 2019, from https:en.wikipedia.org/wiki/1968_in_the_Vietnam_War.
2. Wikipedia contributors. (2019, August 22). Draft Lottery (1969). *In Wikipedia, The Free Encyclopedia.* Retrieved 13:12, August 23, 2019, from https:en.wikipedia.org/wiki/Draft_lottery_(1969).
3. The Vietnam Veterans Memorial, The Wall-USA, "Names on the Wall," www.thewall-usa.com/names.asp.

CHAPTER 4
From Books to Boots

1. Eleanor Roosevelt quote, Goodreads, accessed via the following website on May 30, 2019, www.goodreads.com/quotes/119060-the-marines-i-have-seen-around-the-world.

2. Wikipedia contributors. (2018, August 25). USS Bauer. *In Wikipedia, The Free Encyclopedia*. Retrieved 19:30, July 30, 2019, from https://en.wikipedia.org/wiki/USS_Bauer.

3. The Vietnam Veterans Memorial, The Wall-USA, "Names on the Wall," www.thewall-usa.com/names.asp.

CHAPTER 5
A Black and White America

1. Gerald F. Goodwin, "Black and White in Vietnam," July 18, 2017, New York Times, www.nytimes.com/2017/07/18/opinion/racism-vietnam-war.html.

2. Wikipedia contributors. (2019, August 6). The Murders of Chaney, Goodwin, and Schwerner. *In Wikipedia, The Free Encyclopedia*. Retrieved 16:30, August 26, 2019 from https://en.wikipedia.org/wiki/Murders_of_Chaney,_Goodwin,_and_Schwerner.

3. "Gulf of Tonkin Resolution," updated June 7, 2019, accessed August 18, 2019, www.history.com/topics/vietnam-war/gulf-of-tonkin-resolution-1.

4. Vietnam and All Veterans of Florida State Coalition, "Facts vs. Fiction…The Vietnam Veteran," accessed August 23, 2019, www.vvof.org/factsvnv.htm.

CHAPTER 6
Leaving Home

1. The Vietnam Veterans Memorial, The Wall-USA, "Names on the Wall," www.thewall-usa.com/names.asp.

CHAPTER 7
First Impressions of 'Nam

1. The Vietnam Veterans Memorial, The Wall-USA, "Names on the Wall," www.thewall-usa.com/names.asp.

CHAPTER 8
The War in the Bush

1. "Vietnam Tunnel Rats (28 photos and story)," accessed August 26, 2019, from https://thechive.com/2016/01/14/vietnam-tunnel-rats-28-photos-story/.
2. James Elphick, "How 1/9 Marines Became 'The Walking Dead,'" October 25, 2016, Real Clear Defense, https://realcleardefense.com/articles/2016/10/26/how_19_marines_became_the_walking_dead_110260.htm.
3. Wikipedia contributors. (2019, May 21). Operation Hickory. *In Wikipedia, The Free Encyclopedia.* Retrieved 13:27, August 23, 2019 from https://en.wikipedia.org/wiki/Operation_Hickory.
4. Ibid.
5. "Battle for Ben Het Special Forces A-Camp June 23, 1969," Newsrep, June 23, 2017, accessed on August 23, 2019, from https://thenewsrep/84326/battle-ben-het-special-forces-camp-June-231969/.
6. Robert A. Rosenblatt and Richard T. Cooper, "Last Soldier to Leave Vietnam is Feared Dead," September 16, 2001, Los Angeles Times, www.latimes.com/archives/la-xpm-2001-sep-16-mn-46461-story.html.

CHAPTER 9
The War in the Air

1. Ripcord Association website, "Ripcord Facts," ongoing updates and publications, www.ripcordassociation.com/facts-about-ripcord.
2. The Vietnam Veterans Memorial, The Wall-USA, "Names on the Wall," www.thewall-usa.com/names.asp.

CHAPTER 10
The War on the Rivers

1. The United States War Dogs Association, Inc., "War Dog History – Vietnam," accessed via the following website on August 1, 2019, www.uswardogs.org/war-dog-history/vietnam/.
2. The Edison 64 website accessed via the following website on January 4, 2020, www.edison64.org.

CHAPTER 11
The War on the Roads

1. "Convoy Mission Overview – Vietnam," April 24, 2008, accessed via 720th Military Police Battalion Reunion Association website, www.720mpreunion.org/history/project_vietnam/convoys/overview/overview.html.
2. The Vietnam Veterans Memorial, The Wall-USA, "Names on the Wall," www.thewall-usa.com/names.asp.

CHAPTER 12
The War on the Bases

1. Matthew M. Burke, "The Bloody Battle of Khe Sanh," Stars and Stripes magazine, November 17, 2014, www.stripes.com/news/special-reports/vietnam-at-50-legacy/the-bloody-battle-of-khe-sanh-77-days-under-siege-1.314627.
2. Ibid.
3. Richard Cunningham, "The Dogs of the Vietnam War," New York Times, October 3, 2013, www.nytimes.com/2017/10/03/opinion/the-dogs-of-the-vietnam-war.html.
4. Ibid.
5. The Vietnam Veterans Memorial, The Wall-USA, "Names on the Wall," www.thewall-usa.com/names.asp.

CHAPTER 13
In Support of the Troops

1. Anthony DiPietro, "Vietnam, The MedEvac Helicopter and the Wounded Soldier," March 8, 2018, www.americanveteransaid.com/newblog/vietnam-the-medivac-helicopter-and-the-wounded-soldier/.
2. Matthew M. Burke, "For Those who Prepared Vietnam's Fallen, a Lasting Dread," November 9, 2014, Stars and Stripes, www.stripes.com/news/special-reports/vietnam-stories/features/for-those-who-prepared-vietnam-s-fallen-a-lasting-dread-1.309701.
3. "1968 USS Pueblo captured," updated July 27, 2019, accessed on August 26, 2019, www.history.com/this-day-in-history/uss-pueblo-captured.
4. Erwin Rommel quote accessed on June 20, 2019, www.azquotes.com/author/12582-Erwin-Rommel.

5. "1957-1975: The Vietnam War," blog posted by Steven (no last name), on September 8, 2006, https://libcom.org/history/1957-1975-the-vietnam-war.

CHAPTER 14

Oddities of the Vietnam Experience

1. "Military Lyster Bag," October 12, 2011, www.olive-drab.com/od_medical_other_lyster_bag.php.
2. The Vietnam Veterans Memorial, The Wall-USA, "Names on the Wall," www.thewall-usa.com/names.asp.

CHAPTER 15

In Memory of Our Fallen Heroes

1. The Vietnam Veterans Memorial, The Wall-USA, "Names on the Wall," www.thewall-usa.com/names.asp.
2. Ibid.
3. Susan Sward, "After Vietnam/20 years of sorrow/immeasurable Losses/Porterville still struggling with legacy of war sacrifice," April 27, 1995, SFGate, www.sfgate.com/news/article/AFTER-VIETNAM-20-years-of-Sorrow-Immeasurable-3035349.php.
4. Wikipedia contributors. (2019 June 23). Operation Allen Brook. *In Wikipedia, The Free Encyclopedia*. Retrieved 19:50, August 1, 2019, from https://en.wikipedia.org/wiki/Operation_Allen_Brook.
5. Jesse Greenspan, "Which Countries Were Involved in the Vietnam War?" June 17, 2019, History, www.history.com/news/vietnam-war-combatants#section_7.

CHAPTER 16
Going Back to the World

1. The Vietnam Veterans Memorial, The Wall-USA, "Names on the Wall," www.thewall-usa.com/names.asp.

CHAPTER 17
Opposition, Even at Home

1. The Vietnam Veterans Memorial, The Wall-USA, "Names on the Wall," www.thewall-usa.com/names.asp.

CHAPTER 18
The War's Impact on the Family and Friends of the Veterans

1. The Vietnam Veterans Memorial, The Wall-USA, "Names on the Wall," www.thewall-usa.com/names.asp.

CHAPTER 19
Lessons of Vietnam from Those Who Were There

1. Robert S. McNamara, "In Retrospect: The Tragedy and Lessons of Vietnam" (Vintage Books 1995), pp. xx.
2. Ibid., 321-323.
3. National League of POW/MIA Families, "Number of Americans Still Missing and Unaccounted-For By State," website accessed August 23, 2019, www.pow-miafamilies. org/number-of-americans-still-missing-and-unaccounted-for-by-state.html.

CHAPTER 20
The War Never Ends

1. Clyde Haberman, "Agent Orange's Long Legacy for Vietnam and Veterans," New York Times, May 11, 2014.
2. The Vietnam Veterans Memorial, The Wall-USA, "Names on the Wall," www.thewall-usa.com/names.asp.

CHAPTER 21
Where Are They Now?

1. The Vietnam Veterans Memorial, The Wall-USA, "Names on the Wall," www.thewall-usa.com/names.asp.

CHAPTER 22
The Author's Opinion and Reflections

1. Wikipedia contributors. (2019, August 16). Tet Offensive. In Wikipedia, The Free Encyclopedia. Retrieved 18:45, August 20, 2019, from https://en.wikipedia.org/wiki/Tet_Offensive.
2. William Tecumseh Sherman quote accessed via the following website on July 29, 2019, https://brainyquote.com/authors/william-tecumseh-sherman-quotes.

EPILOGUE

1. United States Department of Veteran Affairs, "National Veteran Suicide Data: 2016 Update," June 10, 2018, https://www.mentalhealth.va.gov/mentalhealth/suicide_prevention/data.asp.
2. Phil Luciano, "Luciano: Former Marine reservist launches Buddy Check 22 effort to wish a vet well," August 19, 2015, Journal Star, htps://pjstar.com/article/20150819/NEWS/150819206.

CPSIA information can be obtained
at www.ICGtesting.com
Printed in the USA
LVHW021417210720
661198LV00001B/11